Peter Scratchley, Clement Kinloch-Cooke

Australian Defences and New Guinea

Peter Scratchley, Clement Kinloch-Cooke

Australian Defences and New Guinea

ISBN/EAN: 9783337314118

Printed in Europe, USA, Canada, Australia, Japan

Cover: Foto ©Andreas Hilbeck / pixelio.de

More available books at **www.hansebooks.com**

AUSTRALIAN DEFENCES

AND

NEW GUINEA

COMPILED FROM THE PAPERS OF THE LATE

MAJOR-GENERAL

SIR PETER SCRATCHLEY, R.E., K.C.M.G.

*Defence Adviser to the Australasian Colonies
and
Her Majesty's Special Commissioner for New Guinea*

BY

C. KINLOCH COOKE, B.A., LL.M.

of the Inner Temple, Barrister-at-Law

WITH AN INTRODUCTORY MEMOIR

London
MACMILLAN AND CO.
AND NEW YORK
1887

I DEDICATE THIS BOOK
TO
LADY SCRATCHLEY

IN AFFECTIONATE REMEMBRANCE

OF HER LATE HUSBAND

PREFACE.

I HAVE endeavoured in these pages to place on record the work done by the late Major-General Sir Peter Scratchley, in connection with Australian Defences, and as Her Majesty's Special Commissioner for New Guinea.

The opinions of a man, whose suggested System of Defence for our Australasian Colonies has been, in its salient points, actually adopted, can scarcely fail to be of public interest in the mother-country; and I am authorised by the Colonial Secretary of State to say that he fully recognises Sir Peter Scratchley's important services to the Empire, more especially those in connection with the defences of Australia.

The account of New Guinea not only gives the most recent and accurate information respecting a comparatively unknown territory, but affords an insight into the opinions of one who possessed both experience and knowledge of the people and politics of Australasia.

The *Memoir* includes extracts from Sir Peter's

Crimean and Indian Mutiny Diaries. In these he makes many interesting allusions to his friend General Charles George Gordon, and other Engineer Officers who took part with him in those campaigns.

My thanks are due to many of Sir Peter Scratchley's friends and brother officers who have given me valuable advice and assistance. Amongst them I would mention Field Marshal Lord Napier of Magdala; the Hon. Sir Arthur Gordon; Major-General Sir Charles Warren; Major-General Sir Henry Gordon; Sir Robert Herbert; Sir Frederick Abel; Major-General Nicholson; Major-General Clive; Mr. Henniker-Heaton, M.P.; the Rev. James Chalmers; and Mr. G. Seymour Fort, Sir Peter's Private Secretary. For the information contained in *New Guinea Notes* I am indebted to Mr. G. R. Askwith.

By the kind permission of Mr. Knowles, the Editor of the *Nineteenth Century*, I am able to reproduce the Chart which was designed to illustrate an article contributed by me to that Review.

And finally, I would especially thank Mr. Philip Scratchley for material aid in the composition and construction of the *Memoir*, and for his kind help in revising the matter relating to his uncle's work in New Guinea.

C. KINLOCH COOKE.

2 GARDEN COURT, TEMPLE:
April 1887.

CONTENTS.

	PAGE
MEMOIR OF SIR PETER SCRATCHLEY, AND EXTRACTS FROM HIS CRIMEAN AND INDIAN MUTINY DIARIES	1

AUSTRALIAN DEFENCES.

CHAPTER		
I.	GENERAL DEFENCE	39
II.	NAVAL DEFENCE	58
III.	COAST DEFENCE	76
IV.	TORPEDO DEFENCE (DEFENSIVE AND OFFENSIVE)	83
V.	LOCAL FORCES (*a*)	103
VI.	LOCAL FORCES (*b*)	122
VII.	NEW SOUTH WALES	145
VIII.	VICTORIA	159
IX.	SOUTH AUSTRALIA	177
X.	QUEENSLAND	185
XI.	WESTERN AUSTRALIA	195
XII.	TASMANIA	213
XIII.	NEW ZEALAND	224
XIV.	TORRES STRAIT	243
XV.	THURSDAY ISLAND	250

CONTENTS.

NEW GUINEA.

CHAPTER		PAGE
XVI.	THE POLITICAL SITUATION	. 261
XVII.	EARLY DIFFICULTIES	. 271
XVIII.	ENGLAND'S NEW COLONY .	. 280
XIX.	SIR PETER'S DIARY	. 303
XX.	NEW GUINEA NOTES .	. 359

APPENDICES.

A.	PAPERS RELATING TO AUSTRALIAN DEFENCES	. 375
B.	PAPERS RELATING TO NEW GUINEA .	. 410

MAPS.

THE AUSTRALASIAN COLONIES AND THE PACIFIC ISLANDS .	*Frontispiece*
THE NEW GUINEA PROTECTORATE .	*to face page* 261
PORT JACKSON .	. 148
PORT PHILIP .	. 160
THE ENTRANCE TO PORT PHILIP	. 161
BRISBANE .	. 187
KING GEORGE SOUND	. 196
HOBART .	. 215
LAUNCESTON AND PORT DALRYMPLE .	. 217
AUCKLAND .	. 230
WELLINGTON	. 231
TORRES STRAIT AND THURSDAY ISLAND .	. 246
NEW GUINEA AND ADJACENT ISLANDS, SHOWING THE POLITICAL DIVISION OF TERRITORY BETWEEN GREAT BRITAIN, GERMANY, AND HOLLAND	. 263

MEMOIR.

PETER HENRY SCRATCHLEY was the youngest son of the late Dr. James Scratchley of the Royal Artillery, and was born in Paris on August 24, 1835. Dr. Scratchley, after serving for many years in India and other quarters of the globe with the distinguished corps to which he belonged, was appointed Inspector of Military Hospitals. Being, late in life, required to proceed in his turn to the West Indies, he decided, having at that time a wife and young family, to retire from the army, and to start in private practice. Dr. Scratchley had already attained to eminence in his profession as the writer of various medical works, of which one became famed as the 'London Dissector,' and went through numerous editions. While considering where to settle down, it was suggested to him that Paris, the Paris of 1830, offered a good opening for an English medical man. Thither he accordingly proceeded with his family, and as consulting physician to the Embassy, and holding other official posts, speedily found himself in an extensive and lucrative practice.

Of himself and his early life Peter Scratchley's Diary contains the following record:—

Arthur [his elder brother] and Peter Clutterbuck were

my godfathers. Peter Clutterbuck gave papa 300*l*. for having made him my godpapa. About eight years old I had the typhus fever, during which I was sixteen days dumb, caused, as mamma always said, by my having sworn very much once during my delirium. I continued ill for thirty-three days. I was a miserably thin and slight boy and very short. About this time my eyes got bad, and I suffered from ophthalmia for two years, when I went to a French school kept by a M. Lemeignan-Mathé, Rue du Faubourg St.-Honoré. I was only a day boarder, and used to go to the 'Collège Bourbon.' While at college I never worked at all, and used to be set to do lines. I used to sit up till twelve o'clock working at them. I remember also how we used to throw books at the masters' heads when in school. I was only ten years old when I went to school. I remained there till the year 1847.

Dr. Scratchley died in the early part of 1848, at a time when the whole of France, and especially Paris as its centre, was convulsed by political changes. On the death of her husband Mrs. Scratchley returned to England, where she had two elder sons settled, one in the Church and the other as an Actuary. The question soon arose as to what was to be done with the boy Peter. His mother wished him to enter a civil profession, but fortunately, as it turned out, the wiser counsels of an elder brother prevailed, and it was decided to remind Lord Palmerston of an offer he had previously made, to recognise Dr. Scratchley's professional services by obtaining a nomination for one of his sons to Woolwich. Lord Palmerston and James Scratchley had been in the same form together at Harrow, and the Prime Minister, who had already shown his warm friendship for his old schoolfellow, promptly responded to the request made to him, and young Peter Scratchley, while still under fifteen years of age, received his nomination as a Gentleman Cadet at the Woolwich Academy.

Peter Scratchley is described by his friends as being at this time a somewhat reserved and thoughtful boy, not prone to say much, but quick and observant, and one who displayed in a striking degree that marked attachment to duty, which may justly be said to have been his distinguishing characteristic through life. An instance of the influence which this instinct (for so it may be called) had on his character, was shown in the untiring devotion with which, at the early age of twelve, he tended a dying elder brother through a long and painful illness.

Owing to delicate health he was decidedly backward, it is said, at the age of thirteen, knowing little but French, which, however, he spoke with fluency and a true accent. Before entering the Academy he was sent to study with a tutor at Woolwich, Dr. Bridgman, and made rapid progress. No doubt he formed at an early age the habit of steady, resolute work, which continued with him throughout his life. In his Diary he states :—

> I passed fourteenth in my Probationary or entrance examination, and joined the Academy on February 1, 1850. The first half-yearly examination I passed fifteenth or sixteenth from the Fourth Academy into the Third. I remained in the Third Academy during this second half-year, and got up to second. The third half-year (1851) I passed second into the Second Academy. I remained there during the fourth half-year and gained my place up to third. In the fifth half-year I passed third into the First Academy. Remained there two half-years

(1852), and in February 1853 I passed third into the Practical Class or Arsenal. There I remained for one year. The second half-year in the examination I gained one place, so that the list stood thus: Wrottesley, Scratchley, Watson, Hale, Rideout, &c.

Towards the end of his course at the Academy, he was prevented from reading for a considerable time by an accident, which nearly cost him the sight of an eye, and confined him to a darkened room for many weeks. Notwithstanding this serious drawback, however, to his studies, he passed out of the Academy at the head of the list (April 1854), and obtained a commission in the Royal Engineers. He thus speaks of the occurrence in his Diary:

On September 6, 1853, I was out at drill, and in playing with my sword I struck a stone, and it flew up and I was blinded. My eye continued bad for three months. I remained in the Cadet Hospital, where Dr. Jarratt attended me, and I then went up to London and consulted Dr. Alexander, Oculist to the Queen. In February 1854 I returned to the Academy, and was placed first on the list, but was told I must keep my place at the head. I did so, and we got our commissions as follows:— Scratchley, Kelsall, to Royal Engineers; De Winton, Hamilton &c., to Royal Artillery. By this illness I lost four places, as Hale, Dumaresq, Longley, and Lempriere got their commissions in the Engineers before me. I was gazetted on April 21, 1854, and on June 20, 1854, I was promoted to First Lieutenant. From Chatham I proceeded, by order of the A. A. G., to Dover. I was then ordered to the Crimea, where I kept a regular diary.

At the Academy he contracted many friendships, some of them destined to be lifelong, with men who afterwards became distinguished officers. Amongst them was Charles George Gordon, with whom that early acquaintance ripened, in subsequent years, into intimate friendship. Although Gordon was Scratchley's senior by some two years, they had many traits in common which naturally disposed them to a mutual liking, and as years passed on and the slight difference in age (which at the Academy was not without importance) practically vanished, they came to hold each other in high esteem. Their paths in life, however, were widely different. The career of Gordon was brilliant and meteoric, almost eccentric in its orbit, terminating in a violent death; that of his friend was less conspicuous, but none the less marked by steadfastness of purpose and devotion to duty.

Lieutenant Scratchley was attached to the 4th Company, Royal Engineers, with which he also served later on during the Indian Mutiny. He left England on July 24, 1855, for the Crimea, where he arrived on August 13 of that year, and remained until June 11, 1856, being present at the siege and capture of Sebastopol. Although barely twenty years of age, his work in the trenches before Sebastopol was characterised by coolness and skill, qualities which were equally noticeable at the final assault upon the Redan, in which he also took part.

Soon after the retreat of the Russians from Sebastopol, Lieutenant Scratchley was employed in surveying the enemy's works and destroying their dockyard establishments. He was then selected to accompany the expedition to Kinburn, on the Black Sea, and was present at the capture of that fortress with his Company. Subsequently he was engaged in constructing defensive works for the better protection of the British troops, in which he was occupied when peace was concluded. For his services in the Crimea he was awarded the Crimean Medal, with clasp for Sebastopol, and the Turkish War Medal.

His experiences during the Campaign are modestly narrated in the Diary he kept at the time, and will be best described in his own words:—

CRIMEAN DIARY.[1]

August 13, 1855.—Arrived at Balaklava at 6 P.M. Anchored outside the harbour. Saw flashes, resembling those of lightning, caused by the firing of guns at Sebastopol.

[1] *List of Officers R.E. and Assistant Engineers doing duty at my time:*—

Lieut.-Gen. Sir H. Jones, K.C.B., went home Sept. 15; Lieut. Cowell, A.D.C., went home Sept. 15; Lieut.-Col. Chapman, C.B. (Col.), went home Oct.: Major Bent (C.B., Lieut.-Col.), Director L attack; Capt. Keane (Major), home Oct., returned; Major Bouchier (C.B., Lieut.-Col.), B.M. and A.A.G.; Capt. Browne (C.B. Major), wounded, home, D.R.A.; Capt. Montague (Major), prisoner, returned Sept.; Capt. Cooke (Major), Survey and Director, R.A.H.; Major Staunton (Lieut.-Col.), home Oct., returned Feb.; Capt. De Moleyns (Major); Capt. Ewart (Major), B.M. and Adjutant : Capt. Nicholson (Major); Capt. Sedley (Major), home, wounded; Lieut. Ranken (Major); Lieut. De Vere (Major), home Oct., returned Feb.; Lieut. Brine (Capt.), sick list Sept. 8; Lieut. Fisher, telegraph (Capt.); Lieut. Elphinstone, wounded 8th, home (Capt.); Lieut. Cumberland, two days before 8th not present; Lieut. Neville, after 8th A.D.C. Gen. Barnard; Lieut. Lennox, after 8th Adjutant R.L.M.; Lieut. Leahy, D.A.Q.M.G.; Lieut. Anderson, Constantinople, after 8th returned; Lieut. Graham (Capt.); Lieut. Gordon (went to Turkish boundary); Lieut. Edwards, two days before 8th; Lieut. Donnelly, after 8th A.D.C. to Lieut.-Col. Lloyd; Lieut. Somerville, died Aug.; Lieut. Dumaresq; Lieut. Scratchley; Lieut. Kelsall, constant after 8th; Lieut.-Col. Lloyd, C.R.E. after Jones's departure; Col. Gordon, C.B., C.R.L.M. after 8th; Lieut. James, returned from prisoner Dec. 23; Capt. Lambert, Jan. 15; Capt. Barry, Jan. 15; Capt. Schaw, Jan. 15; Lieut. Stopford, April 10 (Capt.); Lieut. Goodall, April 10; Lieut. Gossett, April 10.

Assistant Engineers:—Capt. Anderson, 31st, killed Sept. 5; Capt. Wolseley, 46th, wounded Sept. 8; Capt. Penn, R.A., returned to duty Sept. 13; Major Campbell, 46th, returned to duty Sept. 13.

August 14.—Landed and went into Balaklava, but remained during the night on board ship. The crowded harbour looked very extraordinary, especially as everything was so very new to me.

August 15.—Landed and went up to camp. Slept in Dumaresq's tent. Our camp within the range of the Russian guns.

August 16.—Got up. Went to see the field of the battle of Tractir, fought between the Russians, French, and Sardinians. The Russians were severely defeated, leaving many wounded and dead. Saw the poor fellows lying all over the plain—very shocking, but was not so much moved as I expected. War is a stern necessity.

August 17.—Bombardment commenced at 8 A.M. Never heard such an infernal noise in all my life. The shot and shell came pouring into our camp last night. Far from pleasant. However, slept soundly. On duty in the trenches to-night. Went down at 4 P.M. Fire not very hot. Found my way down to the general hut. Elphinstone of 'ours' on with me. Did not witness any casualty.

August 18.—Remained in camp, being tired of my night work. In the evening the Ruskis fired tremendously as they expected an attack.

[*August* 19 and subsequent days were passed on duty, chiefly in the trenches, but without incident, except he records that he bought three horses at an auction for 55*l*. 10*s*. the lot.]

August 26.—Poor Somerville very ill. Stopped with him, and went, in the afternoon, with him in a litter to Balaklava to see him on board the *Imperador* steamer going to Scutari. I am afraid he will not be able to return, although, poor fellow, he wishes sadly to do so. Heavy firing in the evening.

August 27.—Camp duty. An attack expected against the 'Sardines' at Baidar on the Tchernaya, and a sortie against the French.

August 28.—Nothing extraordinary except that the Russians destroyed a French magazine in the Mamelon. (It was originally a Russian one.) It is reported the French lost 200 men and

600 wounded. The explosion was terrific and woke everybody all over the camp, and destroyed some of the French batteries, and wounded twenty-five of our men. Some of the timbers were seen to fly to an immense distance into our Right Attack.

August 29.—On duty in the trenches in the evening. A few casualties and a heavy fire of musketry and shells. Reconnoitred with Elphinstone in advance of the breaking out of the fifth into the sixth parallel, and found the ground very rocky. Proceeded with two men about fifty yards, and were just returning when a Russian picket of half a dozen men fired on us and wounded one of the men. We were only about fifteen yards from them, and if they had not been frightened we should have been taken prisoners, or perhaps been killed. Of course we returned to the trenches, and they ceased firing. The working party were obliged to be withdrawn on account of the casualties. Had two or three narrow escapes from shells bursting.

August 30.—As I thought, the Ruskis made a small sortie on the Right Advance. Dumaresq, who was on duty, says that the picket that was in advance retired immediately, and so did the working party, and the Ruskis of course filled up the trench. A few men were killed, and they retired.

August 31.—The Ruskis made another attempt at a sortie on the Right Advance. The trench was again destroyed.

September 1.—I went to see a theatre in the sailors' camp. It was capital, though I hardly thought it was quite right to have it.

September 2.—I was on duty in the trenches in the day-time, and also on camp duty. Firing very heavy against the quarries. Left Attack and the French did not fire a bit. A magazine in the flag-staff battery blew up. I should not think this was Sunday, as everything goes on in the same way, except the morning service. Another sortie in the evening and the men ran. Reports confirm my opinion that the men are beginning to lose their hearts underneath these failures and this overwork.

September 4.—An attack from the lower picket ravine expected on our Right Advance. Anderson of the 31st, an

Assistant Engineer, killed last night. Poor fellow, I liked him very much.

September 5.—Bombardment commenced this morning. On duty in the trenches to-night. Firing very light. Very few casualties. Got on very well with the advanced sap, and amused myself firing with Jones of the Artillery at the Russians in the ravine.

September 6.—Bombardment was much slacker last night from want of ammunition. Buckley of the Guards killed in advance of the Right Sap. It is becoming absolute madness to venture out.

September 7.—Bombardment continued. It is expected the French will attack to-morrow. On duty in the trenches with Stanton. Heard that poor Bill [Somerville] died of fever at Scutari. Wrote home.

September 8.—To-day was fixed for the assault of the Redan and Malakoff. It began at 12.15 P.M., when they began firing as hard as they could. I was in front of the 'Lime-kiln.' The Malakoff was taken, as the Russians did not expect an assault, and ran. We attacked the Redan, as a feint, and after hard fighting were repulsed. The French were repulsed at the Little Redan, Central Bastion, and the Bastion-du-Mât (Flagstaff), and the Quarantine Bastion. They lost about 12,000 men, we 2,000.

September 9.—The Russians during the night evacuated the Redan, and we took possession at 6 A.M. It is disgraceful how the attack of yesterday failed. The Highlanders, who were the supports, were on the third and fourth parallels, and the Guards were in reserve, in rear of the 'Lime-kiln,' and it would have taken them one hour to march up.

September 10.—On duty in the Redan. Put out several fires that were near magazines. Buried thirty or forty Russians who were lying dead. Went out into the town barracks and flooded a magazine, which they had intended to blow up. Our soldiers were not allowed to take any plunder, so the French took it all.

September 11.—A very windy rainy day. The place one

mass of mud. Thunder and lightning at night. There are a good many incendiaries picked up here and there. They say they are Russian criminals who are promised pardon if they keep up the work of devastation. Five of them were found by Rideout after the explosion of one of the magazines in the Redan. Three of them were dead—two alive—having been buried by the fall of the earth. A general order came out to-day congratulating the army on its success, and a brigade order from Jones [Lieut.-General Sir Henry Jones, K.C.B.] thanking us for the way we had done our duty. I expect we will get a year's pay for our trouble. I am sure I hope so. The Russians sank their remaining steamers.

September 14.—I marched eighty-five men of different regiments to 'Mother Seacole's' on the railway with two sergeants. They were all drunk, and I never had such trouble. However, I harangued them and appealed to their feelings as British soldiers, and I managed to get them there safe.

September 16.—I believe we are never going to do anything. I cannot say I look forward to spending the winter here.

September 18.—Left camp for Sebastopol Dockyard with fifty-six men, four non-commissioned officers, and one bugler.

September 20.—Set the men to work at the shafts. The masonry of the docks perfect, but the stones very soft, and would wear away in short time.

September 21.—Same hard work looking after men. Got up at 5 A.M. like yesterday, and worked till night. Dined yesterday with General Wyndham, Governor of Sebastopol.

September 22.—To-day the siege train marched in. In the usual way that we do things, they came in with colours flying and drums beating and in broad daylight. The consequence was the Ruskis began firing. The second shell killed a man in the Buffs.

September 25.—Lost a rifle found in the Redan. Stolen by a Frenchman.

September 26.—I am very sorry I lost my rifle, as it is the only thing I had worth having out of Sebastopol.

September 27.—An explosion in one of the creek magazines to-day, killing and wounding some men.

October 1.—Reports flying about that the Ruskis are in full retreat and Czar Alexander dethroned. I hope the former is true, as it will save us much trouble next spring.

October 2, 1855.—Ordered to hold myself in readiness for embarkation at Balaklava with the fourth company, Captain Nicholson, Charlie Gordon; Major Bent, R.E., to be C.R.E.

October 4.—Started from camp at 7 A.M. Embarked that morning on board the *Indian* S.S.

October 11.—Odessa is a very fine town, with large massive buildings. The people seem very busy, and I have no doubt very much frightened.

October 12.—It was intended that we should start last night to arrive at Kinburn Fort and land there, but the sea became very rough. The wind, however, went down, so we might have landed this morning. To-day was very fine.

Sunday, October 14.—Got under way about 7 A.M. with the *Arabia* in tow. The fleet proceeding towards the north of Kinburn, and we to the south.

Monday, October 15.—Landed at 10 A.M. We pitched our tents by 7 P.M.

Tuesday, October 16.—Last night I entrenched the sixty-third on our left; made a pretty good trench. The night was very dark. To-day made small redoubts to the right and left, advanced pickets, each to be armed with two guns *en barbette*. Worked till late at night.

Wednesday, October 17.—Continued the redoubt. At 8 A.M. the fleet bombarded the fort, and after a terrific fire of six or seven hours it gave in. It was a splendid sight; the finest I ever saw in all my life. The garrison, twelve to thirteen hundred, surrendered with the honours of war. They were most of them small men—young and old—evidently the worst part of the Russian troops. To-day I also worked at our entrenched position. An attack expected from the Imperial Guard, who marched from Warsaw intending to proceed to Sebastopol; but hearing of the 'fall,' they were expected here.

Thursday, October 18.—Continued the redoubts; but the completing of our intrenched position was discontinued.

Friday, October 19.—Shifted our camp to the village; the English taking the south and the French the north side (which is the best).

Saturday, October 20.—To-day almost all the allied troops, with the exception of 2,000, went on a reconnaisance of six days. Charlie Gordon went on the Q.M.G. staff. I would have liked to have gone.

Sunday, October 21, *to Sunday,* 28.—Employed in Kinburn Fort, repairing the buildings to convert them into barracks. The French officers were very civil. To-day we embarked on board the *Indian.*

Sunday, November 11.—Landed at Razatch, and slept (in camp) on shore.

Monday, November 12.—Marched up to camp from Razatch. A long march, only took two and a half hours. Had a bad toothache.

Thursday. November 15.—Memorable day. About 2 P.M. a magazine in the French right siege train, by the windmill, blew up. Our shell magazine was destroyed. Eight artillerymen killed and many wounded. All the huts and tents round about were blown down, and the shell and shot flew up in all directions. A truly magnificent sight. I believe the French have lost a great many men.

Friday, November 16, 1855.—We turned out at 5 A.M. expecting an attack. The fire at the Right Siege train went out in the right. I went over with the 4th Company to repair damages, but had such a bad toothache that I returned, getting Charlie Gordon to do my work. Had tooth out.

Thursday, November 22.—Winter commencing; still under canvas.

Saturday, November 24.—Moved into my quarter-of-anofficer's hut, next to Ranken. A good change. Received my Crimean medal.

December 2, 1855.—Went into Sebastopol to meet Montague about making sections of Russian works for a report to be sent in.

Wednesday, December 19.—My hut is fearfully cold, 8° during sunrise. My sponge, ink, &c. frozen—in fact, everything. I had hardly had my bath when the sponge I had been using got as stiff as possible.

Friday, December 21.—Armed with a French pass I went to the Quarantine Fort and took some angles for the survey. Fort Constantine appeared unpleasantly close. Wrote home.

Christmas Day, 1855.—Took the Communion. In the afternoon took a walk over to Inkerman. We were five or six walking, and the Ruskis fired two or three shots at us. We had a dinner up in our new mess hut. It passed off very well. Thirteen at dinner.

Monday, December 31.—Surveyed from Fort Artillery to Quarantine Fort. Sat up to see the new year in and the old year out.

Friday, January 11, 1856.—Went out triangulating. Left off the Left Siege attack and commenced another. Wrote home. Went to the theatre. Yesterday went out on a paper hunt. Had a fine run.

Monday, January 21.—Sketching by Kamiesch Lines. There are two reports flying about :

(1.) That peace is nearly settled by Russia accepting the proposals of Austria (doubtful !).

(2.) That a battle was fought at Baidar between French and Ruskis. Ruskis, 30,000 men, defeated—400 prisoners (very doubtful !).

Tuesday, January 22.—Drawing indoors, weather being bad. Peace news confirmed to-day.

Wednesday, January 23.—Went out sketching. In the evening we had two live generals to dinner—Generals Barnard and Crauford and A.D.Cs. Peace news certain.

Thursday, January 24.—Did not go out sketching. Peace said to be certain.

Tuesday, February 19.—Yesterday was a cold, miserable day, blowing a fierce gale N.E. There were thirteen at table, viz.

Gordon, Bent, Ewart, Cooke, 'Nick,' Ranken, Schaw, Charlie Gordon, Dumaresq, Gimlinton, Combe, Lennox, and myself—an unlucky number (as it turned out, poor Ranken was killed at the docks afterwards).

Friday, February 22.—Corps meeting to-day about monument to be erected to the fellows who have fallen during this war. Great discussion, and, as generally happens on such occasions, nothing was agreed upon, and the meeting was adjourned.

Sunday, February 24.—To-day the army (25,000) was reviewed. A splendid sight. The Highlanders and Guards looked splendid.

Monday, February 25.—Packed up preparatory to moving to Cossack Bay, between Balaklava and Karance. Went to the 1st Division Theatre—very good.

Tuesday, February 26.—Marched down to Cossack Bay with 8th Company. Fine day for the march. Slept in a single tent. We had a snowstorm that night. Tent not very cold.

Wednesday, February 27.—Had my tent covered with another, which made it much warmer. Selected position for Lines.

Friday, February 29.—Poor Ranken was killed last night while employed destroying the 'White Buildings.' He was crushed by the fall of one of the building walls. He was not found till 5 A.M. this morning. Poor fellow, I liked him excessively. He is a fearful loss to us.

Saturday, March 1, 1856.—The preliminaries of an armistice were settled on Friday, 29, and it was to be until the 31st. Works of defence to be continued and destruction of Sebastopol.

Wednesday, March 5.—Miserable work for tents. Went round to Balaklava. Some parts of the hills waist-deep with snow.

Thursday, March 6.—Nasty day. South-west wind turned into a gale in the morning. Expecting my tent to come down every moment.

Monday, March 10.—Change in the weather—warm spring day.

Wednesday, March 12.—Beautiful fine warm day. Spring regularly set in, I hope. Laid out the Batteries, &c. to-day, and sketched the ground around them. Peace news expected to-morrow.

Thursday, March 13.—Telegraphic message came to-day to suspend all work at the lines. Reason not known. Nothing known about the peace.

Monday, March 17.—Commenced working at wharf at Leander Bay.

Tuesday, March 18.—Still working at wharf.

Sunday, March 23.—Rumoured that Lord Panmure has resigned, and that Lord Hardinge retires, and that the Duke of Somerset becomes Minister of War.

Monday, March 24.—This day there were races on the Tchernaya plain. Went to see them. It was a beautiful day, and I should think that from 50,000 to 60,000 men were present. The Russians were invited, but General Luders declined on the plea that peace was not settled.

Tuesday, March 25.—Reported that peace had been signed. Working at big plan.

Wednesday, March 26.—General McMahon's (French) 'Corps d'Armée' was inspected to day.

. . . .

Tuesday, April 8.—Moved to ground on the west of the 82nd. Camp above Balaklava, so as to be nearer to the works in Balaklava.

Thursday, April 10.—Charlie Gordon is repairing the old Inkerman bridge that was burnt when the Allies came. Our fellows went over to the north side and invited the Russian sapper officers to come and dine with us. They come on Saturday and are to cross over at Fort Paul, where we are to have horses ready for them.

Saturday, April 12.—The Russian Engineers dined at our mess to-day.

Thursday, April 17.—General review of the army before

General Luder's Staff. The French Army was reviewed in the morning.

Wednesday, April 23.—I was ordered yesterday to take over the command of the 8th Company R.E.

Saturday, May 3.—To-morrow I hope to start on my trip to the interior of the Crimea.

. . . . .

Friday, May 23.—Stopford takes the command of the Company from me—rather a bore, as I lose contingent.

Saturday, May 24.—Queen's birthday. Review of part of the army and distribution of part of the French war medals.

May 28.—Gave over command of 8th Company to Devere, my old captain. Saw Colonel Crauford. He is an old friend of the family. Stopford came down to our camp to command 3rd Company.

May 31.—Went to the Alma with Lennox and Leahy.

June 1.—Returned from the Alma early, having slept in an orchard on the banks of the river—slept in the open.

. . . . .

June 11.—Embarked on board s.s. *Peninsula* for England at 10 A.M.

. . . . .

Sunday, July 6.—Arrived at Spithead.

After his return from the Crimea, Lieutenant Scratchley was employed on engineering works at Portsmouth for over twelve months.

Upon the outbreak of the Indian Mutiny in 1857 he was ordered to the front with the 4th Company, R.E., and embarked for Calcutta on October 2 of that year. On arrival he at once proceeded with his Chief, Lieutenant-Colonel Harness, R.E. (afterwards Sir Henry Harness, K.C.B.), to Cawnpore to join General Wyndham, who had been left behind by Sir Colin Campbell to keep open communication while the last-named officer was relieving Sir James Outram at Lucknow. Lieutenant Scratchley served throughout the Oude campaign from October 1857, and was present at the actions near Cawnpore as Acting Adjutant of Royal Engineers under General Wyndham. The following extracts are taken from his Diary :—

November 29 to December 1, 1857.—Shut up in Cawnpore Fort with the enemy bombarding. Sir Colin Campbell arrived with his army and formed camp on the other side of the Ganges. The enemy shelled the camp. Some of the 93rd were killed, and Colonel Ewart (our Ewart's brother) wounded.

December 2.—Left Cawnpore Fort with the C.R.E [Colonel Harness] for headquarters' camp (Sir Colin Campbell's).

December 5.—The Gwalior force sent about 300 men across the Canal, and made a demonstration on our left. The cavalry of the army and three batteries moved out, and a cannonade ensued for two and a half hours or more. Very unsatisfactory work. One gunner and one horse killed. Returned to camp.

Sunday, December 6.—Present at the Battle of Cawnpore and defeat of the Gwalior Force. This morning, at 8 A.M., the tents were struck and the army prepared to attack the Pandies. The ball was opened by a violent cannonade from the intrenchment (where General Wyndham, with the force under him, was), which was not answered by the enemy. We advanced steadily until we came upon the enemy's camp, which was deserted, tents, &c., being left standing. We halted for a short time. In the meantime the cavalry, with some artillery, had been sent to turn the enemy's right flank. The pursuit was continued on to the Kalpee road. During the pursuit the C.R.E. was ordered to take a message to Brigadier Grant (who had been detached with a small force to attack the 'Subaddar Tank,' and cover our communication with the rear), and I went with him. After advancing several hundred yards we got into a road which led up to a mudhouse. When within fifty yards or so of it, the Pandies commenced firing at us. We retreated unhurt. I cannot praise them for their shooting. As we were going I heard a great deal of firing from two Companies of the 38th, who had been sent to attack the three guns annoying them. When we returned these guns had been taken in style. Sir Colin and the column returned about 6 P.M., and we bivouacked in the open.

. . . . .

December 13.—Took command of the Company from yesterday, Nicholson being made Chief Engineer to Head Quarters on that date.

Lieutenant Scratchley served with the 4th Company R.E., in the subsequent operations with the Commander-in-Chief's army, and accompanied the columns under Brigadier-General Walpole through the district of Stayah as Commanding Royal Engineer. He was attached to a Company of Royal Engineers during the operations before Lucknow and the defence of Fort Jellalabad, and accompanied the storming party which attacked the Begum's palace. He was Orderly Officer to General Sir Robert Napier (Lord Napier of Magdala), Chief Engineer, during the siege and capture of Lucknow. He served during the subsequent operations with General Grant's Force in Oude as Adjutant of the Engineer Brigade, and was present at the action of Baree. As Commanding Engineer, he accompanied the flying columns that were sent to clear the country of the rebels, under the command of General Wetherall, and was present at the famous assault which resulted in the capture of the strong fort Kussin Dampoor. During later operations in Oude, 1858-9, he commanded the 4th Company R.E., under General Grant, and took part in the passage of Gofra. He was specially mentioned by Lord Clyde, General Wyndham, and General

Wetherall in their despatches, and included by General Napier in the list of officers deemed deserving of Honourable Mention. He was awarded the Indian Medal and Clasp for Lucknow at the close of the Campaign.

In October 1859 Lieutenant Scratchley was promoted to the rank of Captain, and in January 1860, General Napier offered to make him his Aide-de-camp; but this offer he was compelled to decline, for the reasons explained in his Diary :—

January 13, 1860.—Received a telegram from Brigadier-General Sir Robert Napier, K.C.B., about coming on his staff as A.D.C. Telegraphed back to Gwalior that I could not leave my Company as I commanded it. In fact an A.D.C-ship would have suited me admirably, if I had not been going with the Company.

January 21.—About five miles from Doomree, Brigadier-General Napier and Captain Lumsden came up to the Train. I got out and walked to the Dak Bungalow with them. General Napier was very civil to me. I explained to him about the A.D.C-ship. He seemed to agree with me He spoke very kindly.

Captain Scratchley was much disappointed when he found that his Company was not to go with the expedition under General Napier to China, as his Diary records :—

February 11, 1860.—I received the unpleasant news that the 4th Company has to go to Mauritius; of all places the one I dislike most, when war is going on in China. I wish Napier would give me another chance of going with him.

Lord Napier thus speaks of him in a letter to Mr. Philip Scratchley :—

38 Cornwall Gardens, S.W.: April 13, 1886.

Dear Mr. Scratchley,—I often heard of Peter Scratchley's visits to my mother, who was much attached to Doctor and

Mrs. Scratchley, but did not meet him till he came to Lucknow with his company of sappers for the duties of the siege in 1858.

He acted during the short siege as my orderly officer. He was most punctual and strict in the performance of every duty, and impressed me with the assurance that he would be found thoroughly reliable and trustworthy in the performance of any difficult duty, and I considered him able and clever.

He was very reserved indeed, and apparently severe in disposition.

I believe I must have applied to have him included in the China expedition of 1860, for which he was at first ordered; but a demand for his company was made in another direction, and when I was on my way to Calcutta I passed him on the road with his company of sappers; he was disappointed, but, with characteristic self-control, turned to his new duty without a word of complaint or regret.

I was very greatly pleased to read of his appointment to be the High Commissioner of New Guinea.

The corps and the country have lost a very valuable officer by his untimely death.

Believe me, dear Mr. Scratchley, yours sincerely,

(Signed) NAPIER OF MAGDALA.

About this time (1860) the Government of Victoria applied to the Imperial Government for an officer of Engineers to superintend the erection of defences in that Colony, and Captain Scratchley, then twenty-five years of age, was selected for this important post. He says:—

March 13, 1860.—Received orders thus:—'Captain Scratchley with a detachment, to be taken principally or wholly from the 4th Company, will proceed to Melbourne, Victoria, and report his arrival to the Governor for employment on the Colonial Defences.'

For three years and a half Captain Scratchley was actively employed in devising a system of defence for Victoria, during which period he also took a prominent part in the Volunteer movement, and acted as Honorary Lieutenant-Colonel of the Volunteer Artillery and Engineers. His evidence given before the Royal Local Commission, appointed to report upon the best means of defending the Colony, shows that he had correctly grasped the situation. The works he advised failed to secure the sanction of the Victorian Parliament, owing to a change in the Ministry, and he consequently returned to England at the end of 1863. The following correspondence shows how highly his services to the Colony were appreciated:—

Victoria Volunteer Office: Melbourne, September 18, 1863.

Sir,—I have the honour to express my regret at losing the services of Captain Scratchley, R.E., now under orders for Europe. Captain Scratchley organised and trained the Volunteer Engineers, and has been since 1861, Honorary Lieutenant-Colonel of the Royal Volunteer Artillery. The large portion of his time which Captain Scratchley has given for the benefit of these portions of the Force makes me anxious that his services should be recognised. I desire therefore to place on record my thanks for the valuable assistance he has, as an officer of the garrison, been allowed to give me in connection with the duties of the Force under my command.

(Signed)   W. A. D. Anderson, Colonel-Commandant
of Volunteers.

The Major of Brigade, &c., Melbourne.

Government House: Melbourne, September 24, 1863.

Sir,—I have the honour to request that you will convey to Captain Scratchley, of the Royal Engineers, the thanks of the

Military Department of this Government, for the 'services he has rendered in devising and controlling Works of defence for this colony, and in the establishment of a Colonial Military Store Department.' It will also be very satisfactory to the Government, if you will make known the opinion it entertains of Captain Scratchley's services to His Royal Highness the Field-Marshal Commanding-in-Chief.

(Signed) C. H. DARLING.

Brigadier-General Chute, Commanding H.M. Forces.

Melbourne: September 25, 1863.

SIR,—This letter will be presented by Captain Scratchley, R.E., who is returning to England to rejoin his corps, after carrying out his plan of fortifying Port Philip as far as the Local Government has decided to do so for the present.

It was my intention, had I continued a few days longer in the administration of the Government, to have forwarded, on receiving Captain Scratchley's final report, a full account of the armed system of earthworks he has constructed around the shores of Hobson's Bay, and to that end I had paid them a special visit, but under present circumstances I shall confine myself to stating that in my opinion, and in that of all military men whom I have consulted, they are well devised for mutual support, and as complete and effective as the means placed at his disposal admitted.

I may add, having just returned from Sydney, that notwithstanding the far superior facilities for defence afforded by Port Jackson, Captain Scratchley appears to me to have accomplished for 30,000l. (exclusive of the armament) more than has been effected there with double or triple the expenditure.

The Victorian Ministry have, I understand, requested my successor to communicate to the Imperial authorities the high sense they entertain of the services rendered by Captain Scratchley to the Colony, and I have no doubt Sir Charles Darling has written accordingly; but as I am, of course, better cognizant both of the value of these services and of the many difficulties with which he has had to contend whilst rendering them, I have thought it only proper to write these few lines in support of any recommendation which the Duke of Newcastle may think proper to make to the War Department in his favour.

They will serve at the same time to introduce an officer, who can give His Grace the amplest and most recent information on many questions connected with the Defence of the Colony of Victoria.

(Signed) HENRY BARKLY.

C. Fortescue, Esq., M.P. &c.

War Office: April 22, 1864.

SIR,—I am directed by the Secretary of State for War to transmit to you, for the information of His Royal Highness the Field-Marshal Commanding-in-Chief, the accompanying copy of a letter which has been addressed to the Under Secretary for the Colonies by Sir Henry Barkly, late Governor of Victoria, in which he expressed his sense of the great value of the services rendered by Major Scratchley in the construction of the Fortifications at Hobson's Bay.

(Signed) EDWARD LUGARD.

The Military Secretary, Horse Guards.

Referred to the Deputy Adjutant-General of Royal Engineers, who is informed that H.R. Highness has expressed to the Secretary of State for War, his satisfaction at receiving so favourable a report regarding Captain Scratchley.

(Signed) W. F. F.

Horse Guards: April 29, 1864.

Noted, returned to the Military Secretary, Major Scratchley having been informed of H.R. Highness the Commanding-in-Chief's satisfaction at receiving this report.

(Signed) FRED. E. CHAPMAN, Colonel Deputy Adjutant-General, Royal Engineers.

Horse Guards: April 29, 1864.

In the following year (1864) Captain Scratchley

was promoted to the brevet-rank of Major for his services in India. During the next six months he commanded a Company of Sappers at Portsmouth, but at the end of that period the Government, wishing to secure his services at Headquarters, appointed him Assistant Inspector of Works for the manufacturing department of the War Office under Col. Inglis, R.E. After a short time he became Chief Inspector, which office he held for twelve years. Major Scratchley was in that capacity much associated with Sir Frederick Abel, C.B., F.R.S., the Chemist to the War Department, in a great variety of work. The latter writes of him thus:—

I had not come in contact with Scratchley since he was my pupil at the Royal Military Academy in 1852-4 until he entered upon his duties at Woolwich in 1864. As a Cadet I had found him industrious, but extremely reserved in manner. On renewing my acquaintance with him in 1864 I found that this natural reserve, which had certainly not diminished, led those who only knew him superficially to consider him haughty and almost unsociable. But he was just and considerate to all employed under him, his reserve vanished with the formation of friendships, and those who learned to know him became warmly attached to him. The important and very extensive duties which he had to discharge as the Director of Construction and Engineer officer-in-charge of many important works connected with the War Office manufacturing establishments at Woolwich, Enfield, and Waltham, the School of Gunnery at Shoeburyness, &c., were performed by him with marked ability and success. He was associated with me in several subjects of enquiry of very special nature, such as the disposal of sewage by irrigation in connection with the Government establishment at Enfield, and the elaboration of a system of manufacture of hydrogen gas for balloon-service in the field, and he devoted himself zealously to the acquisition of the special scientific knowledge essential in dealing with such matters.

Colonel Scratchley was the first Officer to avail himself of an arrangement made between the War Office and the Mint for the instruction of Officers of the Royal Engineers in assaying. He spent several months of the year 1875 in the Royal Mint Laboratory, and Professor Chandler Roberts-Austin, the Chemist to the Mint, says, 'he entered upon the work of assaying, which demands the exercise of minute accuracy, with singular zeal and interest, and acquired considerable skill as an assayer.'

In 1874 Major Scratchley was promoted to Lieutenant-Colonel, and in 1876 was selected by Lord Carnarvon, upon the recommendation of the Secretary of State for War, to act in conjunction with General Sir William Jervois [1] in the important work of advising the Australasian Governments upon the best means of defending the Colonies against foreign aggression. In 1878 Sir William Jervois became Governor of South Australia, whereupon Colonel Scratchley was appointed Commissioner of Defences,[2] and remained in Australia until the beginning of 1883, visiting the different Colonies from time to time. The position, although responsible, was one scarcely to be envied, as he was continually harassed by the ever shifting policy of the Colonial Governments. It happened more than once that after he had taken much trouble to prepare a scheme of defence, which was approved by the party in power, the Government went out of office, and the next ministry refused their sanction, unless the estimated cost was reduced. Sometimes fresh plans were

---

[1] Now Governor of New Zealand.
[2] In New South Wales, Victoria, Queensland, Tasmania, and South Australia.

insisted on, and when, after much trouble and delay, these were made, the original scheme was selected. The choice depended upon the caprice of legislators and the ebb and flow of public enthusiasm.

In 1879 Colonel Scratchley was awarded a C.M.G. 'for his valuable services in connection with the Defences of Tasmania,' and was afterwards (1885) made K.C.M.G. for services in Australia. These services are referred to in the following Dispatches:—

Governor Weld to the Earl of Carnarvon.

Tasmania, Government House, Hobart Town: Jan. 19, 1878.

My Lord,—I have the honour to report for Your Lordship's information that His Excellency Sir William Jervois and Lieut.-Colonel Scratchley, R.E. arrived in Tasmania on the 30th ultimo in order to report upon the Defence question.

. . . . . .

I should also be gratified should your Lordship see fit to express in the proper quarter our appreciation of the services of Colonel Scratchley, who whilst here was indefatigable in examining into everything connected with the Defence Department, and who made many valuable suggestions.

I trust that his services may be permanently retained by the Australian Colonies to superintend the carrying out of works recommended by Sir William Jervois.

I have &c.

(Signed) FRED. WELD, Governor.

The Rt. Hon. the Earl of Carnarvon.

Downing Street: March 21, 1878.

Sir,—I am directed by the Secretary of State for the Colonies to transmit to you for the information of the Secretary of State for War a copy of a despatch (No. 1. Jan. 19,

1878) from the Governor of Tasmania respecting the recent visit of Sir W. Jervois, R.E., and Lieutenant-Colonel Scratchley, R.E., to report upon the Defences of the Colony.

I am to call attention to the remarks of the Governor in respect of the services rendered by Colonel Scratchley on this occasion.

I am &c.

(Signed) W. R. MALCOLM.

The Under-Secretary of State, War Office.

Horse Guards, War Office: April 17, 1878.

SIR,—I am directed by the Field-Marshal Commanding-in-Chief, to inform you that a letter has been received from the Colonial Office covering a copy of a despatch from the Governor of Tasmania, respecting the valuable services rendered by you in reporting upon the Defences of that Colony, and to acquaint you that His Royal Highness has been pleased to express his great satisfaction at receiving so favourable a report.

I have &c.

(Signed) J. GRANT,
Deputy Adjutant-General, R.E.

Lieut.-Colonel P. H. Scratchley, R.E., Melbourne.

War Office: April 17, 1878.

SIR,—With reference to your letter of the 21st ult., covering a copy of a despatch from the Governor of Tasmania respecting the valuable services rendered by Major-General Sir W. Jervois, K.C.B., and Lieut.-Colonel Scratchley, R.E., in reporting upon the defences of that Colony, I am directed to acquaint you for the information of the Secretary of State for the Colonies, that both Secretary Colonel Stanley and H.R.H. the Field-Marshal Commanding-in-Chief have expressed their great satisfaction at receiving so favourable a report, and the officers have been informed accordingly.

I have &c.

(Signed) RALPH THOMPSON.

The Under-Secretary of State, Colonial Office.

In 1881 Colonel Scratchley visited Thursday Island at the request of the Imperial authorities. Some details connected with his visit, given in the following letter written to his son Victor, then a boy of eleven years, are interesting :—

R.M.S. Chyebassa, at sea, Nov. 18, 1881.

MY DEAR BOY,—I left Thursday Island yesterday. It was very hot on the second day, because the wind from the southeast, which blows steadily for nine months in the year, had dropped. I spent the day on board a ketch, which is smaller than a schooner. We sailed about for nearly eleven hours, and were very tired on getting home. I wish you had been there, as you would have enjoyed seeing the crew working the sails and ropes. The water was quite calm, and the breeze steady, except toward the evening, when I think it must have taken us two or three hours to go six miles. We had to tack when going against the wind. We had a crew of four men. The ketch had a tonnage of twelve tons. The old man who owned the boat showed us a letter written some forty years ago by a sailor who was the only survivor from a murderous attack made upon the crew of a ship he was in by the natives on the coast of Queensland. It described the attack by the natives, the way they got on board, and by pretending to come to trade, they deceived the captain and crew. They suddenly rose upon them and tomahawked all except this man, who described in the letter how after being wounded he hid himself below. The daughter of the native chief saved him. He lived for some time on their island, then he was rescued. We were also told of the emigrant ship, that was bringing 300 or more Chinese to Victoria in 1858, during the gold fever, which was attacked by a large number of natives in canoes. The ship was captured, and the Chinese taken on shore. They were surrounded by a stockade, and it is believed that the whole of the wretched men were eaten. Each day a few were killed, roasted, and eaten. This was done in the sight of the survivors. One Chinaman escaped; it is supposed that the natives did not think he would be good eating. Of course things are not so bad now, as the natives have been very severely punished after each massacre. At any rate there are no hostile cannibal blacks near Thursday Island. In New Guinea there are some, but that is ninety miles off. I saw at Thursday Island a Malay boat, a proa it is called, in which nine men drifted for 1,000 miles, and were thirty-two days at sea. They only had rice and a few fowls on board. They kept the fowls until the end. Each day they caught rain-water (it was the rainy season) and boiled the rice, *drinking the water only*. They kept on day after day reboiling the rice. When they arrived at Thursday Island they were mere skin and bone, but quickly recovered under kind treatment.

My trip has been very interesting. Near Thursday Island I saw ant-hills on shore six feet high. I wonder whether your books will tell you anything of this. I am told that besides sharks, there are alligators in the sea in certain parts. This is very curious, as I always thought that alligators only lived at the mouth of rivers, or in them. Read and find out about them.

On board our ketch there was a turtle about three feet across. He had been caught the day before. He had just escaped from a shark, which had nearly bitten off one of his— I forget the name for the legs of a turtle. The poor creature is now lying on his back, tied up. He now and then tried to free himself, but being on his back could not. The turtle-soup you used to drink was made in Queensland from turtles. I am told that when the shark wants to attack a turtle he dives below it, turns over, and then rises to make a snap. A shark has to turn on his back to attack people. I was told that sharks are very easily frightened. At the pearl fishery station, near Thursday Island, we were told on our arrival that a poor native swimmer had lost his leg by being bitten by a shark. He had been lying in a barn for twelve days. Our doctor from the ship went on shore and made it all right, giving the native chloroform. The magistrate told me that one day he was out in his cutter sailing, and suddenly felt as if the boat had struck on a rock. They tacked, and found it was a large turtle floating on the top of the sea. They are much given to that sort of thing. The natives in India attack sharks by diving under them and stabbing them. This morning a Chinese boat came off. It was the queerest thing I have seen for a long time. There were five Chinamen, each with an oddly-shaped straw hat on; each had an oar tied to the side of the boat, and a rudder which looked a thousand years old. The sails were quite different from our sails, and the boat was very like the Malay proa I have already told you of. I also saw at Thursday Island a native canoe with *calico* sails. These canoes are made out of trees, the insides being burnt out. On each side of the canoe there is an outrigger very tight, which prevents its upsetting. You will remember your Cingalese canoe.

Good-bye, my dear boy.

    Ever your most affectionate father.

               P. H. S.

I shall be back soon.

In October 1882 Colonel Scratchley was retired from the Army with the rank of Major-General, and upon his return to England, in the early part of 1883, he was appointed Adviser on Defences for New South Wales, Victoria, Queensland, Tasmania, and South Australia, in which capacity he rendered signal service to the Imperial and Colonial authorities in solving many important questions connected with the defence of the Australasian Colonies. However, his services in this respect came to a somewhat abrupt end towards the close of 1884. The Government having at last determined to protect a part of New Guinea, it was necessary to place at the head of affairs a man possessing Colonial experience.

Everything seemed to point to General Scratchley

as the man best qualified to act as her Majesty's representative in this part of the world. His ability for great work had been proved. His popularity in Australia was well known at home, and considering the soreness then existing between the Colonies and the mother-country, owing to the half-hearted policy displayed by the Government regarding the annexation of New Guinea, and the fact that the Colonies were paying the expense, it was very necessary to send out some one whose past career would render him acceptable to the Colonists. The appointment was pressed upon him, and accepted. In November 1884, General Scratchley once more left England to further the interests of his country in another hemisphere.

On the voyage out he was never idle. When not reading or writing he was walking or conversing. In the tropics he was up soon after five and retired early. He ate and drank little, and in every way endeavoured to keep up his physical condition for the work that lay before him. Essentially a family man, he was never so happy as when seeing after the wants of his wife and children. Nor were his attentions entirely given to his kith and kin; strangers in misfortune were to him as brothers. He was particularly kind to one young fellow on board, whom he nursed through a serious illness.

A somewhat remarkable incident on the voyage may be recorded here. On Christmas Eve, the night being perfect and the sea like glass, General Scratchley, seated on the quarter-deck, told his intimates how, in a dream the night before, he saw his friend Charles

Gordon, who appeared to be in great trouble and danger, although for what reason was not apparent. A few weeks later the world heard of the hero's death. Within twelve months it heard of the death of his friend.

Sir Peter Scratchley carefully considered those working under him, and, though strict, was never severe. Still he exacted from his subordinates the amount of work he judged them capable of doing, and refused to recognise an idle man in any way. Though tolerant in his judgment of men, he never forgave dishonesty of purpose, or placed further confidence in any one who had once deceived him. Thorough himself in all his work, he expected thoroughness in others. The maxim ' What is worth doing at all is worth doing well,' was carried out in every detail of his life. Whether it were letters or despatches, if, when written, they did not express what he meant to say, he would write them over and over again, until they appeared to his mind entirely satisfactory. It is not intended to imply by this that he liked entering into minute matters, but his every action exhibited a determination to do well whatever he undertook to perform. This trait is characteristically illustrated in a letter General Scratchley wrote to his brother (the Rev. Charles Scratchley) concerning the latter's sons :—

> It may, I suppose, be said that I have been successful; but whatever success I may have attained I attribute to the circumstance that, whatever I had to do, I have endeavoured to do not only well, but to the very best of my power. Whoever follows this plan will in time attract the attention of his superiors, and get on. Tell this to your sons.

He was also heard to remark on one occasion, 'I hate details, but whenever it is necessary for me to master them, I do.' Curiously enough, this characteristic was also to be found in his friend General Gordon, who not unfrequently altered his tactics and dictated new directions on the eve of a battle. Throughout his career General Scratchley, strong himself, was never unmindful of the weakness of others; yet neither the pressure of circumstances nor the force of temptation had any weight with his sense of justice. He would punish the individual who erred from the path of duty, whether it were public or private, at all hazards, but having once passed judgment, not unfrequently with a sternness approaching almost to severity, he would afterwards encourage the culprit by deeds of kindness and words of advice.

In everything he displayed untiring energy and fixity of purpose. Independent to a degree bordering sometimes on indifference, he would act from experience rather than rule. Tact coupled with fearlessness carried him successfully through many important undertakings, where others more erratic and less bold would have failed. His manner, though at times brusque and offhand, was manly and refined. But his forethought for others was often remarked by those about him. Practical instances of this trait in his character were seen in his personal inspection of the arrangements made for the crew of the ship that took him to New Guinea, and again in his care of a petty officer who was ill from fever. Sir Peter Scratchley personally saw that his wants were attended to, and frequently visited him, and not only sent him in a special steamer to Sydney, but also took much trouble in making arrangements for his comfort upon his arrival there. His interest in the man never flagged, and when ill himself from the same fearful malady, he called his private secretary to his side and asked him to write and tell the officer how sorry he was that he had not shown greater sympathy with him during his severe illness.

The most decrepit native was treated by him with the same amount of kindness that he bestowed on the hale and hearty. Hence it is not a matter of surprise that he won in a very short space of time the confidence and love of the natives of New Guinea. 'Alas for New Guinea!' said Mr. Lawes,[1] when he heard of Sir Peter's premature death; 'she has indeed lost a true friend and father.'

Mr. Chalmers thus writes: 'The General was a grand man; I loved and trusted him. Poor New Guinea has lost a true and loyal friend, and one in whose hands native interests were safe. The General did too much hard mental and physical work.' An instance of his kindness to the native children was shown when one day some fishing canoes came alongside the *Governor Blackall*. A little girl, between five and six years old, seated in one of them, attracted his attention. He sent one of the crew to bring her on board, and himself presented her with beads and a looking-glass—gifts which greatly pleased the little thing, and caused much chatter about the new arrival that night in the native village.

---

[1] The Revs. W. J. Lawes and J. Chalmers are the Heads of the London Mission in New Guinea.

Other instances of Sir Peter's kind treatment of the natives will be found recorded in the part of this book devoted to his work in New Guinea. Suffice it to say here, that by the exercise of tact and judgment coupled with generosity and kindness, Sir Peter sowed seeds of friendship for white men in the hearts of those who formerly feared and hated them.

This life, so devoted to duty, was destined to be closed prematurely by jungle fever, contracted in New Guinea; the same deadly form of disease to which, early in this century, his maternal grandfather, Captain Roberts, Commandant of Colombo, had fallen a victim in the jungles of Ceylon.

Sir Peter Scratchley died at sea on December 2, 1885. The greatest sorrow was expressed throughout Australia at his untimely death. His body was conveyed to Melbourne and there received the honour of a public funeral, which was attended by delegates from the other Australasian colonies. The body was afterwards brought to England and interred in Old Charlton Cemetery.

AUSTRALIAN DEFENCES.

CHAPTER I.

GENERAL DEFENCE.

THE Australasian Colonies are favourably situated for defence against foreign aggression, and no hostile power is likely to incur the expense, or run the risks involved, in sending out an expedition for the purpose of gaining a permanent footing in that part of the world. At the same time it is extremely unwise to disregard the possibility of such an attempt being made, more especially in the event of the mother country being unable to render any assistance. The Colonies should therefore look the question fairly in the face, and in any event be prepared to protect themselves. 'No one who is acquainted with Australia,' said Sir Peter Scratchley, ' can deny that it possesses the best material for establishing, in an economical manner, a sound system of self-defence, and should the Colonies delay the adoption of ordinary precautions, they will remain exposed to the risk of a successful raid by a well-armed cruiser, which would be productive of the most serious consequences.'[1]

He considered that the influence which torpedoes, especially of the offensive class, must have upon all

[1] This opinion was expressed before the present schemes of defence were adopted.

defensive arrangements in the future was scarcely appreciated in Australia. 'It is admitted,' he said one day, when addressing a technical audience on the subject, 'that their introduction simplifies and reduces the cost of coast defence to a very large extent; but it is not generally recognised that offensive torpedoes may be brought to such a high degree of perfection as to render it necessary to abandon the construction of ironclads, and resort to unsinkable unarmoured ships of great speed and heavy armament. Until this point is reached, however, defensive torpedoes must be the main element of protection, wherever the question of cost is of paramount importance; but at the same time it is to be distinctly understood that no scheme of coast defence by torpedoes, whether offensive or defensive, can be considered complete, unless the torpedoes are supported and protected by guns and a land force. A good system of submarine mines is a paramount necessity for an efficient defence, and nothing must be allowed to stand in the way of establishing and maintaining in Australia the requisite organisation in as complete a manner as possible, as without torpedoes [1] a reliable defence of the Australian Colonies cannot be carried out.'

The Russians employed torpedoes during the Crimean war for the defence of their ports in the Baltic, but without success. The Confederate States of America, however, used them to some purpose, and their employment had a marked influence upon the naval opera-

---

[1] The employment of torpedoes in the scheme for Port Jackson enables New South Wales to depend upon a single or outer line of defence instead of two lines. See p. 151.

tions of the Northerners during the latter part of the War of Secession. From that time up to the present, the attention of every European nation, and also of the United States of America, has been directed to the subject. Great Britain, possessing special facilities and experience in the manufacture of electrical cables, explosives, and other appliances for submarine defences, soon took the lead in this as in other branches of defensive warfare; but foreign Powers rapidly began to show equal activity in the matter, and now there is scarcely a foreign port of any importance which, in time of war, would not be found well protected by means of torpedoes.[1]

In planning any complete system of Australasian defence the external or naval defence for the protection of commerce must not be overlooked. As a matter of economy, Sir Peter Scratchley considered that small armaments of the heaviest guns,[2] both on land and sea, should be adopted, as only a moderate force is necessary to secure their efficient working. 'Any country,' he said, 'that selects the heaviest guns, the most powerful armoured forts, and the most perfect system of defensive and offensive torpedoes on the smallest scale, secures at once for itself an undoubted superiority for very many years to come, and avoids the constantly recurring expense of making changes in order to keep up with the times.' The main object in view when planning the defence of a port is to prevent an enemy's ships from entering, hence the first line

[1] For further information on this subject, see chapter on *Torpedo Defence*.
[2] An instance of this policy is to be found in the adoption by the Italian Government of 100-ton guns for their navy.

of defence should naturally be established as near the entrance as possible. For this purpose the natural configuration of the land in the Australasian Colonies is favourable.

Several persons think that to secure a really reliable defence, Australia should depend entirely upon a permanent force. Sir Peter Scratchley believed that this was a wrong view, and, being satisfied from what he had seen of Volunteers in England as well as in Australia, encouraged everything that tended to promote the efficiency of a Volunteer force in the Colonies.[1]

'Knowledge and experience,' he remarked at a Colonial inspection of Volunteers, ' are more than ever the moving springs of all naval and military operations, and the Australian Governments should not delay in establishing proper schools of instruction. A still greater necessity for this step exists in consequence of the local forces in Australia being almost entirely composed of Volunteers. Further efforts should also be made to train every officer in the theory as well as the practice of his duties, while facilities ought to be afforded to the non-commissioned officers and men to gain similar knowledge. All exercises should be conducted exactly as they would have to be put into practice in time of war, and should be rehearsed as frequently as possible upon the actual ground to be occupied to resist an attack, in order that every officer and soldier may know his exact place and what is expected of him, and in this manner only can the inherent defects of a Volunteer organisation be counteracted.'

[1] For further information on this subject see pp. 107-9.

Now as to the modes of attack to which the Australasian Colonies are exposed. They may be briefly summarised thus: An enemy might—

(i.) Despatch one or more cruisers to make a descent upon the coast, or operate against her commerce. A squadron intended for such an operation would probably consist of three or four vessels, one or two of which might possibly be ironclads. These vessels, eluding our cruisers, and appearing suddenly before one of the capitals or chief towns, might capture the merchant ships lying in the harbour, intercept any of the numerous ships conveying gold and colonial produce, or, under threat of bombardment, demand a payment of many millions of money. Supplies of coal might be procured from any unprotected coal depôt.

(ii.) Endeavour to force his way into a port, or blockade the entrance.

(iii.) Attempt to capture the batteries with a view to permanent occupation, or land a force with the object of meeting the local troops assembled to arrest his advance.

(iv.) Attempt to bombard an exposed town from the open sea.

These attacks Sir Peter Scratchley considered could *only* be provided against by a combination of military and naval defences.[1]

The schemes of defence set forth in the following pages, for the several Australasian Colonies, were based upon the suppositions:—

---

[1] Sir Peter Scratchley adopted the data thus laid down in his recommendations for the defences of New Zealand, so far as the fortification of the principal harbours was concerned.

That there was no probability of an expedition on any extensive scale being despatched against Australia, so long as Great Britain retained command of the seas.

That, in the event of Great Britain being engaged in hostilities with any great maritime Power, a sufficient watch would be kept by the Imperial Navy, to intercept, or follow up, an expedition directed against Australia.

The schemes aim at fortifying the principal harbours and approaches to the capitals by batteries and torpedo defences, provide field forces where required to resist a landing of the enemy, and recommend armed vessels (in some cases armoured) and torpedo launches, not only for the general defence of the towns on the sea coast, but also for the protection of local commerce, and as a provision against bombardment.

Notwithstanding the soundness of these views, General Scratchley found people in Australia who either did not believe in the necessity for any defence whatever, or who proposed to throw the burden upon the mother country. The number of persons holding these opinions is, however, rapidly diminishing. Again, he met individuals who, being in favour of a policy of inaction, advocated submission to the enemy with the view of buying him off, expecting that their losses would be made good out of the indemnity they assumed the mother country would be able to extort from the defeated enemy.

In fact, in the course of duty, he came across an extraordinary diversity of opinion on the subject. This is greatly to be regretted, because it leads to half-hearted measures, frequent changes in military policy, and in the long run prevents the question of defence being dealt with in a thorough, comprehensive, consistent and businesslike manner. Economists, he observed, oppose a large expenditure on defences, and prefer to run a certain risk and a possible disaster, involving the loss of enormous sums of money if the enemy were successful, rather than face the difficulty in good time, and, by incurring the necessary expenditure, effect what may fairly be looked upon as an insurance upon the property of the country. This may without impropriety be designated 'the penny wise and pound foolish' policy, a policy that leaves to chance what should be carefully planned beforehand, and which can only result in disgrace and disaster.

Some people in Australia think the Colonies would be unable to hold their own against a determined enemy; an impression that gained ground, no doubt, owing to the incomplete and desultory character of former [1] defence preparations. This belief, however, is fast disappearing now that the Colonial Governments have determined to follow the advice given at their request by the highest authorities. Others say that Australia is not worth attacking; while a few are of opinion that the colonies cannot afford the expense of self-defence, and therefore it would be better to separate from the mother country, rather than remain liable to attack whenever Great Britain may be at war with a foreign Power. The first argument may be dismissed at once as absurd. The second apparently seems more

[1] Preparations made before 1877.

feasible; but recent events show that the friendly relations between the mother country and her colonies are fast becoming closer and closer, and that therefore any plan of defence involving separation would now meet with little or no support.

Sir Frederick Weld,[1] speaking at Launceston some years ago upon 'The Relation between England and her Colonies, and their Duties in reference to Defence,' referred to these points as follows:

England will no doubt defend us, but it is impossible that her fleets should be everywhere, and you cannot expect her single unarmoured ships of no great size to lie in ports where they would not be assisted in case of need by batteries, and might be caught in a trap by a superior force. Were such a ship, for instance, lying at Hobart Town, and were there reason to suspect a probable visit from a more powerful enemy, it would be clearly her duty to put out to sea, where she could escape, or manœuvre, unless there existed a local system of defence with which to co-operate. It must also be remembered that it may often be the duty of a naval commander to keep his force well in hand, ready to direct it on any point that might be threatened, or himself to attack an enemy, for offensive operations are often the best defence. I think that it may be reasonably expected that in a war England would be able to prevent any powerful expedition being directed against the colonies. Such an expedition could not be fitted out and get to sea secretly; it would probably never get to sea at all; and if it did, it would almost certainly be taken or destroyed. I doubt not also but that England would take vigorous measures, by the employment of swift cruisers, to protect commerce and to capture hostile cruisers or privateers; indeed, we already hear that she is prepared to do so; but the seas are wide, and even in the old days of sailing vessels, at the end of last century and

---

[1] Sir Frederick A. Weld, K.C.M.G., was then Governor of Tasmania. He is now Governor of the Straits Settlements.

beginning of this, when we had clouds of cruisers and privateers of our own on the seas, we never did absolutely succeed in clearing them of small hostile cruisers and privateers, though we did clear them of hostile fleets. We must not forget Paul Jones; and we all remember how much injury the *Alabama* inflicted upon the commerce of the Northern States before she was met and captured, though several vessels were solely occupied in her pursuit; therefore I do think that it is probable that some vessels of that class, for which telegrams tell us a national subscription is now being raised in Russia, may succeed in eluding English cruisers for a while, and may attack and levy subsidies upon, or, in default, plunder, British settlements that are not ready to resist them.

Are we worth attacking? The bullion in the banks would be a rich prize, as has been noted in Russian newspapers, which have lately published the colonial bank returns; but the bullion in the banks would by no means be necessarily the measure of the subsidy required—the measure of the ransom would be the measure of the strong man's cupidity and the defenceless man's fear. Moreover, the destruction of shipping and of stores, the interruption of commerce, the collapse of public works and of public and private credit, would only be remedied by time and by the imposition of heavy taxation. I once asked an eminent merchant what he would do under the circumstances; and he said, 'Well, it might happen, and, if it did, I think I should arrange my affairs as well as I could, and move off to safer quarters.' I said, 'Would it not be wiser to pay a small insurance in the form of defence, and make things safe?' Remember, too, that to pay subsidies and ransoms is the surest way to invite future visits. It is a policy as fallacious as it is disgraceful; it has ever had the same result; it is like offering a premium for robbery. And further, bear in mind that, having once bought experience, people would raise an outcry for defence—for locking the door after the purse was stolen, and very little left wherewith to buy a lock.

This remarkable address, coming from an old New

Zealand colonist, who had become acquainted with the subject in its different aspects,[1] attracted much attention at the time. It is worthy the consideration of all who take an interest in the question of Australasian defence.

When the annual expenditure of a country has to be reduced, the attention of its rulers is but too often directed to retrenchment in the military expenditure. 'In Australia, in times of peace, with no immediate danger, and with so many persons indifferent to the subject of defence, no hesitation is shown in making the reduction.' The military engineer, therefore, in devising a scheme of defence for the Australasian Colonies, has to consider the cost fully as much as the requirements. ' His function,' said Sir Peter Scratchley, 'is not only to study the resources and necessities of the country to be defended, but also to ascertain from the Government the amount that can be fairly expended for establishing and maintaining a system of defence. In other words, he must cut his coat according to his cloth. The problem presented to the military engineer is how to establish and maintain a reliable defence, organised with the resources available for the purpose, at the lowest possible cost.'

It has been stated that the military engineer has little or nothing to do with the expenditure, and that his duty should be confined to advising what is requisite for an efficient defence. Sir Peter thought the process should be reversed, and that the Australasian Parliaments should severally decide what annual expenditure each colony could afford for defence purposes for a term of

[1] In his capacities of colonist, Colonial Minister and Governor.

years, and agree to have peace and war establishments for the defence forces, together with reserves which can be embodied in time of war. The hand-to-mouth policy which unfortunately prevailed for so long a time was the natural outcome of dealing with the defence question from year to year, and he considered it unreasonable to expect satisfactory results, unless some security was offered that a fair trial would be given to any approved scheme. The military authorities of the Colonies ought not to lose sight of the fact that they are providing for a defence organisation different from that of any other country, inasmuch as it may never necessarily have to bear the test of war. They should carefully consider the peace arrangements as much as the war requirements. 'Once,' said General Scratchley, 'the necessary defensive measures represented by the capital expenditure have been provided, they must endeavour to arrange for their maintenance with local means which are readily available. But whether the defensive arrangements are on a large or small scale, the details must be entirely planned or marked out during peace, and nothing must be left to chance, for in proportion to the degree of preparation in time of peace, will be the power of efficient defence in case of war.'

The tendency of English-speaking races is to disregard this maxim, and place too much reliance upon pluck and readiness of resource. The secret of German superiority in recent times is without doubt to be found in their recognition of this axiom. A lavish and needless expenditure will invariably result from neglect of preparation. Indeed too much stress cannot be laid upon this aspect of the question, and if this advice is followed, there will probably be no recurrence of that uneasiness which of late years has so frequently alarmed the Australasian Colonies, whenever there is a chance of England being engaged in a European war.

General Scratchley considered the true value of fortification was not understood in Australia. Speaking on the subject he said: 'Fortification is unquestionably the most economical way of securing a place from attack. It enables the defenders to utilise their defensive powers in the most effective manner. It leads to direct economy, not only in the first cost, but in the maintenance of the defences. Where fortification is not resorted to, a very large expenditure has to be incurred in the provision of floating defences, and in the maintenance of naval and military forces. This heavy expenditure goes on from year to year, without adding to the defensive power of the country. On the other hand, with fortification, once the first cost has been incurred, the annual cost of maintenance is insignificant, and the defensive resources are ever present and immediately available.'

One of the objects of acting on the defensive is to gain time. Addressing the Queensland Volunteers on this point, he observed that field fortification was a means to this end, and that as Australia will be more or less unprepared, everything that may tend to retard the operations of the enemy by sea or land will be so much gain. 'At the same time,' he said, 'the maxim that the attack is often the best defence must never be lost sight of, and field defences must invariably be so planned as to admit of the free movement of the defenders, and nothing must be allowed to stand in the way of their being able to assume the offensive at the right moment. Fortified positions may be strong independent points of support in the rear of a force, to secure its communications; or strong self-contained defensive positions upon the line of the enemy's advance, in which the defenders would await his attack; or, again, in which an over-matched or defeated force may continue a resistance no longer possible in the open field. There is much for Australia to learn from recent wars, and especially from the last Russo-Turkish War. General Valentine Baker, who commanded a Turkish force in Bulgaria, remarked that

> the extraordinary value of a system of shelter trenches or light field fortifications was constantly exemplified during the war. I never once during the campaign saw a position which had been lightly fortified in this manner taken by a front attack by either one side or the other. The moment the Turkish soldier moved into a position near the enemy, even if it were possible that he might only remain in that position for one day, the pack-horses carrying the shovels and pickaxes were immediately brought to the front, and there and then each battalion entrenched itself; with this result, that if a Turkish army advanced, it left behind it a succession of entrenched positions on which to fall back in case of a reverse. The system of shelter trenches adopted by the Turkish army varied as they gained experience. It was singular to note the extraordinarily small loss suffered by the men, even if exposed for hours to a continuous and heavy fire of artillery. The same system was used for guns with an equally good effect, and gun-pits sunk almost to the level of the earth were found to be most practically useful.

If a soldier is taught to throw up shelter trenches wherever he rests, and consequently to leave those trenches for more forward positions as opportunity offers, there is no falling off in his willingness to attack. It is true that, conscious as he will be of the value which he himself derives from entrenchments, he may hesitate to attack with vigour positions so entrenched; but, in my opinion, his reasoning is both just and natural and commanders, who in the future urge their men forward to frontal attacks upon previously prepared and entrenched positions, simply court disaster and defeat.

'Positions are generally open to turning movements. This is a point which engineers must not lose sight of in planning the fortification of positions between Sydney and Broken Bay, as well as other points on the coast.'

'The infantry must be capable of doing every kind of work required for its own security without relying on the engineers, who will have to devote their time to fortifying the key points of a position. The infantry will have to construct rifle-pits, trenches for compact bodies of troops to fire from, and trenches intended for shelter only.'

'The construction of gun-pits will fall upon the field artillery. All this points to the necessity of imparting instruction to the artillery and infantry in field defences. By first training the engineers carefully to a thorough knowledge of the work, there would be no difficulty in carrying out such a course of instruction. This opens out another very important question as to the arrangements for supplying the infantry with tools. This can be done by adopting the pack-horse, a mode of transport with which Australians are well acquainted. After deciding upon the general plan of defence the salient points should be the first to be fortified, and, in making the necessary connections between these points, the main object should be to obtain a certain amount of immediate cover for the infantry and artillery, this cover being afterwards improved should time be available.'

'As regards obstacles, they may be used either in conjunction with defensive works, or in the open field to stop an advance or to increase the difficulties of a night attack. In Australia, where the country is much wooded and long ranges cannot in consequence be secured, and the enemy has only a short distance to pass over under fire, obstacles are especially valuable. They will perform their part if only they retard the progress of the enemy's advance and break up his formations. Natural features of the ground can be readily converted into serious obstacles by cutting wet ditches, making deep cuts and holes in shallow water, and rendering steep places precipitous. *Abattis* formed of limbs of trees laid close together are particularly suited to the Australian bush. Entanglements made with wire and placed in front of the ditches of a redoubt, or where the rapid advance of the enemy must be checked, can be employed to a very large extent. They require little skill, and can be very expeditiously constructed. Ordinary post and rail fences would also be found to be very useful obstructions. Palisades, *trous-de-loup*, or pits with stakes at the bottom, barricades, fougasses, and especially mechanical mines for very important points, should be introduced in the field defences. The mere knowledge of the fact that carefully fortified positions had been selected to resist his progress, would render it most improbable that an enemy would attempt to land; but to gain this degree of preparation no line should be lost. The roads, tracks, and country generally over which the enemy may be expected to advance, must be carefully reconnoitred and studied.'

'Plans giving the fullest detailed information are essential. When these plans are issued, officers of the several arms should be invited to reconnoitre roads and tracks, to study the ground, and submit projects of attack and defence for the consideration of the commander, who would then issue his instructions to his officers selected to prepare the positions, whenever war was declared.'

In organising a system of the defence for a country, care must be taken so to combine the several parts as to produce a complete and harmonious whole. This is what Sir Peter Scratchley did when he came to the conclusion that the best scheme of defence for the Australasian Colonies was one including the following defensive elements in due relation to each other:

On Land.

1. Defensive works.
2. Guns.
3. Torpedoes—defensive or stationary, offensive or locomotive.
4. Obstructions—passive and active.
5. Military forces—cavalry, artillery, engineers, torpedo men, and infantry.

At Sea and Afloat.

6. Floating Defences
 - Defensive
   - Armoured—Floating batteries.
   - Unarmoured—Gun-boats.
 - Offensive
   - Armoured—Ironclad vessels.
   - Unarmoured—Swift cruisers, torpedo-boats.

The first step aimed at was to devise a means of protection against the minor attacks of cruisers, by the employment of defensive and offensive torpedoes, in combination with guns on land and gunboats armed with heavy guns. At the same time he advocated that more powerful defensive works at sea should be begun, and arrangements for repelling a landing in force organised. As great difficulty would be experienced in maintaining a large force of trained gunners without incurring a very heavy expenditure, he considered that the defensive works should be designed on the smallest scale compatible with efficiency and so as to include modern improvements. The guns required for the protection of the submarine mines should be mounted in inexpensive works, but those intended to check and beat off vessels attempting to force a passage should be protected so as not to be silenced by the enemy's fire.

Leading public men in the Australasian Colonies have given much consideration to the question of defence, and there can be no doubt that, if aided in the future as they have been in the past by the advice of competent Imperial officers, they will be able to arrive at a satisfactory conclusion as to the proper measures to be adopted in each case. The system of defence advocated 'does not involve any large expenditure of money without adequate results; and there are no real impediments which cannot be readily overcome, provided the Colonial Governments approach the subject in a broad and liberal spirit.' Considering, however, the difference of opinion which exists, even among acknowledged authorities, as to the relative merits and importance of each element of a complete system of defence under various circumstances, Sir Peter considered it preferable to start from a common basis, and leave the decision to the officers entrusted with the duty of advising.

In some instances, he acknowledged, it would not be practicable to provide the several elements in the order advocated. For example, 'where the channel to be defended is narrow and well defined, with suitable sites for guns, it would be preferable to establish a system of submarine defence, combined with the heaviest armament on land, to the exclusion of unarmoured gunboats; while on the other hand, if the channel is broad and a large expanse of water has to be protected, the best combination would be to employ heavily armed gun-boats to support the submarine defences, with torpedo vessels as auxiliaries. Again, as in the case of Port Phillip, where the channels are broad and numerous, and there are other points besides the entrance to be defended, no doubt a turret-ship, and one or more gun-boats with torpedo vessels, will be considered to be most advantageous. In every case, however, such of the elements of defence as are omitted for the present may be added in future years, when the power and efficiency of the defences will be increased in proportion as each element is added; while, long before the full development is reached, the defensive arrangements will be sufficient to repel any attack that may reasonably be expected for many years to come.'

Lastly, General Scratchley wished the Colonies to bear in mind that although they cannot afford to be satisfied with the best of existing defensive appliances, yet, by the exercise of foresight and enterprise, they must endeavour to reduce within the narrowest limits the constantly recurring expense of keeping pace with the improvements in naval and military science.

CHAPTER II.

NAVAL DEFENCE.

'Every complete scheme of coast defence consists of two parts, which must be combined to produce the best results.' The Australasian Colonies are fortunately situated in respect of the first part, that of acting on the offensive in the open sea, as it is practically undertaken by the mother-country; while their own interests should naturally induce them to provide the other, or defensive part, themselves. With regard to this latter step, Sir Peter Scratchley considered that each Colony should undertake the entire charge and responsibility of its own defensive arrangements, and so lessen the difficulties surrounding the Imperial Government in providing adequate protection for Australasian commerce in time of war, and increase the chances of effective assistance being afforded to the Colonies by the mother-country, in the event of their being attacked. 'According to the completeness and thoroughness of the defensive measures adopted will the naval supremacy of the British Empire be strengthened, and the Australasian Colonies themselves directly benefited, as increased freedom and power will thus be afforded to the Royal Navy, for encountering any hostile expedition that may be despatched against them.'

It is evident that the efficiency of the Australian squadron would be seriously impaired if it were liable to be called upon to render assistance to individual Colonies. This squadron has too extended a sphere of action to do more than cruise in search of hostile ships and afford general protection to Australasian commerce, although it would appear, if the Admiral 'received reliable information of any intended attack, it would be his duty to render assistance so long as he did not impair the efficiency of his force in carrying out the main objects for which it is provided by the mother-country.' Here it may be pointed out that Sir Peter deemed it 'imperative that the instructions given to the officer in charge of the squadron should be in specific terms, and well understood by the Australasian Governments, so as to ensure combined action and avoid misunderstanding from the fact of the responsibilities undertaken by the mother-country and her Colonial dependencies, respectively, not being clearly defined.'

Although Sir Peter Scratchley looked upon the progress made in the military defences of the Australasian Colonies as highly satisfactory, he considered that much remained to be done in the matter of their naval defences. In his opinion the several Governments should combine and establish one general scheme of naval defence, to be worked in conjunction with the Imperial Navy.

Admiral Tryon has lately been endeavouring to bring about a combination of this kind, but the difficulty of cost has hitherto proved insurmountable. Not long since the Governors of the Australasian Colonies addressed to Mr. Edward Stanhope, then Colonial Secretary of State, a joint telegraphic message requesting information as to what steps the Admiralty proposed to take for strengthening the naval defences of the Australian station, in the event of England being involved in a European war.

The Colonial Governments and the Admiralty, although united as to the necessity of augmenting the permanent naval forces in Australian waters, are unable to agree upon the apportionment of the cost; and, even if this question were satisfactorily adjusted, probably two years would elapse before the new vessels required could be constructed and sent out. Meanwhile the Colonial Governments are of opinion that it is a matter of urgency that the Australian naval squadron should be strengthened, in view of their being suddenly called upon to protect the merchant shipping. Under the present system the Australasian Colonies must necessarily be in time of war a source of weakness and anxiety to the mother-country, whereas if the several Colonies acting together were to combine with Great Britain in keeping up a joint system of naval defence, the combination would directly strengthen the defensive power of the Empire, and go far to assuage the present uneasiness that exists in Australia.

'Whenever there has been a chance of Great Britain being involved in war with a naval power, the Australasian Colonies have hitherto taken alarm, and expense has often been incurred on defensive measures which would be inefficient if war had actually taken place.'

The feeling of alarm, however, ceases when war no longer appears imminent, and the question of defence fails once more to occupy a prominent position in Australasian politics.

Opinions differ as to the nature of the attacks to which the Australasian Colonies are exposed; but at the same time both naval and military authorities concur as to the absolute necessity of fortifying the harbours of the capitals, together with such other ports and coal depôts as may afford places of refuge and shelter in case of need.

Sir William Jervois deemed it necessary that the Colonies should be prepared to resist the attack of a squadron composed of three or four vessels, one or two of which might be ironclads, and capable of landing a force of about 1,200 men. In this opinion Sir Peter Scratchley entirely concurred. Sir William thus remarks upon the nature and degree of attack to which the Australasian Colonies might be subjected:

> In the event of Great Britain being engaged in hostilities with any great maritime Power, the enemy would retain the most powerful portion of his fleet in European waters, or in the Atlantic, for the protection of his country or for operations in the immediate neighbourhood of hostilities. If he sent his fleet, or any considerable portion of it, on an expedition against the Australian Colonies, a sufficient part of our Home fleet would in turn be set free to intercept it, and our squadrons in the Pacific, on the China, the Australian, and Indian stations, might, if necessary, be concentrated to oppose it.
>
> But whilst the bulk of the enemy's naval forces would be occupied in the immediate scene of action in Europe or America, he might no doubt despatch one or more cruisers to operate against our maritime commerce, or make a descent upon any of

our colonial possessions; and the Australian Colonies, owing to their wealth and prosperity, would, if undefended at certain points, be tempting objects of attack.

A squadron intended for such an operation might consist of some three or four vessels, one or two of which would probably be armoured, and might issue from the Russian ports of Vladivostok or Petropaulovski, from the French port of Saigon, from San Francisco, or from some other quarter. Eluding our cruisers, and appearing suddenly before Sydney, Melbourne, Adelaide, or in Moreton Bay, it might capture the merchant vessels lying in the harbours, intercept any of the numerous vessels conveying valuable shipments of gold, or under threat of bombardment, or after actually firing into one of the large towns, demand and obtain a payment of many millions of money.

Or this object might possibly be attained by an enemy landing a small force in the vicinity of one of the places named, if the configuration of the country were favourable to such a plan, and if steps were not taken to prevent it.

Admiral Wilson states that the defence question must be considered ' under the supposition that England retains her command of the seas, for were she to lose it, as a matter of course the Colonies would go too; and the defence and force required to maintain independence of a foreign Power would necessarily be totally different from what, under present conditions, is required.'

It has been suggested as possible that during war a squadron of fast frigates, including even an ironclad, might escape the vigilance of our fleet and make a descent on the Australian coast. There is no doubt that such is *possible*, but I cannot allow that it is reasonably probable, and it appears to me that we have to deal with probabilities more than possibilities.

But to examine this branch of the subject, it must be remembered that, in these days of steam and telegraphic communication, the *locale* of every war ship in the world is known, and that, as a matter of fact, the moment war is declared, each and every ship of any power would be watched by our cruisers. Still there is the possibility of enemies' ships evading our vessels, or we may be beaten in action, and so leave them uncontrolled, but even then it is by no means clear that they could or would make an attempt at attack.

My reason for arriving at this conclusion is that no war ship has yet been built which can steam 2,500 miles at full speed, except some light steel vessels, and it is but reasonable to conclude that enemies' vessels attacking these Colonies could only hope for success by dealing a sharp unexpected blow, therefore speed is an essential element in the calculation.

Another point is that, although coal is abundant in Australia, no judicious commander would attempt such an expedition as we are now contemplating on the chance of picking up a coal ship at sea, or of being able to get it by capture from the shore. Thus we find that a war ship could not, with a reasonable hope of success, make a descent on an enemy's coast at a greater distance from a coal depôt than is represented by (say) two-thirds of her full speed coal power.

If my hypothesis be correct, an examination of the chart will show that there are few places within the limits prescribed from which cruisers could be sent. The three nearest possible enemies' ports, belonging to first-rate Powers, from which ships of war could be despatched, are—

Petropaulovski, distant from Melbourne		.	5,900 miles
San Francisco	,, ,,	.	6,800 ,,
New Caledonia	,, ,,	.	1,550 ,,

The last-named place need hardly be included, as no armament of any strength could be prepared or assembled there without the knowledge of the Colonies.

It might be argued that war ships would be preceded by coal ships, and replenish at one of the numerous islands in the Pacific; but against such a premise must be set the delay it would entail, and the amount of arrangement and preparation, which would seriously diminish the chances of the attacking force, while it would give ample time for places likely to be the scene of attack to prepare. There are, it is true, some coaling depôts amongst the Western Pacific Islands belonging to Germans and Americans; but as these are quite unprotected by batteries, and would at once be destroyed by the regular navy in the event of war being declared by or with the nations to which they belong, they cannot be looked upon as depôts for war purposes.

He concludes by observing that the probable class of vessels to be expected in time of war, and which the Colonies should be prepared to meet, are armed merchant vessels, possessing great speed and coal vitality. Such vessels, if well commanded, might do immeasurable damage both to shipping and exposed ports, and could more easily evade the watchful eye of our cruisers and consuls abroad, while from their coal capacity they might be fitted out at remote ports, and pass unobserved, disguised as traders, over half the world.

General Scratchley admitted the force of Admiral Wilson's arguments, but refused to accept his conclusions. 'Were such recommendations to be adopted, uncertainty and risk would be introduced in the defence preparations of the Australasian Colonies.' He was, however, entirely in favour of providing defences capable of securing the principal ports of Australia against the more formidable attacks contemplated.

Admiral Hoskins,[1] although doubtful as to the practicability of ironclads attacking Australia, believes in the possibility of a sudden raid by a flying squadron

---

[1] Admiral Hoskins was Admiral Wilson's predecessor in command of the Australian squadron.

capable of landing a force of over 1,000 men. He insists upon the necessity of fortifying all important points in Australia, in order that the navy may be free to operate at sea in the best manner possible for the general defence of the Colonies. In his opinion the Imperial squadron could not undertake the defence of any Australian port, and each Colony should defend its own harbours.[1]

These officers agree that the defences of Australia must be planned on the assumption that Great Britain retains command of the seas. 'If this should not be the case,' General Scratchley admitted, ' a larger expenditure will have to be incurred by the Colonies, and the present defence arrangements somewhat modified.' This assumption, however, is not universally accepted. Some advocate preparations ' on a scale sufficient to repel large expeditions, which would be undertaken with a view of destroying Australasian commerce and of occupying portions of the Australian continent.' They insist upon the necessity of the Australasian Colonies being prepared to fight an enemy single-handed, and argue that the contingency of the mother-country being at war with several foreign Powers, whose combined navies would keep the Imperial navy fully employed in Europe and elsewhere, is within the bounds of possibility, if not probability.

Admiral Wilson, acting upon his estimate of the danger to be apprehended, condemned the defence measures recommended by Sir William Jervois and Sir Peter Scratchley in the following terms:

[1] For Admiral Hoskins' own words on this subject, see p. 70.

It appears to be useless to advocate a system which, though it may be perfect from a military point of view, is too expensive either to be adopted, or, if adopted, to be kept up in a state of efficiency.

Again :

It is, to my mind, in a combination of the two (fortifications and ships) security will be found; but where money is limited —as it is in new countries, and where the attacking force can never, so long as we hold the seas, be anything more than one or two armed merchant vessels—expensive fortifications, such as are being constructed at enormous cost throughout these Colonies, absorbing all the money available for defensive purposes, I contend are out of place.

Sir Peter Scratchley considered that opinions so strongly expressed, whether supported or not by sufficient arguments, would have a prejudicial effect upon public opinion in Australia, and raise a doubt in the minds of the Colonial Governments. They are opinions from which he entirely dissented. Looking at the wealth, the revenue, and the resources of the Australasian Colonies, he was of opinion that the expenditure proposed for the establishment and maintenance of the defences was not more than these flourishing communities could afford to pay in return for security against attack, although he frankly admitted that there was ample room for economy in the matter of organisation.[1]

Although Admiral Wilson objected to the expenditure on fortifications, he recognised the necessity for them in the case of such places as Sydney, Glenelg (Adelaide), Brisbane, Auckland, Wellington, and Hobart,

---

[1] It should be noted too that the expenditure for the defence schemes was approved by majorities in the several Legislatures.

as 'fortified places are important as ports of refuge, and as stations for coaling.' Admiral Hoskins has laid down very clearly that, on such a wide and extended station as the Australian Colonies, no place is safe from an isolated attack which is not properly fortified and protected by its own local defences, thus practically indorsing Sir Peter Scratchley's recommendations, so far as they concern the defence of the principal Australasian harbours.

The important question of maintaining fortified coal depôts at Thursday Island, King George Sound, Fiji, and elsewhere, is not yet settled. It has been suggested to construct earthworks[1] at these places when war is imminent, and for this purpose to maintain at Sydney a reserve of two hundred marines. Sir Peter Scratchley, however, feared that extemporised defences of this character would be of no value whatever when the distances between the places to be suddenly defended were taken into account and the small number of men to carry out the preparations was considered. He strongly advocated the necessity of placing all defence arrangements in the Australasian Colonies on a permanent basis to start with, and on a scale suited to their resources, but capable of expansion in the future.

Admiral Wilson's recommendations before the *Sydney Royal Commission*[2] were to the effect that, besides any batteries that might be erected, gun-boats for harbour defence, torpedo launches, and the guns and appliances

---

[1] The guns to be kept in store at the naval headquarters, and the sites selected for batteries purchased.

[2] See pp. 152-54.

for arming merchant vessels in time of war, should be kept ready for use at the principal ports of the Australian Colonies. These merchant vessels would, with the Imperial Navy, aid in the general defence of commerce and seaboard. For the manning of these ships, as well as for the naval harbour defences, he recommended the establishment of naval brigades, under the supervision and instruction of officers of the Royal Navy. He further urged that the Australasian Colonies should jointly agree to establish these auxiliary naval defences, which would be under the orders of the senior officer of the Imperial Navy in time of war, and yet be subject to the control of the several Governments in time of peace. Nothing in these proposals would, in Sir Peter Scratchley's opinion, interfere either with what has already been done in the way of defence preparations, or with the recommendations contained in the schemes of defence set forth in the following pages. On the contrary, the naval measures suggested, he considered, would immensely increase the defensive power of the Colonies, and could be provided by degrees and at any time.

In Admiral Wilson's recommendations relating to the naval defences of the Colonies, although the military expenditure was strongly condemned, no naval estimates were submitted. Taking as a guide the estimate handed in to the *Sydney Royal Commission*, the expenditure on the *personnel* of the naval contingents recommended for the Australian station would amount to 76,000*l*. a year.[1] In the absence of a clear understanding as to

---

[1] Reckoned by Sir Peter Scratchley. It is fair to state, however, that

whether this large sum was to be incurred in addition to, or partly in substitution of, the military expenditure, it was, of course, impossible for Sir Peter Scratchley to form a correct opinion upon the proposal. He was, however, decidedly of opinion that, although the Colonies would be willing to spend a fair amount of money for naval defence, they would not be prepared to go the length suggested. At the same time he advised that the matter should be ventilated, and more definite proposals laid before the Australasian Governments.

'The large expenditure proposed supports the objection so often urged against the adoption of *floating* in the place of *fixed* defences.' Referring once to the common impression that naval men, artillerists, and engineers will, each in their turn, show a preference for their own arm, and advocate its employment for defence purposes to the exclusion of others, Sir Peter said, ' This is quite a mistake. No engineer, artilleryman, or sailor that I have ever met, who really knew his business, ever thought of taking this one-sided view.'[1]

As an indication of the importance which naval authorities attach to *fixed* defences, Admiral Hoskins,[2]

nearly two-thirds of the *personnel* proposed was required for manning the armed steamers which would be commissioned on the outbreak of war. In estimating the amount Sir Peter did not include the cost of maintaining the *matériel* of the naval defences, which would comprise ' seventeen gunboats, eleven torpedo boats, and forty-four improvised torpedo launches ;' nor was the first cost of providing this *matériel*, or the armament and fittings for the steamers, taken into account.

[1] He advocated the use of *fixed* only where they would effect the object in view more economically than *floating* defences.

[2] See also Sir William Jervois's remarks on p. 164.

when discussing the question of Australasian defence, held that

the principal duty of the commander of a naval force is to meet a hostile squadron wherever it can be found, and endeavour to stop its ravages *in limine*, and not by dividing and shutting up his ships in the different ports, to give the enemy the command of the sea and the power of attacking them separately in detail. He has a right to expect that the principal ports shall be protected by land forces and batteries, either afloat or on shore, sufficiently strong to protect them against an ordinary cruising squadron, and by heading it off, or delaying it, to give him a better chance of intercepting it, and also to afford him a refuge and shelter in case of his being worsted or overpowered in a sea-fight. To call on ships to protect the ports, instead of the ports the ships, is to invert the obligation and prevent their performing their proper duties. Should the enemy not send a squadron to these seas, but only single cruisers, acting independently against our commerce, corresponding steps would, of course, be taken; but even then, to enable detached vessels to act with vigour and success, it would be necessary for them to have fortified places to fall back upon in case of need.

Here it is distinctly pointed out that, unless the Colonies are prepared to help the navy, the navy cannot assist them in their defence.

Sir Peter Scratchley thought that the proposal to place any floating defences maintained by the Colonies directly under the supervision of the Australian squadron was worthy of serious attention, as therein 'lay the only security for maintaining the ships, crews, and naval reserves in a really efficient condition.' All local forces, whether naval or military, must suffer deterioration, for reasons too obvious to require demonstration, and how to counteract this is only one of the many difficult problems connected with the defence organisation of these Colonies which press themselves upon the attention of Australasian statesmen.

Briefly then, Sir Peter Scratchley admitted the desirability of organising sea-going defences for the protection of Australasian commerce, in order to reinforce the Imperial squadron in time of war; but thought that the nature of these defences should be considered as following upon the suggested schemes of land defence, and not as antagonistic to them.

In the second column of the following tabulated statement will be found the principal harbours and other places in the Australasian Colonies which Sir Peter considered should be taken into account in a well-considered

Colony	Principal harbours and other places	Points d'appui or coal depôts for Shipping and Navy
QUEENSLAND	Thursday Island (Torres Strait)	Thursday Island
	Cooktown	*Cooktown*
	Townsville	*Townsville*
	Keppel Bay (Rockhampton)	*Keppel Bay*
	Moreton Bay (Brisbane)	Moreton Bay
NEW SOUTH WALES	Port Jackson (Sydney)	Port Jackson (Sydney)
	Newcastle	
	Botany Bay	
	Wollongong	
VICTORIA	Port Phillip (Melbourne)	
	Portland	Portland
	Warnambool	
	Belfast	
SOUTH AUSTRALIA	Glenelg (Adelaide)	Glenelg
	Port Victor	*Or Port Victor*
WESTERN AUSTRALIA	Freemantle (Perth)	
	King George Sound	King George Sound
TASMANIA	Hobart	Hobart
	Launceston	Launceston
NEW ZEALAND	Auckland	Auckland
	Wellington	Wellington
	Port Lyttelton (Christchurch)	
	Port Chalmers (Dunedin)	
	Bluff Harbour	*Bluff Harbour*

scheme of military and naval defence; in the third column those places suggested as *points d'appui* for the Imperial navy,[1] and such auxiliary Colonial naval defences as may be organised.[2]

Various authorities have from time to time advised the fortifying of most of the harbours and other places above mentioned. Sir Peter, however, added Cooktown and Townsville, as he considered these two ports could be easily defended, and were admirably placed for the general naval protection of the coast of Queensland, being links of the chain connecting Torres Strait with Keppel Bay. Indeed, it would be very unwise, in any scheme of naval defence that may be ultimately adopted, to ignore these two ports, seeing that the distance between Thursday Island and Moreton Bay (Brisbane) is 1,400 miles.

The only important places in Australia [3] which are not likely to be fortified for some time to come are the ports of Cooktown in Queensland; Belfast, Warnambool, and Portland in Victoria; and Port Victor in South Australia. A small Volunteer Artillery corps has been established at Townsville, and if Sir Peter Scratchley's suggestion is carried out, when the breakwater at that port is completed, a small work will be placed at its head to command the anchorage and protect the town and harbour.

[1] When employed in its proper sphere of protecting commerce and trade, and keeping up communication with Europe and British Possessions in the East and elsewhere.

[2] The ports in the third column—excluding those in italics, which were added by Sir Peter Scratchley—were also selected by Admiral Wilson for coal depôts during war.

[3] Excluding Western Australia and Thursday Island.

Should it be decided to fortify the ports above mentioned as suitable for coal depôts, General Scratchley considered that naval defences would have to be established in all the Colonies, and that naval reserves[1] would be required at King George Sound, Adelaide, Melbourne, Hobart, Launceston, Sydney, Brisbane, Auckland, and Wellington. He strongly supported Admiral Wilson's recommendation regarding armed merchant steamers, and considered that if his scheme were put before the Australasian Governments on its merits, apart from the shore defences, the majority of the Colonies would enter into a general agreement on that basis.[2]

At the Intercolonial Conference[3] held at Sydney in 1881, where all the Colonies were represented, a discussion was raised on the subject of naval defences by Mr. Morgan, the Premier of South Australia. 'Mr. Morgan no doubt intended that special vessels belonging to the Imperial navy should be set apart for Colonial service, and take the place of the ironclads recommended for South Australia and New South Wales, and the small unarmoured vessels suggested for Victoria and Queensland. Many feel that a purely Colonial navy can never remain thoroughly efficient or keep pace with modern improvements; and Colonial opinion generally coincides with what Admiral Wilson has said on this subject.'

[1] These reserves would man the gun-boats, torpedo-boats, launches, and armed merchant vessels.

[2] The Anglo-Australian mercantile marine is very numerous, and every day improves in quality and speed, so that no difficulty would be experienced in securing the required number of vessels.

[3] For extracts from the published proceedings of the Conference, see *Appendix* A.

Sir Peter Scratchley had good reason to believe, therefore, that the proposal to provide Colonial naval reserves and equipments of guns, for manning and commissioning merchant steamers on the outbreak of war, would meet with ready acceptance in Australia, 'provided the Governments received an assurance that the employment of this class of vessels was to be preferred to Mr. Morgan's proposal, which would be very costly, and yet not provide a sufficient number of vessels.'

In order to move the Australasian Colonies to consider a federal scheme of naval defence, Sir Peter considered the lead should be taken by the Imperial Government, and the outline of a scheme suggested.

NOTE.

The naval assistance afforded to the Australian Colonies, New Zealand, and Tasmania, during the past five years (1881–86) in regard to ships, &c., is as follows :—[1]

Colony	Vessels	Nature of Assistance given
Victoria	2 second-class torpedo boats	Construction inspected and payments certified to by Admiralty officers.
	Torpedo boat *Childers*	Casual inspection during construction, and certificates for payment granted.
	Gunboats { *Victoria* / *Albert* }	
	50 feet steam life pinnace	Construction inspected and payments certified to by officers of Portsmouth Dockyard.
Tasmania	Second-class torpedo boat	Do. by Admiralty officers
South Australia	Gunboat *Protector*	Do. ,,
Queensland	Gunboats { *Paluma* / *Gayundah* }	Do. ,, Work was also done at our Dockyards on these two vessels at the expense of the colony
	Second-class torpedo boat	Construction inspected and payment certified to by Admiralty officers
New South Wales	*Wolverene*[2]	Tons Dispt. I.H.P. A screw corvette 2,540 1,490. Presented to the colony in 1881 for use as a training ship

[1] So far as known in the Ship and Dockyard branches.

[2] Statement showing description and value of naval, victualling, and medical stores on board H.M.S. *Wolverene*. Where practicable, actual prices, as new, have been taken; in other cases approximate values only inserted :—

 Naval Stores :—
  Boatswains'   £3,624
  Carpenters'   2,067
  Engineers'   1,234
  Gunners'   432
           — £7,357
 Victualling Stores   162
 Medical Stores   51
    Total   £7,570

CHAPTER III.

COAST DEFENCE.

THE subject of coast defence, when considered in connection with Australia, Tasmania, and New Zealand—exposed as these countries are to formidable attacks by sea—is one of much importance. Having already dealt with Sir Peter Scratchley's views generally on this point, in the previous chapters, I do not propose here to treat the matter at great length, but the following particular remarks made by him on the subject may not be without interest.[1]

The defences of the Australasian Colonies are planned so as to secure the capitals and principal harbours from attack by a squadron of several ships, of which one or more might be ironclads. For this purpose, floating, or what may be termed naval, defences are being provided as auxiliaries to the coast batteries. These naval defences should be classed under two heads :—

(I.) *Naval Harbour Defences.*

Ironclads, although adding very largely to the effective power of any scheme of coast defence, are so

---

[1] I have collected Sir Peter's remarks on the subject and arranged them under his own headings.

costly that they cannot be generally recommended for the Australian ports. If introduced, however, it would be most important that they should possess seagoing qualities, and be capable of assuming the offensive, in order to attack and pursue hostile ships blockading a port. For purely defensive purposes unarmoured gunboats are to be preferred, as being less costly to build and maintain, and as requiring smaller crews. Whether ironclads will be able to maintain their superiority either for offence or defence, is a point upon which it is impossible to speak with any degree of certainty; but, considering the great advance attained in offensive and defensive torpedoes, which may fairly be expected to continue, and that we may be on the eve of a great revolution in naval warfare, the employment of unsinkable ships, with protection provided for the guns and other vital parts, must be considered.

All authorities on the subject of coast defence agree in recommending the employment of heavy guns, mounted upon small vessels of light draught, unprotected by armour, to supplement the fixed and floating defences of a port or harbour, and vessels of this class have been introduced into the Imperial service, and are being adopted by foreign Powers. These gun-boats are not intended to take the place of forts, on land or in the water, in those cases where the latter have to be resorted to for securing an effective defence; but it is considered that whenever it is not possible to carry into execution a complete system of defence at once, they should rank as next in importance to stationary torpedoes as an element of the system. The fact that they can be constructed to carry the 38-ton gun, which is capable of piercing the armour of any ironclad afloat at the present date, is only one of the many arguments which can be adduced in favour of their adoption for the Australian Colonies. Their small cost, too, when compared with that of armoured turret-ships, the few men required to man them, and the moderate expenditure necessary for their maintenance, are all points worthy of the most careful consideration wherever the question of erecting forts or of providing and maintaining turret-ships cannot be entertained. They may be employed to act either singly or in numbers, in support of land or other fixed defences or in conjunction with turret-ships, and, under certain circumstances, could attack the vessels of the enemy lying off the entrance to a port. If stationed inside the entrance they should be protected by an advanced line of torpedoes, and if advancing to the attack they might be covered by steamers of great speed, adapted to discharge any kind of locomotive torpedo; while in time of peace these gun-boats should be hauled up on shore, and could be easily and economically maintained in a thoroughly efficient state.

The principal objection to their employment is due to the fact that they are vulnerable to the fire of small guns, owing to their being entirely unprotected by armour; but, on the other hand, as they would almost invariably open fire when end on to a hostile vessel, they would present but a very small mark to the enemy's guns. It has been proposed to plate their bows so as to render them proof against the fire of moderately large guns and thereby make them nearly as effective as small ironclads. The unsteadiness of the platform from which the gun is fired is a defect common to all floating defences, and, although not to be disregarded, is not a serious objection, as in most situations these gun-boats would manœuvre in moderately calm water, and the superiority of their armament would enable them to engage the enemy with great effect at long ranges.

The best vessel for the purpose is one of moderate size and speed, with a small draught of water, and armed with one or two heavy guns. Boats of this type are being built in England, and have been introduced in the British and foreign navies.

One of the most suitable is the gunboat of the *Alpha* type, carrying one 8-inch gun forward and one 6-inch aft, both B.L. new type chambered Armstrong guns. The boat is built entirely of steel; its principal dimensions are as follows : [1]

	feet	inches
Extreme length	118	6
Breadth	27	0
Draught of water	7	6
Displacement	319 tons.	
Indicated horse-power	180	
Estimated speed	10 knots.	

Besides the heavy guns there are two 9-pounder B.L. new type guns and two machine guns. The engines are of the most improved type; they and the boilers are placed below the water line. The bunker capacity is equal to 200 hours' full-speed steaming. The boat sails well. Several boats have made the voyage from England to China. For the sea voyage

[1] This was written by Sir Peter Scratchley in 1882.

they are rigged, and when equipped for fighting the rigging is dispensed with, so as to reduce the visible bulk of the boat. These boats can be utilised in time of peace for Government service along the coast.

Besides gun-boats, torpedo-boats are now considered to be necessary for harbour defence; and, where the choice has to be made, they should be provided before the gun-boats. There are numerous classes of torpedo-boats. They vary in size from the small boats of 13 knots' speed, 58 feet long, costing 2,000*l.*, to the 20-knot boat, 110 feet long, costing 10,500*l*. The larger boats are intended to go to sea, and will stand rough weather. They also carry machine-guns. . . . Of course to obtain the best results two or three boats are required; but where economy has to be exercised the presence of one boat would have a very great moral effect on the enemy's proceedings. Where suitable steam launches are owned by private parties, they should be surveyed and registered for use in time of war. This is a matter which should be looked into at once. The number of men required to man torpedo-boats is very small.

(II.) *External Defence of the Seaboard and Commerce.*

Under this head should be classed swift cruisers and armed merchant vessels, which would form part of a federal naval defence maintained by all the Colonies.

In 1882 Sir W. G. Armstrong & Co. forwarded to the Government of New South Wales a memorandum on their *Protected Barbette system of mounting and working Coast Guns*.[1] This memorandum was submitted to Sir Peter Scratchley, who after much care and consideration put his ideas and criticism into writing.

The 'Protected Barbette' System for mounting Guns in Coast Defences.

The views contained in the memorandum on this subject from Sir William Armstrong & Co. are generally correct. When they were submitted to Sir William Jervois and myself in 1878, their soundness was recognised, and we decided to adopt the system in the Australian Colonies, wherever *new* guns had to be mounted in the coast batteries. A battery on the 'protected barbette' system is in course of construction at Middle Head, to receive two 25-ton guns purchased last year from Sir William Armstrong & Co., and should additional guns be provided for the batteries of Port Jackson, it is proposed to mount one or more of them at South and Middle Heads on the same plan. Batteries of the same type have been constructed at Adelaide and Brisbane, and are now being built at Hobart and in Victoria. The system, however, does not admit of universal application, any more than that unarmoured ships will do all the work of ironclads. That the system is greatly superior to the present plan of mounting guns *en barbette* must be admitted. In the plan hitherto adopted, the gunners are very much exposed, especially when loading—the operation which takes most time ;

[1] This memorandum will be found set out in *Appendix A*.

in Sir William Armstrong's plan they are well under cover; and, excepting the man who aims the gun, the gun detachment is screened from the enemy's view. But, if we take as examples the extreme points of South and Middle Heads in Port Jackson, where it is necessary to mount additional guns it will be found that at these two points the lateral range is very great (over 250°), the sites are cramped, and their height above the sea is small, conditions which are not favourable to guns mounted *en barbette*. These are two cases where some kind of overhead cover, such as cupolas, should, if practicable, be provided to protect the guns and gunners against shell and machine-gun fire.

Although the bombardment of Alexandria is an event which could not under any circumstances occur in Port Jackson, much valuable information concerning the vexed question of *coast defences v. ships*, will no doubt be obtained. I think the lessons to be learnt from that bombardment are that in order to render coast batteries thoroughly reliable, a portion of the guns must be protected so that they cannot be silenced; and that highly trained artillerymen to man the guns are absolutely necessary.

CHAPTER IV.

TORPEDO DEFENCE (DEFENSIVE[1] AND OFFENSIVE)

TORPEDOES, both defensive and offensive, are relied upon to so great an extent in the systems of defence suggested for the various Australasian Colonies, that no account of Sir Peter Scratchley's connection with that work would be complete that did not include some reference to his views on this important subject. I have, therefore, collected together and arranged in narrative form various opinions expressed or written by him on this subject during the period he was advising the Australasian Governments.

Even before submarine mines were recognised to be valuable weapons of defence, it was an accepted axiom among naval and military men that guns alone, unsupported by obstructions, would not effectually prevent vessels from steaming past a battery or fort at moderate ranges. Passive obstructions in the shape of booms, sunken vessels, and barges were generally supposed to form part of the defensive arrangements of a port; but, owing to the great cost, want of durability, and

[1] Or *submarine mines.*

unwieldiness, the provision of these booms was never seriously provided for. The employment of sunken vessels to close a channel was only intended as a last resort, and should on no account be adopted when time and the necessary appliances for torpedo defences are available. To say nothing of the permanent injury which may result to the channel so obstructed, the cost of restoring it for navigation, and the impossibility of estimating the damage which might be done, there is an obvious objection in the fact that the obstruction exists for both the enemy and the defenders. It is necessary to direct especial attention to this mode of obstructing a channel, because it has often been urged as a simple way of providing for the defence of the West Channel of Port Phillip.[1] Considering how easy and economically this channel can be closed by a battery and torpedoes, it would be the height of folly to think of such a plan.

These defensive weapons have passed out of the theoretical stage, and their utility and reliability have been practically tested in actual warfare. If success has been attained in former years with comparatively crude torpedo defences, what may not Australia, New Zealand, and Tasmania expect from the present perfected arrangements? Yet in face of the proofs that can be produced as to the reliability of submarine defences, attempts have been made to throw doubt upon their efficacy. Some critics assert that naval officers undervalue their employment, as they can readily be removed by counter-mining and other well-

[1] See p. 162.

known means. Now the very reverse of this opinion prevails amongst naval authorities, who admit that only in very special cases will it be possible to attempt to force a passage defended by torpedoes, provided they are adequately protected by strongly constructed forts or batteries.

Experimental attacks upon defensive torpedoes have to be conducted without that all-important element of defence—guns firing at the ships and boats; consequently they prove nothing. Such experiments are useful as affording the navy an opportunity of practice, and to the engineers they disclose the weak points in the working of a system of submarine mines; but what can be done with ease during peace could only be achieved in time of war by sacrifices of life and material.

Of recent years all appliances have been much simplified, and the details of working have been very carefully elaborated. Experiments are still being carried on in almost every country. In England several companies of the Royal Engineers are specially trained to take the charge of the submarine defences of the Imperial ports and harbours at home and abroad.[1] There is a special school of submarine mining at Chatham; while at Portsmouth, besides the military submarine mining depôt, a naval torpedo school exists for the instruction of officers and men

---

[1] *R.E.—Submarine Mining Companies.*—4th Company, Chatham: 21st ditto, Chatham; 22nd ditto, Gosport; 27th ditto, Halifax, N.S. (2nd Section, Bermuda); 28th ditto, Gravesend; 30th ditto, Plymouth; 33rd ditto, Gosport (2nd Section, Hong Kong); 34th ditto, Malta; 35th ditto, Chatham; M ditto (Depôt Co.), Chatham.

of the Royal Navy; and already militia submarine mining corps[1] are established to act as auxiliaries to the Royal Engineers—in fact, the arrangements for training both officers and men, and carrying on a systematic course of experiments, are very complete, and the Imperial authorities fully recognise that there is no finality in anything relating to torpedo warfare.

The submarine defences of England are being placed on a very satisfactory and permanent footing. A broad line of separation has been established between offensive and defensive torpedoes, and the conclusion arrived at by the War Office, on this point, was that the former of necessity belonged to the navy, as they were required for attacking ships and floating defences generally; whilst the latter, being intended purely for defensive purposes, should be placed under the charge of the military authorities. At first sight one is disposed to think that because the torpedoes are laid in water, necessitating the employment of steamers, barges, boats, and other naval appliances, seamen are more likely to be fitted by their training for undertaking the charge of them. A little consideration, however, removes this impression. Defensive torpedoes, being fixtures, worked and maintained from the shore, under the protection of batteries or forts, form part of the land defences of a place, and therefore must be under the immediate and undivided control of the military commander.

---

[1] *Southern Submarine Mining Militia.*—The Hampshire, 1st and 2nd Company, Gosport; the Devonshire, 3rd Company, Plymouth; the Kent, 4th Company, Chatham.

In exceptional cases, such as the protection of a disabled or inferior fleet, which cannot take refuge under land defences, a system of defensive torpedoes may have to be extemporised and guarded by the fire of the ships. But such cases are exceedingly rare, and never likely to occur in Australia. The experience of the Imperial service, and of European nations generally, support the view that the custody and working of submarine defences in the Australian Colonies should be entrusted to special corps, organised for the purpose, and composed of professional electricians, skilled artificers, and persons accustomed to the use of mechanical appliances, assisted by seamen and handy men possessing a general knowledge of seafaring matters. To ensure the proper working of submarine defences, the corps entrusted with them must be rendered thoroughly efficient by regular and systematic training. The success of the torpedo defences in Australia will depend not only upon the knowledge and experience of both officers and men, but also upon the degree of preparation beforehand. The mistake is not to be made of supposing that a torpedo defence can be readily extemporised.

The popular notion of a torpedo is a kerosene oil tin filled with an explosive, fitted with a fuse, and attached to a piece of coated wire, which, when placed in the water, is made to explode by electricity, the whole constituting a very simple and easily managed arrangement, which any one, be he landsman or seaman, can easily undertake.

What is the real fact? Simple as the application of submarine mines undoubtedly is, there is probably no defensive weapon which requires more careful manipulation, more experience and practical knowledge on the part of the officers and men placed in charge. Not only must the necessary appliances for instruction be provided, but the men must be frequently exercised in laying out portions of the systems of mines in the actual positions they will occupy in time of war. Experiments must be encouraged, and every effort made to keep pace with modern improvements. If, at any time, retrenchment should be called for in the annual expenditure for the maintenance of a system of defence, the pruning knife must not be applied either to the submarine mining or the artillery arrangements. These two defensive elements represent the essentials of the defence organisation. It needs no demonstration to show that torpedoes without guns to protect them, or that batteries without torpedoes to bar the channels, will not prevent an enemy's ships from entering a harbour. These two branches of defence are absolutely inseparable and of equal importance, so much so that I am inclined to think that it will be advisable to secure the close connection which should exist between the artillery and the submarine defences by attaching the Torpedo corps to the Artillery force.[1]

[1] A committee has very recently been sitting on this question, and it has been decided to leave submarine mining arrangements in the hands of the Royal Engineers.

DEFENSIVE[1] TORPEDOES.

The primary object to be attained by their employment is either to prevent an enemy's ships from passing through a channel in which the mines are laid, or to protect certain waters where ships could take up positions for purposes of bombardment. If judiciously laid and thoroughly efficient, submarine mines will compel the enemy's ships either to retire and blockade the port, or to undertake the task of silencing the fire of the defenders' guns, when the mines would have to be removed in order to force an entrance.

To render stationary torpedoes really effective, it is absolutely necessary that they should be adequately protected by guns in suitable defensive works; otherwise a passage could be cleared through them either by *countermining*, *creeping*, or *sweeping*. These operations, although very difficult and risky, may no doubt be undertaken by a determined enemy, and no system of torpedo defence can be considered to be efficient which does not provide against them.

Countermining is the term applied to the operation of destroying the defenders' submarine mines by the explosion of heavy charges in their proximity. It is asserted that countermines can be laid by the aid of steam launches with the requisite accuracy, except in channels properly guarded and swept by artillery fire. *Creeping* is the operation of removing electrical cables, mines, and other obstructions in the water, by dragging

---
[1] Or *submarine mines*.

for them along the bottom by means of grapnels, technically termed creepers. *Sweeping* is employed to ascertain the position of mines by dragging a rope, technically termed 'the sweep,' up or down a channel.

For forcing a passage through mines countermining is the best, but creeping and sweeping could also be attempted so as to clear as large an area as possible. Apart from the protection afforded by guns, these operations may be counteracted either by providing an advanced system of mines or by dummy mines, chains, and other obstructions in the water, while electrical lighting of the channels must be adopted during the night.

There are two classes of submarine mines :—

i. Electrical { Observation { (a) Ground.
{ Electro-contact. { (b) Buoyant.

ii. Mechanical.

It is not possible to lay down any absolute rules for the employment of the different kinds, but the following observations will serve as a guide to the choice of the most suitable mines:

Ground Mines

consist of iron cases, containing charges varying from 250 to 500 lbs. of gun-cotton, laid at the bottom of a channel, and are best suited for the defence where free navigation for friendly vessels has to be preserved, and in waters where there is great variation of tide but the depth does not exceed forty to fifty feet at any state of the tide. They are often so fitted as to be able to be fired either by observation or by contact, and in groups, as twin mines, or singly, and should only be adopted under conditions such as are found in Port Jackson and at Newcastle in New South Wales, where the navigable channels are narrow and well defined, and favourable sites exist for the observing and firing stations, and where an enemy's vessel could scarcely pass, except almost over a submerged mine. There is, in fact, a degree of uncertainty inseparable from this mode of firing, owing to inaccuracy in the instruments used, errors of observation by the men employed, and the consequent possibility of the circuit not being closed by them at the correct moment. It should be observed that the effect of large charges fired under water is much more circumscribed than was formerly supposed, and consequently considerable accuracy as to the relative positions of the ship and mine must exist if the former is to be damaged.

Buoyant Mines

are similar to the ground mines except that the charge floats at any required depth below the surface, and is kept in position by heavy sinkers. They are employed where the depth of water is too great for ground mines, and are fired in the same manner.

Electro-contact Mines

are intended to float about twelve to fifteen feet below the surface of the water, and can only be fired by contact. They are laid at shorter distances from each other than the larger mines—preferably 100 to 150 feet apart, and in several rows at least 120 feet apart, the intention being that no ship of moderate size should escape striking one or more of them in passing through the channel. They are growing very much into favour on account of their small cost and the certainty attending their employment, and are admirably suited for closing the portions of a channel which need not be kept open for navigation, and as advanced mines where observation mines are adopted.

Mechanical Mines

are arranged to explode upon being struck; they require no cables, and are altogether cheaper and more convenient than electrical mines. They must also be placed so that ships cannot avoid striking them. They can be readily extemporised, and their charge should be about 100 lb., the same as for electro-contact mines. The main objection against their employment at present is a certain risk in laying them down, and the difficulty of recovering them without first exploding the charges, an operation which sometimes may lead to a loss of life. Strong hopes, however, are entertained that a mine is to be produced which will be safe both to lay and to remove. It is evident that as these mines are always in action, they cannot be laid in channels which have to be used by friendly ships, and the general opinion is that they should only be employed for closing the minor channels of a port, or as a last resort if the electrical mines are not to be had.

The plan of attack which would probably be

adopted by an enemy, who attempted to force a channel defended by torpedoes, now requires consideration. Having obtained as much information as possible on the subject, the hostile commander would have to decide whether he was strong enough to force the passage. He would then determine the width of the passage he intended to clear through the defenders' mines and obstructions. Assuming that he was provided with all the necessary appliances, and that he had a sufficient number of steam launches, the first operation would be to creep with exploding creepers, so as to destroy the electrical cables of the defenders' mines; the next, to send forward the countermining boats, which, if successful in exploding the countermines, would be followed by the attacking ships. At the same time, if booms protected the lines of mines, they would have to be breached with charges attached to them from fast steam launches.

Provided, of course, that the enemy possessed a sufficient number of launches and steamers which he was prepared to sacrifice, that he was able to follow up the attack very quickly, and that circumstances of wind and weather were in his favour, it is not difficult to conceive that he might succeed in forcing his way through the mines; but the chances of success must be entirely based upon the assumption that the defenders were culpably negligent, that they were utterly unprepared or taken unawares, or that they were unprovided with the necessary guard-boats to enable them to attack the enemy's launches as they commenced their operations. Moreover, as I have already remarked, I do not think that it would be possible for any enemy attacking the Australian Colonies to bring with him appliances superior to those which we should possess, if only the right steps are taken to provide them. To reach this state of preparedness, careful forethought and patient elaboration in time of peace are needed.

OFFENSIVE TORPEDOES.

Under this designation should be classed any torpedo employed for the purpose of attacking an enemy's ship, whether from on shore or from ships. There are several kinds of offensive torpedoes. The Lay, the Von Scheliha, and the Erickson, which belong to one particular class of locomotive torpedoes, being all steered and controlled from a distance. They differ from each other in important details, and have not been found suitable for the Imperial service. The Whitehead, also a locomotive torpedo, which, after projection, is no longer under control, and therefore subject to the action of currents until it has run the distance for which it has been adjusted. There are also the Harvey and other towing torpedoes, which do not carry any source of motive power, together with the outrigger and drifting class, and also plunging boats. The Harvey torpedo is not in favour, as all towing torpedoes require very great skill in their employment, and it is necessary for the vessel using them to approach within forty yards from the ship attacked. The outrigger torpedo is attached to a spar projecting from the boat or vessel carrying it, and the distance at which it can be used is limited by the length of the spar, which can be conveniently handled, and it is exposed, like the towing torpedoes, to the enemy's fire. Opportunities for using it from boats may not often occur, yet it is a weapon which is likely to be largely employed now that steam launches of great speed are being introduced. The success of outrigger torpedoes will mainly depend upon the practicability of getting near the ship to be attacked without being seen. Speed, therefore, is of paramount importance.

Plunging boats for attaching torpedoes to the bottom of a ship, by means of the crew on board of them, have not been tried in England because they are considered to be so destructive to life, and have proved unsuccessful when experimented with by foreign nations.

The Whitehead torpedo, which consists of a steel cylinder pointed at both ends, and is propelled at any required depth below the surface by compressed air at high pressure, is now being issued to all fighting ships of the Royal Navy. Special launches of great speed have been built to carry the Whitehead torpedo. Although the effective range of the Whitehead will be limited when fired from ship against ship, there can be no doubt that for the defence of narrow channels, whether fired from the shore, rafts, or barges, it will be an invaluable submarine weapon. It can be fired from a tube, placed on the deck of a vessel, or below the waterline.

The Lay torpedo,[1] an American invention, intended

---

[1] Colonel Beaumont, R.E., strongly advocated the employment of this class of offensive torpedoes, and submitted designs for boats in which the motive power was compressed air at very high pressure.

to carry a much heavier charge than the Whitehead,
is a submarine boat, propelled under water by liquid
carbonic acid, but steered from the shore or ship by
an electrical cable paid out from the boat. It has a
cylindrical hull with conical ends, and is constructed
of light steel. It varies from twenty to thirty feet in
length, and from two to four feet in diameter, and is
propelled by a screw, the engine, ten to forty horse-
power, being worked by the expansive force of carbonic acid or ammoniacal gas. Through the propeller
shaft, which is hollow, passes the electrical cable,
which pays itself out, and by which the boat is steered.
A coil of cable is placed within the torpedo. There
are horizontal rudders to regulate the depth at which
the torpedo is to travel under water, also guide-rods,
one fore and one aft—by which the position of the
torpedo is determined by the operator. At night these
rods show an electric spark in the direction of the
operator, the light being invisible to the enemy. The
shore end of the electrical cable is attached to a key-
board connected with a powerful battery for generating
the electrical current. The cable is composed of
several insulated wires; one is used for starting or
stopping the engines, another steers, another regulates
the depth below surface, another elevates or lowers the
guide-rods, one is devoted to exploding the torpedo;
thus every part of the machinery in the boat is under
the control of the operator on shore, for whose information tell-tale dials register the action of every part.
The valves, which regulate the admission of the carbonic acid gas into the cylinders of the engines, are

opened and shut by means of the electrical current. The charge for destroying the enemy's vessel can be detached and lowered underneath it, and the boat returns back to land to receive another charge. The accuracy of this torpedo boat is said to be marvellous, but the speed has not so far exceeded seven to eight miles an hour. Mr. Lay has, I am told, made great improvements in its construction, but they have not, I think, been submitted for trial in England.

Messrs. Brennan and Calvert, of Melbourne, have invented a very ingenious locomotive torpedo, about the size of a Whitehead, in which the motive power is derived from two wires, coiled upon drums inside the machine, which are placed on a shaft that works twin screws in the tail. On starting the torpedo, the wires are unwound from the drums inside on to larger drums on shore, which are rotated by steam, and so the torpedo is propelled forward. At the same time control is retained over the torpedo, deviation from the course being obtained by means of a break, which retards the revolution of one of the drums on shore at will. I have witnessed trials of the torpedo which have been attended with success, and the inventors have wisely decided to submit the torpedo to the Imperial authorities.[1]

In the Colonies spar torpedo boats will in many cases be required to take the place of defensive mines, such, for instance, as the New Zealand harbours, where submarine defences will be expensive. For the defence of such important capitals as Melbourne and Sydney,

[1] This is now being done.

however, offensive torpedoes will have to be largely employed to supplement the submarine mines and obstructions in the channels. The Whitehead is still recognised to be the best locomotive torpedo at present in use, although the certainty of its action cannot always be counted upon; but if the Brennan comes up to the expectations of the inventor, it is likely to be adopted on account of its comparative simplicity; and, knowing the time and money which have been expended upon the invention, together with the perseverance shown by Messrs. Brennan and Calvert in overcoming the difficulties which are to be met with in such matters, I cannot but hope that their exertions will be crowned with success. Should the invention receive the approval of the Imperial authorities, there will be many openings for it in connection with the defences of the Australian ports.

Whatever shape these offensive torpedoes may take, it is evident that spar torpedo boats must be included in the equipment for the defence of every important port, and that they will play an important part in defensive warfare of the future. These boats will, as I have already observed, be employed to protect the submarine mines and obstructions. They would also be invaluable, if held in reserve, to attack the enemy's ships should they have succeeded in silencing the fire of the guns on shore, even if only temporarily.

The mode of attacking a vessel would be somewhat as follows: If a single boat be used, it should approach the enemy's ship as stealthily as possible. At 200 or 300 yards' distance, according to circumstances, the spar should be rigged out, the boat put at full speed, and steered for the point intended to be struck. At about thirty yards off the engines should be slowed, so that the torpedo may be brought into contact without risk of the outrigger breaking off, and the instant the torpedo touches the ship's side it should be exploded. If several boats were available, the attack should be made from different directions, and, when practicable, it should be directed against the vital parts of the ship, viz., the engines, boilers, and screws.

No doubt the attack upon an enemy's vessel with torpedo boats will be a service of great danger, but I am quite satisfied that there will be no difficulty in obtaining volunteers for the purpose amongst the seamen and engineers employed in the ports of the Australian Colonies. The higher the speed of the boats, and the larger the number employed, the greater the certainty of a successful attack, which, as a rule, should be conducted at night or at early dawn.

The advantages to be gained from the employment of spar torpedo boats are many. They are admitted to be most formidable weapons in the hands of daring and determined men. They do not require specially trained men for working them, and can be utilised in time of peace for the Government service, provided they are of moderate size. In many Australian ports there must be many boats which would be well suited to the work; and so it will not be found necessary to purchase special boats.

Should a really reliable locomotive torpedo be invented, which can be controlled from the shore or ship after being launched, it is possible that we may be on the eve of a great revolution in naval warfare, the importance of which cannot be disregarded. So far as the Australian Colonies are concerned, they can afford to wait for the development of these truly infernal machines. They have everything to gain from them in a defence point of view.

At the same time the New South Wales Government has acted wisely in purchasing two outrigger torpedo launches of the Thorneycroft type. These boats are creditable specimens of the nature of work that can be turned out from the shipbuilding yards in Sydney. The employment of these boats is likely to increase, and they may fairly be expected to render much useful service in the event of an attack being made upon Port Jackson, or any other harbour of New South Wales, where extemporised torpedo boats have been provided. I trust, however, the Australian Governments will bear in mind that every new steam launch built for service in time of peace should be designed as far as possible so as to be capable in time of war of being utilised as an outrigger torpedo boat.

The sphere, too, for the employment of torpedo launches can be greatly extended. They should be employed in watching the approaches to a harbour or roadstead. They should attack and destroy any similar hostile craft, or any vessel which may be endeavouring to explore or reconnoitre the different channels, or be engaged in searching for, or attempting to remove, submarine mines and other obstructions. Under favourable conditions of weather and sea, these boats may, if skilfully and daringly handled, carry destruction among blockading ships, either by using spar torpedoes or launching locomotive torpedoes at short ranges. The mere possibility of the defenders being able to attempt such enterprises will, in any case, oblige the blockading ships to keep at some distance away from the port, or even compel them to keep continually moving about, with fires alight ready to manœuvre immediately at full speed, in order to avoid their small but quick and handy assailants.

Again, in the case of a defensive system of submarine mines being destroyed or rendered useless from any cause, a few torpedo-boats kept in reserve, hidden behind a point of land or some other cover, would prove a very formidable and almost irresistible enemy, especially as in forcing a passage a squadron would only be able to steam at a moderate speed, and much of the attention of the officers commanding the ships would be diverted towards the batteries and other defences with which they would have to contend.

On the other hand, an attacking or blockading fleet would find ample employment for a large number of steam torpedo-boats in performing guard duty, in reconnoitring passages and approaches, in searching for and destroying the defenders' submarine mines, and in attacking on dark nights vessels lying in the enemy's harbours.

How to protect ships lying at anchor against hostile torpedoes is one of the most difficult problems which have yet to be solved in connection with naval warfare. If a vigilant watch be kept, some little notice of an intended attack may be obtained, although it is very possible to conceive that on a dark night and under favourable conditions a fast-steaming launch with noiseless engines might succeed in eluding or slipping unnoticed past the boats keeping guard. But if the attack were made by a number of boats manned by daring and resolute crews, and converging upon the vessel from different quarters, it would be no easy or certain matter, even if their approach was observed, to prevent them reaching the ship, or, at all events, arriving within so short a distance as would allow them to launch Whitehead torpedoes against her with probably fatal effects.

Indeed, I place a high value on these accessions to a system of defence, especially for the more important Australian ports which are liable to be blockaded, and for the smaller harbours which, from insufficiency of means, cannot be very strongly defended. The mere knowledge that the defenders possessed these boats would have a great influence upon the proceedings of the commander of a hostile ship or squadron; he would at least hesitate to make an attack, except with extreme caution.

At the same time I am ready to admit that the weak point of torpedo-boats is their vulnerability, and that Gatling guns or case shot may render it almost impossible for one or two boats to reach the ship attacked; but it is when they are employed in considerable numbers, several boats suddenly attacking a single ship from different quarters, that one realises the great capabilities of this offensive weapon as a means of defence.

CHAPTER V.

LOCAL FORCES (a).

Sir Peter Scratchley held that no system of Australasian defence could be considered complete which did not provide for the maintenance of such bodies of trained men as might be necessary for its proper working; yet, in his opinion, the question of organising the Australasian local forces was surrounded by many difficulties.

He strongly advocated that an effort should be made, as far as local circumstances would permit, to bring the organisations adopted in the several Colonies into harmony with each other, in order that, when the proper time arrived, the whole of the defensive arrangements might be placed upon a federal footing and entrusted to the control of an Imperial officer.

Good must result, he considered, from periodical consultations between the various military commanders in the Australasian Colonies. 'By encouraging intercourse and interchange of ideas a spirit of emulation would be introduced in all matters affecting military efficiency, thereby counteracting to a certain extent the tendency towards stagnation that must inevitably occur in colonial forces, where the officers being stationed in one place are deprived of the opportunities and advantages enjoyed by officers of the Imperial army in the ordinary course of duty.' At an Easter training of the local forces in New South Wales he was much impressed, not only with the attention in according to the Commandant of Victoria the full military honours to which his high office entitled him, but also the warmth of welcome from the officers of the Permanent and Volunteer forces. These facts, in his opinion, showed that there existed among the Volunteers of New South Wales a true feeling of soldierly comradeship towards the military forces of a sister Colony, which would bear fruit in the future, when the question of military federation became ripe for settlement. He looked upon a comparison of results obtained under different systems of military organisation as tending to promote military efficiency, but at the same time considered that the Australasian Colonies would not learn much from the experience of other countries—such as the United States and the Dominion of Canada—where the local conditions and defence requirements are totally different.

Speaking on the subject to a Colonial audience he said: 'When the defence schemes are completed, with an experienced officer at the head of affairs, it will then be practicable to introduce uniformity of organisation, and ensure the adoption of improvements which would result from a more complete interchange of ideas between the officers commanding the several Colonies. This officer, acting as military adviser to the Australian Governments, would exercise a direct control over the local forces. In this manner only can there be security for real progress, and in this manner only can the administration of these forces be conducted upon the principles of "keeping all questions relating to the maintenance of military discipline entirely clear of party or political influence." With such an adviser, removable every three or five years, a fresh impetus would be given periodically to the military administration of each Colony, modern improvements would be introduced, the Governments would be relieved from embarrassing military questions, and their recommendations, backed by competent military authority, would command the support of Parliament and of the public generally.'

In fact, he desired to introduce in military affairs a federation for defence purposes, without waiting for that political federation which may not come for many years, or for a war scare, when it is always dangerous to introduce reforms. Military federation will, no doubt, crown the edifice of self-defence which the Australasian Colonies are now building; while when Perth, Adelaide, Melbourne, Sydney, and Brisbane are connected by railways, and the principal Australian ports properly secured, the defensive power of Australia will be so greatly increased as to render the success of any foreign attack practically an impossibility.

The Australian Colonies occupy a large continent, perfectly secure against attack from within, and situated at great distances from any foreign Power likely to be at war with the mother country. They are, however, exposed to attack as an integral part of a great empire; yet this very connection, Sir Peter considered, to a certain extent simplified the problem of self-defence, as, 'except in the contingency of England's naval supremacy being destroyed, the Colonies would not be called upon to fight single-handed against a large expedition.' Once make Australia strong enough to hold her own against foreign aggression, by the establishment of local defences manned by local forces, and a defence organisation is established upon a proper basis, which in years to come, as the country progresses in importance and resources, can be increased or lessened as circumstances may require. 'But Australia must bear in mind that the attacks she may be called upon to repel will be well considered and determined, while the men employed in these expeditions will no doubt be highly trained, well seasoned, and disciplined sailors and soldiers. Any half measures are therefore absolutely dangerous, and it would be preferable to abandon all attempts at defence rather than organise the mere semblance of a defensive organisation.'

In deciding on the strength and composition of the land forces[1] required for an adequate scheme of defence, Sir Peter deemed it necessary that the Colonies should be prepared in all available ways for a raid upon commerce along their coasts, and for an attempt to overpower the defences provided at the principal ports and elsewhere should such an opportunity present itself to the enemy. To oppose such attacks by land, he considered two distinct bodies of men should be organised:

A force composed of paid and regularly trained soldiers.

[1] For a description of the Land Forces in the various Colonies see pp. 142–43.

A force consisting of Volunteers.

The strength, he considered, actually required for each place is clearly set forth in the chapters devoted to the defence of the individual Colonies. Where Volunteer forces are maintained entirely on the English or purely voluntary principle, he thought it desirable to allow a certain percentage in excess of the strength required, so as to make up for any probable deficiency in the numbers that would turn out for duty. Where, however, the system of partial payment prevails, he saw no reason for exceeding the authorised strength. In considering the numbers required, it was assumed that every man in the ranks would be moderately trained.

'But moderate training for the Volunteers,' said Sir Peter Scratchley, 'will only suffice if there is a body of highly trained men, immediately available on the outbreak of war, ever ready to man the defences, and thus affording time to perfect the training of the auxiliary forces. More than this the Australian Colonies cannot afford, and with less than this they should not remain satisfied, if it is desired to have a reliable defence organisation. Circumstanced as the Colonies are, and liable immediately on the outbreak of war to have their ports attacked, it would be simple folly to rely entirely upon bodies of partially trained men, who would be obviously unfitted to take at once their position in the first line of defence.'

Although he considered that each Colony should possess a permanent nucleus of highly trained men, supplemented by auxiliaries enrolled on the Volunteer principle; at the same time he asserted that, whatever form Volunteer organisation in the Australasian Colonies might take, success must depend upon the working arrangements made to carry it into effect, while the superiority of one system over another would depend upon its proved efficiency.

The days are gone by when bodies of armed men were looked upon as mere fighting machines, which fulfilled their purpose so long as they were brave, obedient, and highly drilled. Superior education at one time was not expected among the junior officers. Now things are entirely changed. The modern art of war is a difficult and complicated science, which can only be mastered by industry and intelligence. 'That army will fight by far the best which possesses in its ranks the largest number of intelligent, well educated, well trained, and well disciplined men. Not only must the modern fighting force comprise intelligence and education, but it requires to be well disciplined and well drilled. It is in the latter respects that Volunteer forces are most wanting. Experience and practical knowledge have to be imparted to bodies of men who, of necessity, cannot devote the time required for the purpose. The problem, however, has to be solved, and Australia must not rest satisfied with mere pluck, unskilled and ill-directed.'

Speaking on this point to the Queensland Volunteers, he said: 'A military force cannot hope to be successful in any enterprise unless the officers possess the entire confidence of the men, and this confidence can only be obtained by the officers proving to their men that they are thoroughly acquainted with their work. In the present day the responsibilities of the officers are much increased, and the greater dispersion of the men renders it more difficult for the officers to control the proceedings of their men. Let the officers bear in mind that there is no royal road to military knowledge. A special training is as much required for the military profession as for any other, and 'by study alone can officers during peace fit themselves for real work in war.'

Sir Frederick Weld made the following observations on the subject:—

There is another point that I wish to impress upon those of my hearers who are about to take part in the Volunteer movement. Very much depends, almost everything depends, upon the officers. Now a man is not necessarily fitted to be an officer because he is a gentlemanly man, a good fellow, or even a valuable member of society. These qualities may be advantages, but what is above all wanted, is a man who can unite firmness with tact, who possesses coolness and nerve, who has good sense and military aptitude, and who will give up his time to study and learn his work thoroughly.

'Non-commissioned officers,' said General Scratchley, on the same occasion, 'must endeavour to show themselves superior to the men in knowledge, drill, obedience to orders, attention to details; thus, and in no other manner, will they command their respect and ready support. As for the men, the sole aim and object of training carried on in peace time is to render a man an efficient soldier in the field. The necessity for drill as well as for musketry instruction is obvious. It has been observed that the fire of infantry, armed with breechloaders, has become so formidable of late as to require a complete change in tactics. But the rapidity of musketry fire, leading to waste of ammunition and inaccuracy of aim, is a danger which can only be guarded against by increased training of the men.'

It is considered by some military writers that infantry posted under cover will be much more formidable, either for attack or defence, than artillery. This opinion Sir Peter did not share, for he believed that we shall be forced to adopt the protection of field artillery in the manner so often advocated by Colonel Brackenbury. Major Drury, in an able and well-considered article, suggested that the proposal should be at once considered in Australia. In the Colonies difficulties are experienced in getting men to attend daylight parades. Perhaps employers are to blame in this respect, as 'they do not care to make any sacrifices in order to afford their men facilities for attending drill.' In Sir Peter Scratchley's opinion, this deficiency in daylight drill could only be satisfactorily met by periodical assemblies of the men in camp for a few days' continuous training.

It is, however, fair to state that public opinion in the Australasian Colonies is much divided upon the question of organisation. 'Many think that if the stringency of the regulations for securing efficiency is increased, the payment of fees for compulsory continuous training and for attendance at drill in daylight must be conceded. Some, on the other hand, oppose the principle of payment as contrary to the spirit of a purely Volunteer force on the English model. A few in New South Wales, who object to the stringency of the new regulations, are in favour of the Naval Brigade system, under which the men are paid for attendance at parade.'

The conclusions and recommendations contained in the report upon the financial state and internal organisation of the Volunteer force in Great Britain General Scratchley deemed of special interest to Australasian Volunteers, and many of the recommendations therein suggested have been adopted in the new organisations. Addressing a body of Colonial Volunteers on this subject, he said : 'The most noteworthy recommendation of the report is that which relates to encampments. There is nothing new in this, for any one who has seen Volunteers for a few days in camp will have remarked how quickly the men improve in drill, discipline, soldierly bearing, smartness, and steadiness. After all, this is only an illustration, on a small scale, of the good resulting from practice, in time of peace, of the work to be done by a soldier in war. The Germans have taught the world that the army which has the greatest habit of manœuvring in time of peace will be certain to be successful in time of war. Unfortunately, in Australia, the question of expense is raised as an objection, people forgetting that more is got out of this expenditure on continuous training than out of any other incurred upon the military machine.'

Sir Edward Hamley remarks as follows upon the proper use of camps of instruction :

> The reader will have noted that all important changes of tactics and of organisation have been made in intervals of peace, and that the place has been a camp of instruction. It was

in his Silesian camps that Frederick worked out his system, taught it to his generals, and brought it to perfection. It was in the camp of Vaïssieux that two marshals of the old *régime* devised and taught the new methods, which the French Republican armies so successfully put in practice against the inheritors of Frederick's tactics. It was in the camp of Boulogne that Napoleon modified the new system, and prepared the French army for the triumphs of Ulm, Austerlitz, and Jena. It was in the mimic warfare of their summer exercises that the Prussians were prepared for the triumphs of Bohemia and of France. . . . To this end their practice in these multitudinous details is incessant, and the main business of regimental officers is to learn the capabilities of ground, of all kinds and in all circumstances, and to dispose of their men carefully upon it. The word system is applicable to their training, not as representing fixed methods, but as expressing cultivation of intelligence and preparation by practice for the innumerable contingencies of war.

In a report addressed to the Victorian Volunteer Commission of 1876, by the commandant of the local forces of Victoria (Colonel Anderson, C.M.G.) that officer gives the following outline of the organisation :—

The organisation of the Victorian Artillery avoids many of the difficulties which must result from a small permanent force constantly remaining unchanged in personnel, and stationed in one quarter. . . . On the departure of the Imperial troops the battery was formed from the candidates for the Police force, the Government announcing that in future all the appointments to the police were to be from its ranks ; at the same time the high qualifications for the police heretofore in force were to be continued, recruits having to pass the same examination as to education, character, and physical fitness as former candidates had to undergo. . . . The standard height is 5 feet 9 inches. . . . Crime in the military sense is prevented by the dread of discharge, and so of forfeiting entry into the police, and by the superiority of the class of men who alone can join. . . . It is calculated that three years' service is the average a man will have to perform before passing on to the police or penal departments. It is also calculated that by this system the police &c. will by degrees become serviceable in time of war; and it is possible that the system may be extended to other departments.

Commenting upon this report, Sir Peter Scratchley said: 'The important feature of this proposal is that it tends to identify the force with the people of the country, and the men, after serving for two or three years, are absorbed in the ranks of the civil servants of the State or in civil pursuits. A further and most important advantage is, that the men on leaving the force pass into a Reserve, and remain liable for a term of years to be called out annually for continuous training during a few days, and permanently, if necessary, during time of war. It has been justly observed, by an able advocate of army reform in England, that 'it is the truest economy to make a man a perfect soldier while we are about it, and send him home practically a free man, except in time of war.' This should be the aim of all organisations adopted in the Australian Colonies; but to carry it into effect the officers and non-commissioned officers must be highly efficient, and to secure this efficiency they must be sufficiently paid.'

He was aware that there would probably be difficulties in the way of keeping up the training of the men when in the Reserve, especially of those who might join the Police force, but advised that the system should have a fair and lengthened trial. Indeed, he believed that these proposals opened the way to a complete solution of the question of providing a reliable force for the defence of the Australian Colonies. In Australia the difficulty of attracting to the ranks a superior class of men is much greater than in other countries; and, in his opinion, this could only be removed ' by offering them sufficient inducement to serve for a brief term not exceeding three years, and to continue in the Reserve for a further term.' The inducement he thought should be a promise that those men who had fulfilled certain requirements as to good conduct, education, and physical fitness, should be entitled to employment under the Government in the Police, Penal, Postal, Railway, Customs, and other departments, when vacancies occurred.

'No doubt, in course of time, banks, public companies, merchants, and others, would become candidates for the employment of these men; as no better training for young men, nor a greater test of their qualifications, could be desired, than the three years' discipline and healthy employment in the ranks of the force.' Under Sir Peter Scratchley's system, courts-martial and confinement in prison or cells for grave offences would become unnecessary, as bad conduct would be punished by discharge. The power of dismissal must, however, be vested in the commandant without any interference whatever; indeed, Sir Peter considered this point the keystone of the whole system. With the great inducements offered he thought there would be no difficulty in obtaining candidates for admission to the force. Nor would it be necessary to give high pay; on the contrary, it should be adjusted so as to make the men large gainers on leaving the force. Marriage, he thought, should be freely allowed, but the men should be required, as in Melbourne, to live in barracks as single men, special indulgences being granted them in the matter of leave, provided their conduct was satisfactory.

As to the length of service and mode of training in the Reserve, Sir Peter Scratchley expressed himself thus: 'There should be three classes—the first and second, each with five years as the term of service, and retaining fees of 10*l.* and 5*l.* per annum in return for being called out annually; service in the third class to be optional, and for a further term of five or ten years without retaining fees. The men in the third class would only be liable to be called out in time of war, when bounty could be paid to them whether they were embodied or not. The men in the Reserve, not in Government employ, should be free to reside wherever they desired, and to leave the Colony on giving previous notice, the payment of fees being regulated so as to be always in arrear. Much of the annual training, such as company drill and musketry instruction, would have to be conducted by small detachments, excepting at the capitals and large towns, in order to lessen the inconvenience; but an effort should be made to get the whole force together for a few days in each year, by engaging substitutes to take the place of the Government employés when training. Officials in the employ of Government might also be induced by the payment of small retaining fees to qualify as officers for the Reserve force. The training of the Police should be under the control of the Commissioner, and when brigaded with the paid Regular force it should be under the command of police officers. In the large Colonies it might be advisable to attach permanently to the force a section commanded by a police officer, into which the men intended for the Police would be passed in order to undergo an intermediate training in Police duties, and to which the Police in the Reserve would be attached for the annual training. This section could be utilised to reinforce the Police in times of pressure. In like manner, there would be no difficulty in imparting instruction to the men qualifying for other Government departments. By degrees, as the men joined the Reserve, the strength of the Regular paid force could be reduced year by year until it reached a limit to be agreed upon, thus leading to economy without impairing efficiency.'

Such an organisation, possessing the advantage, not to be had with any other system, of increasing year by year the defensive power of the country, in his opinion, would be found to be the least costly of any mode of raising a force of trained men in the prime of life. It was designed in accordance with the views entertained by the leading military authorities of the day, and is manifestly preferable to 'a system which maintains a costly force—*without reserves*—supplemented by bodies of partially trained men.'

Admission to the force, Sir Peter Scratchley considered, would have to be regulated by an Enlistment Board, composed of the officers commanding the Artillery and other members of the staff, the Inspector-

General of Police, the Superintendents of Civil Establishments, and such other heads of departments as would be concerned in the matter, as in this manner there would be a safeguard against the enlistment of men unfitted for employment. Certain objections were raised to the idea. These Sir Peter met by proposing to place in the hands of the heads of the Civil Departments of the State the power of refusing to enlist men who were not likely to meet their requirements; and by allowing the men in the Police who belonged to the Reserve to be commanded by qualified police officers.

Remarking upon the duties, nature of instruction, and training to be given to the several arms, he said :—

'The officers and men of the Mounted Police, who are intended to act as scouts, should be taught the use of small-arms, and to act as mounted riflemen; they should be carefully instructed in outpost duties, reconnoitring, and conveying intelligence. The remainder of the field force being composed of Volunteers, and the time available for their training being limited, the first care should be to teach every man how to shoot, and the groundwork of his drill.

'The Field Artillery must be thoroughly practised with their guns, sufficient provision being made for the necessary supplies of ammunition. As to drill simple field movements only are requisite. The Engineers should acquire a fair knowledge of field engineering, comprising the construction of entrenchments, shelter trenches, field redoubts, and obstructions, and the hasty repair of roads and bridges. They must be good marksmen, and be ready to take their share in fighting when necessary. The officers must combine a high standard of theoretical knowledge, with the qualification of being able to conduct the practical operations referred to with working parties both civil and military. The strength of the Engineer company being so small, any engineer duties connected with the coast batteries and entrenchments at the Heads may be safely entrusted to the Artillery officers and their men, for the nature of the engineering work required will be of a totally different character from that to be performed in the field. The Torpedo corps stands in a different category from the other arms of the service, although it is somewhat allied to the Engineers as being eminently professional in its character. In England, it has been found necessary to detail certain companies of the Royal Engineers for torpedo duties only, to be supplemented by special Militia and Volunteer Torpedo companies. In Australia, all the officers should be either skilled electricians or civil or mechanical engineers. The men should be selected more for their intelligence than for other qualities, a good percentage of them being telegraphists, electricians, and mechanical engineers. The rough work in the laying of torpedoes, &c., should be entrusted to hired labour if it cannot be found entirely in the corps. The men should be taught the use of small-arms and company drill, as in time of war they must be prepared to defend themselves against boat attacks.

'The Infantry should possess three qualifications, which are absolutely essential for its efficiency: accurate shooting with the rifle, good marching power, and a thorough knowledge of all movements in extended order. As regards the latter point, extended formations in fighting have become absolutely necessary. Arms of precision have acquired such a rapidity of fire and such extreme range that they can now be brought to bear at distances which were considered long cannon range in former days. These changes also affect the tactics of Artillery.'

A popular delusion existed in Australia—and it has not yet entirely disappeared—that 'in the event of a fight the population would turn out to a man, and that the Colonies could trust for defence to bodies of riflemen, similar to the *francs-tireurs* in the Franco-German war.' On this delusion Sir Frederick Weld remarked:

But unfortunately a custom prevails of hanging or shooting any person not in the uniform of a regularly enrolled corps who may be taken in arms; and in the French war the Prussians, by no means an uncivilised enemy, in such cases shot hostages selected by lot from among the unarmed inhabitants when they could not or would not deliver up those who had fired on them, and they levied extra contributions besides. . . . At Bazeilles they gave up the village to the flames, and men, women, and children perished or were slain. But putting aside this little inconvenience, the fact remains that undisciplined men, acting on their own devices, might most often be as much or more in the way of friend as of foe; no Government would be justified in entrusting them with arms unless put under strict control in purely defensive positions, and even then it would be a great risk, and very doubtful gain, if any. I doubt not men's bravery, but I would most strongly impress upon Volunteers that though our race is a fighting race, and comes of 'fathers of war proof,' it is one singularly impatient of control, perhaps even more so in colonies than at home, and therefore I say that obedience and strict discipline and respect to officers are the first and most essential requisites. You may shoot well, you may drill well, you may march well, but unless you bring to your work strict discipline, and unquestioning and implicit obedience, you are a powerful piece of machinery under no control, out of gear, with wheels working wildly in different directions, and, consequently, utterly useless. You may be sure that there is no man who does not better himself by gaining that self-control which is necessary for discipline and obedience, more especially if he gives that obedience because it is a self-imposed duty, possibly to one in many respects his inferior; and if this is a lesson to men, so also, morally as well as physically, it is a valuable training for boys, and I wish all our schools would have cadet corps. I would give every encouragement in my power to them.

When I speak of discipline and drill I do not want undue attention and time to be given to what I call show drill. You must drill to become perfect in the handling and use of your weapons, and you must drill in order that you yourselves may be readily and easily moved and handled for all such purposes as are likely to be practically useful in the particular kind of services which you are likely to be called upon to render.

The sound advice contained in these remarks, coming from a thorough believer in Volunteers, deserves more than passing notice, and must carry weight. Commenting on it Sir Peter said: 'This belief in Volunteers for the defence of these Colonies I entirely share, and as a professional soldier I also insist upon adequate training. I consider Sir Frederick Weld completely disposes of the suggestion to trust for defence to bodies of riflemen, similar to the *francs-tireurs* in the Franco-German War; and I am a thorough supporter of this self-reliant and noble policy which, originally brought from the mother-country, has, I am happy to find, taken root in Australia.'

In remarking on the 'constitution and policy of the Colonies,' Admiral Wilson stated that 'the presence of a permanent armed force ... is distasteful, ... and that fact being the case it is as well ... at once to bow to and recognise as a fact that a permanent military or naval force cannot, under the present circumstances[1] and condition of the Colonies, flourish,' and added that 'the small force maintained in each Colony can never be worth the money expended on it.' On these important points Sir Peter Scratchley held direct contrary opinions—opinions formed after a long and intimate acquaintance with the Australasian Colonies. He saw the necessity for maintaining some sort of permanent military force, a necessity which was recognised by the leading public men and politicians in Australia. The doubt expressed by the same authority that these corps could 'not be relied upon in case of social broils within their own Colonies,' according to Sir Peter Scratchley's experience was not borne out by actual facts. At Newcastle in New South Wales the riots among the miners were promptly suppressed by the despatch of a battery of permanent artillery from Sydney, while at Hobart the Chiniquy disturbances were checked by the calling out of the *unpaid* Volunteer force. Nor should the disbanding of the Artillery corps at Melbourne, Sir Peter thought, be taken as an example in support of this theory, as the measure was condemned alike by leading men and the public generally.

[1] In 1881.

CHAPTER VI.

LOCAL FORCES (β).

ONE of Sir Peter Scratchley's last actions before leaving Australia for England, in 1882, was to draw up a memorandum for the advice of the Colonial Governments, based upon the report of the *Military Defences Inquiry Commission of New South Wales*,[1] over which body he presided. In this memorandum Sir Peter described minutely the various local forces then existing in Australia, Tasmania, and New Zealand, and made various critical remarks and suggestions on the different organisations. These I have arranged and embodied with other notes and memoranda written by him on the same subject, and I propose in this chapter to give a *résumé* of his facts and figures taken from these sources.

MILITARY FORCES.

(1) PERMANENT FORCES.

(a) *Artillery.*

In New South Wales there is a permanent force of artillery, comprising three batteries. Its organisation and constitution are similar to those of the Imperial Army. The men enlist between the ages of eighteen

[1] See p. 152.

and forty for five years, and may re-engage for two or five years. The lowest rate of pay is 2s. 3d. per diem for gunners, in addition to free rations of bread, meat, and groceries, free kits on joining, uniform, &c. Working pay is given to the men when employed on military works. This force is in a highly efficient condition.

In Victoria an artillery corps existed until recently, but its organisation was very different from that of New South Wales. The men were enlisted on the condition that after serving from two to three years they would receive appointments in the Police and Penal Departments, subject to their good conduct whilst in the artillery force. The pay of gunners was 2s. per diem and all found. The men, before enlistment, were examined as to their fitness for employment in these departments by a board of officers, composed of the commandant, the officer commanding the corps, and the heads of the departments concerned. The discipline was very strict, and was maintained by a much simpler code of regulations than in the Imperial service. The commandant possessed the power of dismissal without appeal. The men knew that grave misconduct on their part would be followed by dismissal. There was no crime in the ordinary military sense. The force existed for ten years, and was highly efficient.

(b) *Infantry.*[1]

A small but well trained infantry corps was established some years ago in New South Wales, with the

---

[1] It should be noted that the majority of the Commission referred to above considered an infantry permanent force unnecessary.

same organisation as the present artillery force, but after a few years it was disbanded. The artillery force, which then consisted of one battery only, was ultimately increased to its present strength of three batteries, as it was considered of paramount importance to provide a body of highly trained artillery men immediately available for the batteries on the outbreak of war.

(2) VOLUNTEER FORCES—PAID.
(More properly designated Volunteer Militia).

In New South Wales a force, consisting of artillery (field and garrison), engineers, torpedo corps, and infantry, was established in 1878 on the paid system (10s. for whole-day, and 5s. for half-day drills). The officers and men are paid for attendance at twenty daylight drills, and for six days' continuous training in each year, as already explained. The regulations are of a stringent character.

In South Australia a similar force, composed of artillery and infantry, is maintained on the paid system, the officers and men being paid one-half the New South Wales rates for attendance at daylight drills (5s. for whole-day, and 2s. 6d. for half-day drills), but there is no continuous training. The regulations are much more stringent than in New South Wales, and the men enrol for three years' service.

Both these paid Volunteer (Militia) forces are well-trained and efficient.[1]

---

[1] No reference is made to the New Zealand Militia, as Sir Peter believed that it only existed on paper.

(3) VOLUNTEER FORCES—UNPAID.
(Great Britain, or Capitation Organisation.)

This is the organisation in force in Victoria, Queensland, Tasmania, and New Zealand. The men are not, however, compelled to turn out for daylight drills, and the result is that they very rarely do so. In Great Britain this is not the case: both officers and men cheerfully attend daylight drills, and continuous training in yearly encampments is likely to be adopted as far as practicable. Annual encampments were formerly held in Victoria, but have of late years been discontinued for reasons of economy. In Queensland these encampments are held; in New Zealand occasionally; in Tasmania not at all.

All these Volunteer forces are, more or less, in an unsatisfactory state, if military efficiency only be considered. There is enthusiasm and admirable zeal, together with a strong desire on the part of officers and men to improve; but high efficiency cannot be expected under the present organisation, for the reasons which were fully represented to the Royal Commission.

(4) RIFLE VOLUNTEER FORCE.
(South Australian Organisation.[1])

This is an organisation peculiar to South Australia, which was introduced by Colonel Downes, R.A., the commandant, in 1879. Any twenty or more men may form themselves into a company in any part of

[1] See *Appendix* A.

the Colony. They can elect their own officers. The commandant acts as inspecting officer. The men receive rifles on loan, and are each allowed 100 rounds of ammunition annually. They must perform ten drills per annum, and go through a course of musketry instruction. Targets are supplied for each company, and prizes for rifle-shooting are granted by the Government; uniforms and instructors are provided by the companies. It has been decided to give the companies a capitation allowance of 1*l*. 10*s*. per annum for each effective—in fact, to convert the rifle companies into Volunteer corps on the English model.

This movement, which stands quite outside of the Volunteer organisation of South Australia, has so far been a great success. It meets those cases, which are to be found throughout Australia, of inland towns and districts, where the young men are anxious to join the Volunteer force, but the localities are so distant as not to permit of the men being immediately available for defence against foreign aggression. Time, of course, only will prove whether these Rifle companies can be maintained and governed with success. Much will depend upon the efficiency of the inspecting officer. I must confess a very strong leaning towards the idea, but I fear that the practical result will be to discourage the Volunteer movement for the sake of economy—an appeal which can never be resisted by any Australian Government—without providing an adequate and reliable force for the defence of the country. If regular paid forces, with proper reserves available in time of war, are maintained, I am not prepared to say that the South

Australian defence organisation may not prove in the long run to be that best suited to the requirements of the Australian Colonies.

NAVAL FORCES.

(1) Naval Reserve—Paid.
(*Victorian Organisation.*)

This force is organised on the plan of the English Naval Reserve, and officers and men are paid for attendance at drill, which is compulsory. The men receive 12*l.* per annum. The Reserve is also trained afloat, and is a highly efficient force, being composed of seafaring and other men employed in connection with shipping.

(2) Volunteer Naval Brigade—Paid.
(*New South Wales Organisation.*)

This is also a paid force peculiar to New South Wales. The officers and men are paid rates equal to those of the Victorian Naval Reserve; but they rarely, if ever, drill in daylight, and have never been exercised afloat. The force, as at present organised, is of little value for service afloat, and is not really a naval brigade.

(3) Naval Volunteers—Unpaid.
(*New Zealand Organisation.*)

This force is nothing more than a land volunteer force designated 'Naval Volunteers,' and is organised under the Volunteer Act of the Colony. It cannot, as at present constituted, be looked upon as of much value for service afloat.

COST OF THE SEVERAL FORCES.

As to the cost of the several forces above described, the annual expense per head (officer and man), including staff, instruction, clothing, contingencies, and, in the case of permanent forces, food, pay, &c., but exclusive of ammunition, stores, and equipment, will be found to be as follows :—

		£	s.	d.
Paid Military Forces.	1. New South Wales Permanent Artillery	94	0	0[1]
	2. Victorian (late) Permanent Artillery	86	0	0
	3. New South Wales *Paid* Volunteer Militia 18–20		0	0
	4. South Australian *Paid* Volunteer Force	13	0	0[2]
Unpaid Military Forces	5. *Unpaid* Victorian Volunteer Force	6	14	8
	6. *Unpaid* Tasmanian Volunteer Force	7	10	0
	7. *Unpaid* Queensland Volunteer Force	6	10	0
	8. *Unpaid* South Australian Rifle Companies under	1	0	0[3]
Paid Naval Forces	9. Victorian Naval Reserve	18	0	0
	10. New South Wales Naval Brigade	18	0	0
Unpaid Naval Force.	11. New Zealand Naval Volunteers	not known		

COMPARISONS.

(i.) There is practically no difference between the cost of the *unpaid* Volunteer forces in Queensland and Victoria ;

(ii.) In Tasmania the cost per head is about 1*l.* more ;

(iii.) The South Australian *paid* Volunteer force

---

[1] A small force would probably cost more than 100*l.* per head.
[2] This amount includes about 6*l.* pay per head.
[3] If 1*l.* 10*s.* capitation be added the cost would be under 3*l.* per head.

is organised on a cheap plan, which is due to the low rate of pay given to the officers and men; whilst in New South Wales there is a more costly system, owing to the high rates of pay (which are double those of South Australia) and the continuous training;

(iv.) The South Australian rifle companies, on the original plan, without capitation, cost very little.

FORCES CONSIDERED NECESSARY.[1]

a. Garrison artillery to man the guns in the batteries.

b. Torpedo corps for the torpedo defences, to be affiliated to the garrison artillery.

c. Garrisons to be placed in the batteries to protect them from assault.

d. A field force — composed of cavalry, field artillery, engineers, and infantry—to meet the enemy should he attempt to land.

e. A naval brigade for service afloat in armed vessels, gun-boats, torpedo launches, guard-boats, &c.

EXPENSE.

If expense were no object, it is manifest that paid forces would be the most reliable; but it is idle to discuss the best defence organisation without taking the cost into account. It has been justly observed that expenditure for purposes of defence, and especially for

---

[1] Sir Peter when making these suggestions assumed that the principal harbours could be defended by coast batteries and other defensive accessories. Each Colony must be separately considered.

the maintenance of military and naval forces, is not popular in Australia. The fact is that the community as a whole has never yet been so strongly convinced of the need of effective means of defence as to be willing to incur any large sacrifice for the purpose. We have not yet reached that stage when every one is agreed on the point. The chances of attack appear to be so remote that the risk not only has been, but is now being, deliberately incurred in some of the Colonies, notwithstanding the repeated remonstrances of the various military and naval authorities who have been asked to advise. It appears impossible to persuade many people that defence preparations are nothing more than an insurance against the danger of attack. The difficulty of arriving at the right settlement of what had best be done is often urged as an excuse for doing nothing; and, notwithstanding several war scares, when money has been literally wasted in ill-directed preparations, the question is still left unsettled, and every year uncertainty prevails when the military estimates are under consideration. This uncertainty leads to a hand-to-mouth policy, which is not only fatal to efficiency, but in reality conduces to extravagance, for money is laid out without producing any lasting results by adding to the defensive resources of the country.

ARTILLERY.

A portion of the artillery required for the batteries should be permanently enrolled and paid, 'in order that, in time of peace, they may take care of the guns, magazines, and all appliances, and, on the outbreak of war, there may be a body of trained men immediately available. Universal experience has shown that the skill and precision required for handling the guns in the batteries can only be secured by careful and continued drill as a business, and not by occasional exercise differing very little from a pastime, as in the case of Volunteers.'[1]

The strength of the permanent force will depend on the number of guns mounted in the works, and in every case, for the sake of economy, it will have to be supplemented by an auxiliary force. The question then arises, whether this auxiliary body should be composed of paid or unpaid Volunteers. It stands to reason that better results will be attained with paid Volunteers than with an unpaid or purely Volunteer force, simply because, in the paid force, attendance at drill is not only made compulsory, but it takes place in daylight—two conditions which, according to the opinions of all Volunteer officers in Australia, cannot be enforced with unpaid Volunteers. A more rigid discipline can be insisted on in return for money payment, and, owing to physical tests and medical examination of recruits, a more able-bodied class of men can be obtained. Looking at the fact that the coast batteries are of the first importance in the scheme of defence, the auxiliary artillery must be so organised as to be forthcoming when wanted. For that reason I consider that this force should be on the paid system, especially where a permanent artillery force is not maintained.

[1] See *Appendix* A.

TORPEDO CORPS.

Next in importance, where torpedo defences are established, is the organisation of the torpedo corps. Here again, as this is a special corps, and the class from which the men are to be obtained is very limited, and its services must always be available, and steady drill and practice are as essential as in the case of the artillery, it will be necessary to place them on the same footing as the auxiliary artillery, and pay both officers and men for attendance at drill. Moreover, the officers should receive remuneration, especially when they are professional men. It has been suggested that the torpedo corps should be enrolled for three years, and placed under a Military Discipline Act. In any case it should be affiliated to the garrison artillery, as both corps must work together at all times.

FIELD FORCE.

As to the field force, which is to be composed of field artillery, engineers, and infantry—with possibly a mounted corps—it has been urged that the necessity for payment is not so obvious as in the case of the auxiliary artillery and torpedo corps, and that numbers may make up for the inferior quality. The field force is required to meet attacks on land, which are less likely to occur than attacks by ships on the batteries. The chances of landings being attempted by an enemy are remote, more especially if naval defences are provided, as already explained; and the mere knowledge that field forces were maintained would probably be sufficient to deter the enemy from making any such attempts, which under any circumstances would be attended with great risk of failure. At the same time it is well to consider whether the gain, from enforcing strict discipline and attendance at daylight drill by money payments, is not so great as to justify the additional cost. Again, it may be objected that so much dissatisfaction would result from the non-payment of so large a portion of the Volunteers as the field force that it would lead to a break-up of the force. Five years' experience with Australian Volunteers forces me to support the opinion of their officers, and to recommend, with much reluctance, payment for the whole force, as it is every day becoming more evident that, without the paid system, real military efficiency cannot be attained.

PAYMENT OF FORCES.

Next, as to the amount of this payment. In New South Wales the officers and men receive very high rates of pay for detached daylight drills, as well as for the continuous training of six days at Easter. But it has been recommended that the number of compulsory detached drills should be increased to thirty per annum, besides the continuous training, on the understanding that the present pay of 12*l.* per annum to the men be not exceeded. This is tantamount to a reduction in the rates of pay. It was admitted before the Military Defence Inquiry Commission of New South Wales that the rates were very high,[1] but it was urged that a reduction might have the effect of breaking up the force. The Commissioners, therefore, preferred to increase the number of compulsory drills and the stringency of the regulations. They also recommended enrolment for one year. There is no reason, however, for adhering to the New South Wales rates in those Colonies where the money payment is not at present in force. If it should be decided, therefore, to adopt the paid system, I strongly recommend the adoption of the strict regulations, penalties, term of enrolment for one year at least, and moderate rates of pay in force in South Australia. On reference to Colonel Downes' evidence before the Military Committee it will be seen that this force is a complete success. That officer informed me that recruits can be obtained without any difficulty, notwithstanding the stringency of his regulations and the long term of enrolment (three years). It may also be mentioned that there is scarcely any difference between the rates of wages at Sydney and Adelaide.

Although I admit the enormous advantage of yearly encampments for continuous training—especially in the case of unpaid Volunteers—I concur in the opinion given by some of the military members of that Commission to the effect that the annual continuous training should not be compulsory, or paid for. Considering that a large number of men come from the wage-earning classes, it

---

[1] The fact that the men of the Volunteer Naval Brigade in Sydney were paid 12*l*. per annum, without being subjected either to continuous training, daylight drills, or stringent regulations, induced the Commandant of New South Wales to recommend the same rate of pay, as he feared that he could not get men at a lower rate.

is obvious that, although they can with ease be got to attend detached drills of a few hours' duration on Saturdays, and occasionally for whole days on holidays, they may be unable, without serious loss, to go into camp for six or even a less number of days. If men attend twenty daylight drills in the year, besides drills at night, which need not be paid for, the continuous training is not of such importance as with an unpaid Volunteer force. In fact, there will be time enough, on the outbreak of war, to give the officers and men in a paid Volunteer force this additional training.

The garrisons for the defensive works come under the same category as the field force, and they would be furnished from it.

As to country corps, owing to their distance from the points to be protected, they would not be available for defence purposes, as the attacks on these Colonies are certain to be sudden. The cost of maintaining such corps as Volunteers, with a capitation grant, may be considered to be too heavy. A less expensive organisation can, however, be adopted, similar to that of the rifle companies, as originally established in South Australia without a capitation grant. I would, however, place these companies directly under the Commandant.

NAVAL BRIGADE.

With regard to the Naval Brigade, considering that the officers and men can only be recruited from a limited source—the seafaring class—and from that portion of the community which is employed in connection with the shipping of a port, it is absolutely necessary to give pay. The Naval Volunteer Corps which exists in New South Wales and New Zealand, unless entirely reorganised, can never be of any real value for service afloat. On this point Admiral Wilson gives valuable evidence, which must be followed if any reality is to be given to such Naval Brigades as may be established in the Australian Colonies. The Victorian Naval Reserve is the only Colonial naval force which approaches the standard laid down by Admiral Wilson.

GENERAL REMARKS.

The efficiency of the defence organisation depends entirely upon the efficiency of the officers, and it is hopeless to expect any improvement until they are afforded means of acquiring knowledge. The first step to be taken is to establish a school of instruction, at which all officers should be induced to attend. In all the Colonies I have found that the best officers are eager to avail themselves of every opportunity afforded them, and it will be unwise economy to grudge the small expenditure necessary for the purpose. Military lending libraries, reading and lecture rooms should be established in connection with the school of instruction. The encouragement of lectures and discussions amongst the officers on military subjects cannot but be beneficial.

The nomination or elective principle for the appointment of officers must be abolished (except in the case of rifle companies) if efficiency is to be insured.

LOCAL FORCES.

It does not admit of question that persons are often elected who do not possess the qualifications required of officers.

Matters affecting the efficiency of the military machine in time of war should be considered without delay: such as the supply of ammunition; the supply and distribution of water and ammunition to the troops whilst engaged in the field; commissariat supplies and ambulances, and store arrangements. The supply of ammunition in war time would be best met by the establishment of a central arsenal on the Australian Continent, from which Queensland could draw her warlike stores. For many years, however, all the Australian Colonies will have to maintain sufficient reserves of ammunition for small arms and ordnance; for in time of war it will be impossible to ensure supplies from England. Other subjects will have to be considered in detail by the staff of the local forces. The necessity for a well organised military store department is also of paramount importance. All these things will, of necessity, be on a small scale in Queensland, and it will be quite possible to organise them in an economical manner; but the point to be insisted on is that they should receive attention in time of peace, and not be left for settlement when war is imminent.

The recommendation of the Commission,[1] that an Imperial officer should be appointed Inspector of the Local Forces, and Military Adviser to the several Governments, is of special importance, and a reference to the evidence given will show the very strong opinion

[1] See p. 157.

held by the several commandants on the subject. It is essential for the maintenance of efficiency in military forces that there should be periodical and searching inspections of everything connected with their administration. To obtain this the Australian Government must have an independent officer, in no way connected with the Colonies—an outsider, in fact—whose only aim will be to point out what is required from time to time to maintain efficiency in the defence organisations. The appointment of such an officer would strengthen the hands of the commandants, and be a guarantee that full value was being obtained for the outlay incurred.

No doubt some little advantage might result from the presence of Imperial troops in the Colonies; but, under a proper organisation for the local forces, there is no reason to doubt the practicability of ensuring the requisite military efficiency for dealing successfully with the problem of self-defence, due regard being had to local circumstances and requirements.

The principle of short service and deferred pay, with ultimate employment in the civil departments of the State, will be the best organisation for the permanent force, and, if effectively worked out, it will lead to the formation of a trained reserve available in time of war.

The police force, in the towns near the seaboard, should also be drilled to act as a military body in support of the other land forces, their place being supplied for the time by special constables. If the requisite number of Volunteers cannot be obtained, resort should be had to a Militia, and although a general impression appears to prevail that the Volunteer forces of the different Colonies are not as efficient as they should be, this may be traced to defects in organisation rather than in principle. As far as practicable, the Volunteer portion of the artillery and torpedo corps should be enrolled from the population in the immediate vicinity of the points to be defended; but the men for the field force should be taken from as large an area of country as possible. It is believed that the disinclination which exists among English-speaking races to contribute in person towards the defence of the State, as the duty of every citizen, may be gradually eradicated by cultivating amongst the youth of the rising generation a knowledge of the use of arms and of discipline. This may be partly effected by the introduction of elementary drill in all places of education, and by the formation of cadet corps where the numbers are sufficient.

Every officer should qualify for his position, and the troops should be frequently exercised on the ground likely to be occupied in repelling an attack. The employment of Imperial officers, to act as instructors, would lead to increased efficiency, and, if they were replaced at short periods, little difficulty would be experienced in keeping pace with the improvements made in military science.

SIR PETER'S CONCLUSIONS.

(*a*) An Artillery Permanent Force is most desirable, but is not recommended for the small Colonies. The strength would be too small to secure value for the large outlay.

(*b*) The balance of opinion in Australia is decidedly to the effect that an *unpaid* Volunteer force cannot be sufficiently trained to form a reliable defence force, and that, when the numbers are small, the difficulties of maintaining discipline are greatly increased. It is admitted that good marksmen can be turned out under the unpaid system, but they will not be fit to take the field as efficient soldiers. The popular notion that Volunteers, if good marksmen, and in sufficient numbers, and well commanded, will be able to defeat an invading force, is rapidly losing ground, and is scouted by experienced and thoughtful Volunteer officers throughout the Colonies.

(c) Day-light drills are absolutely necessary in order to attain efficiency.

(d) With an *unpaid* or purely Volunteer force the daylight drills cannot be enforced, and a very large percentage of the men never attend these drills.

(e) Encampments are always necessary, more so in the case of an unpaid Volunteer force. They are sure to be attended by the majority of Volunteers, whether paid or unpaid, and it is not advisable to make attendance compulsory.

(f) When money is available, the paid system should certainly be adopted; but whether the Volunteers should be paid or unpaid is a *question of policy, which can only be decided by Government*.

(g) Where a permanent artillery force is not maintained, the auxiliary artillery should certainly be paid.

(h) Torpedo corps should under any circumstances be paid, being more or less professional corps recruited from a limited class.

(i) The field force (comprising field artillery, engineers, when they are maintained as a separate body from the torpedo corps, and infantry) should be paid, if the country can afford the expense. If not paid, the strength of the field force might be increased, in order to make up by quantity for the inferior quality; but this course is not recommended, as it will be preferable to lay out the extra money for the large force in improving the quality of a smaller number.

(j) If payment for compulsory attendance at drill be adopted, the South Australian organisation should be adopted in preference to that of New South Wales.

(k) The question of land grants to be substituted for money payments should be considered; the system, as hitherto tried, was founded on an entirely wrong basis.

(*l*) Rifle companies on the South Australian plan, *with or without a capitation grant*, are best adapted to country districts; but they must not be established if an *unpaid* Volunteer force is maintained.

(*m*) A school of instruction should be established for officers and non-commissioned officers, the commandant and paid staff acting as instructors.

(*n*) The election of officers by corps should be abolished, except in rifle companies.

(*o*) Reserves of ammunition should be maintained. All questions connected with commissariat and other supplies should be settled in time of peace.

(*p*) An Imperial officer, to act as inspecting officer and military adviser, should be appointed.

In 1884 Sir Peter Scratchley was re-editing some papers on the subject of the local military forces of the Australasian Colonies. Among them were the following tabular statements. If these are read with the foregoing descriptions, which were written in 1882, and compared with the remarks on the present state of the defences of Australia and New Zealand, which will be found set out in the chapters specially devoted to the individual Colonies, a very fair estimate can be made as to the strength and organisation of the military forces in the Colonies at the present time.

Table A. gives a description of the various local forces in the Australasian Colonies.

Table B. gives the strength and composition of the several military forces under the different organisations. The numbers, Sir Peter Scratchley considered, might in some cases be reduced if the paid system should be introduced.

TABLE A.

Colony	Permanent Force	Paid Volunteer Militia	Unpaid Volunteer Force
New South Wales	Garrison Artillery	Field and Garrison Artillery—Torpedo Corps—Engineers and Infantry	Nil
Victoria	Do. (being established)	Do. (about to be established)	Rifle Companies proposed
South Australia	Do. (being established)	Field and Garrison Artillery and Infantry	Rifle Companies
Queensland	Nil	Field and Garrison Artillery Torpedo Corps and Infantry (likely to be established)	Nil
Tasmania	Nil	. . . .	Field and Garrison Artillery—Infantry
New Zealand	Portion of Constabulary to be trained to Garrison Artillery	. . . .	Field and Garrison Artillery—Torpedo Corps—Engineers Infantry

LOCAL FORCES.

TABLE B.

Colony	Paid Forces (total officers and men)					Unpaid Volunteer Force (total officers and men)					Grand Total Paid and Unpaid	Remarks
	Permanent Artillery	Volunteer Militia				Cavalry	Artillery	Engineers	Torpedo	Infantry		
		Artillery	Engineers	Torpedo	Infantry							
New South Wales	319	300	60	100	1,340	—	—	—	—	—	2,119	
Victoria	125 being established	—	—	—	—	125	1,016	250	18	2,191	3,725	
South Australia	50 being established	150	—	—	780	—	—	—	—	900	1,880	
Queensland	—	—	—	—	—	—	250	{60}		755	1,065	Will probably be increased to 1,200
Tasmania	—	—	—	—	—	20	200	{380}		414	634	do. to 850
New Zealand	—	—	—	—	—	732	907	{708}		5,318	7,367	To be reduced to 4,000
Total	494	450	60	100	2,120	877	2,373	708		9,608	16,790	

NOTE.

The number of naval and military officers now employed in the service of the Australian Colonies, New Zealand, and Tasmania, by the permission of the Board of Admiralty and of the War Office, is as follows:—

Number of Officers on the Active List of the Army employed.

—	Colonel	Majors	Captains	Lieutenants
South Australia . . .	1	—	—	—
New South Wales . .	—	1	1	2
Queensland	—	1	2	—
Victoria	—	3	2	1
New Zealand	—	—	1	—
Total . .	1	5	6	3

Number of Officers on the Active List of the Navy employed.

—	Captain	Commander	Lieutenant	Gunners
Queensland	—	1	—	—
South Australia . . .	—	—	—	1
Victoria	1	—	1	2
Total . .	1	1	1	3

Military Officers . . . 15
Naval Officers . . . 6
Grand Total . . 21

CHAPTER VII.

NEW SOUTH WALES.[1]

LOOKING at the map, it is at once obvious that an attack upon New South Wales by a foreign Power can only be made at some point along the coast which forms the eastern boundary of the Colony. This coast, well lighted and easy to navigate, is open to the Pacific Ocean, and extends for about six hundred miles. It consists of cliffs, bold headlands, and undulating hills interspersed with low-lying country and sandy beaches. The prevailing winds are north-easterly in summer and westerly in winter, when the water is comparatively smooth ; but heavy gales of wind occasionally blow from other quarters, and owing to the coast being exposed to the Pacific Ocean a heavy swell breaks upon the shore and renders landing in boats difficult. Numerous harbours, however, capable of accommodating the largest vessels, and many small ports, besides a few open roadsteads and bays, are to be found along the coast.

Port Jackson is the principal harbour of the Colony, and contains a main harbour, with an area of about nine square miles, and a middle harbour, with an area

---

[1] The geographical facts in the chapters on New South Wales, Victoria, Queensland, South Australia, and Tasmania, are selected from the *Preliminary Defence Reports* made in 1877 by Sir William Jervois in conjunction with Sir Peter Scratchley.

of three square miles. To the north of Port Jackson are the harbours Broken Bay, Newcastle, and Port Stephens,[1] and the open roadsteads at Cape Byron, Trial Bay, and Cape Hawke. South of Port Jackson are Botany Bay, Jervis Bay,[2] and Twofold Bay.[3] All of these will admit vessels of large size, although Botany Bay and the bays north of Port Jackson are not safe during easterly gales. The minor harbours[4] are—to the north, the harbours at the mouths of the Manning, Macleay, Clarence, and Richmond Rivers, and Port Macquarie at the mouth of the river Hastings; to the south, the small ports of Hacking, Wollongong, Kiama, Ulladulla, and Bateman's Bay, some of which form outlets for rivers.

Sir William Jervois and Sir Peter Scratchley began their joint connection with the military defences of the Australasian Colonies by inquiring into the steps necessary to be taken to secure the proper defence of the mother Colony.

In view of the facts that no settlements of any importance existed near the sea, and that food supplies in large quantities could only be obtained at Sydney and Newcastle (the flourishing port of the great coal district of New South Wales), they considered that these were the only places likely to be attacked, and consequently the only places that required special local

---

[1] Distant from Sydney about 20, 70, and 110 miles respectively.
[2] 95 miles from Sydney.
[3] 235 miles from Sydney.
[4] The entrances to which are all more or less obstructed by bars which reduce the depth of water to from seven to fifteen feet, and in some cases to below seven feet.

defences. In their opinion Botany Bay[1] should be defended with a view of preventing its occupation by an enemy; but the construction of batteries at Broken Bay[2] was unnecessary.

DEFENCE OF SYDNEY.

The following extracts[3] explain the line of defence suggested for Sydney:

'Apprehensions have been expressed that an enemy might land a force at the head of one of these inlets,[4] and march upon the city; but the approaches to Sydney from these quarters are, however, very different from those leading from Botany Bay. The country between Botany Bay and the town is open, and, as before stated, there are good roads; whereas between Sydney and Broken Bay the country is difficult, covered with bush, and the roads are bad. These roads can be made impassable to an enemy, both at the landings and at other places. There are three converging points at which, in order to meet the improbable case of his making an attempt against Sydney from Broken Bay, special preparation should be made to oppose him —at the Spit Ferry, at the junction of the tracks from Pitt Water and Cowan Creek, and at the junction of the road from Peat's Ferry to St. Leonards and Parramatta. At these points earthworks might be thrown up at the time, trees cut down, interlaced with wires, and other obstacles formed, thus providing strong entrenchments, behind which the field force for the

---

[1] The northern shore of which is only about three or four miles from the outskirts of Sydney, with which city it is connected by good roads.
[2] Situated at the mouth of the Hawkesbury River, about eighteen miles north of Port Jackson. Here extensive anchorage is to be found for ships of any size, and by means of inlets on the southern shore of the bay, called Pitt Water and Cowan Creek, vessels can approach within fifteen miles of Sydney.
[3] From *Preliminary Report on Defences of New South Wales*.
[4] Pitt Water and Cowan Creek.

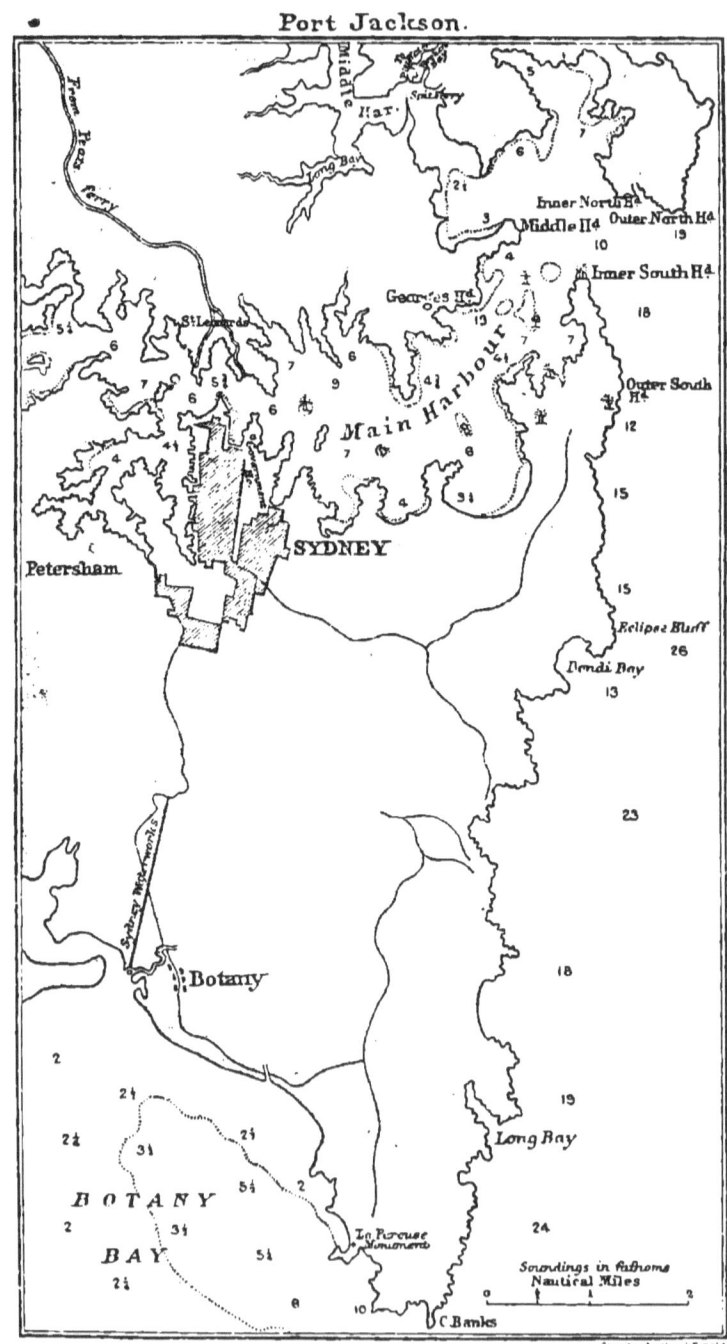

defence of Sydney would be in a position to repel any possible attack from the northward. The difficulties of an attack from this quarter, both as regards the distances to be marched and the obstacles to be overcome, are so great it did not appear at all probable it would be attempted; and it is unnecessary to recommend the construction of batteries for the defence of Broken Bay.

The probability of a hostile force landing to attack Sydney on any part of the coast between Botany Bay and Broken Bay is exceedingly remote, while beyond, either to the northward or the southward, the distances to be traversed and the difficulties to be overcome are looked upon as sufficient safeguards against any such attempt being made. The bays on the coast in the neighbourhood of Sydney are exposed to the rolling swell of the Pacific, and, except during westerly winds, on the duration of which no calculation can be based, are exceedingly unfavourable for the landing of troops. As regards a landing between Port Jackson and Broken Bay, 'an enemy would only be in a similar position to that which he would occupy if he attempted to advance from Pitt Water. The only point between Port Jackson and Botany Bay at which there is a comparative facility for landing is Long Bay, which is protected from all but south-easterly winds. An attempt to land at any of the bays adjacent to Sydney, where, in exceptional cases, landing may be practicable, or an attack from the direction of Broken Bay, must be provided against by a field force, acting from positions affording the readiest access to the points to be defended.'

Now as to the probability of hostile vessels throwing shells into Sydney from outside the entrance to the harbour, this, no doubt, is possible, but it would not be desirable to construct land batteries to prevent this mode of attack. Such defences would only lead to considerable additional expenditure, both on works and men, and after all might not effect their object; whilst the ship fired at would be a comparatively small object and at a considerable distance, on the other hand the place she would be firing into covers several square miles, and every shell thrown into it must take effect, and create considerable consternation. Apart from other considerations, probably the best plan of resisting such an attack would be by spar torpedo boats or vessels constructed for projecting the Whitehead torpedo, which, issuing from Sydney Harbour, might be directed against the enemy's ships.

They considered, however, that steps should be taken for the general defence of the coast, so as to prevent an enemy occupying any of the harbours whence he might issue to attack and capture passing vessels. It is sometimes urged that the defence of these harbours can be best accomplished by torpedoes. This method did not appear practicable, as it would necessitate the construction of batteries at each port, without affecting the proceedings of hostile cruisers, except in the immediate vicinity of the harbours.

Taking all the circumstances into account, Sir William Jervois and Sir Peter Scratchley arrived at the following conclusions—

(i.) The most effective and economical means of providing for the defence of the harbours along the coast, for the protection of local commerce, and to prevent Sydney being shelled by ships lying outside the harbour defences, would be to provide an ironclad vessel superior to any enemy's ship likely to come into Australian waters.

(ii.) Special local protection must be provided for Newcastle.

(iii.) A field force should be provided to oppose an attempt at landing in the neighbourhood of Sydney, or an attack from the direction of Broken Bay, as well as for the support and protection of the sea batteries.

Defences of New South Wales.—Original Scheme codified by Sir Peter Scratchley.

LAND DEFENCES.

PORT JACKSON.

South Head. — Reconstruction and improvement of existing batteries	To be armed with three 10-inch, eight 80-pr. rifled guns, two S.B. shell guns. (Two of the 80-prs. on sea face to be replaced ultimately by heavier guns)
Mid. Head and George's Head. —Reconstruction and improvement of existing batteries	To be armed with five 10-inch, one 9-inch, eleven 80-pr. rifled guns, five S.B. shell guns, ten S.B. 68-prs.
Mid. Head and George's Head. —New batteries	Ditto

BOTANY.

Bear Island.—Enclosed work with barracks	To be armed with one 10-inch, two 9-inch, and two 80-pr. rifled guns. Barracks for garrison

NEWCASTLE.

Signal Hill.—Enclosed work with barracks	To be armed with three 9-inch and four 80-pr. rifled guns. Barracks for garrison

BARRACKS AND RETRENCHMENTS.

Barracks at South and Middle Heads	For garrisons of batteries
Entrenchments at South Head, Middle Head, and George's Head	To enclose batteries

TORPEDO DEFENCES.

Port Jackson	Complete system of submarine mines, with observing and firing stations for both channels at entrance
Newcastle	Ditto, across channel
Botany Bay	Mechanical mines near entrance

MILITARY FORCES.

Regular Artillery Corps . . .	375 officers and men
Volunteer Militia (Auxiliary) Garrison Artillery	200 officers and men
Torpedo Corps	100 officers and men
Volunteer Militia Field Force to repel landings	1,500 officers and men—artillery, engineers, and infantry. (Police to furnish mounted corps)

NAVAL DEFENCES.

Ironclad vessel	For protection of coast and commerce
Torpedo-boats	For harbour defence
Naval Brigade and permanent crew	For ironclad vessel and torpedo-boats

The report of the *Military Defence Inquiry Commission of New South Wales*[1] claims special attention, owing to the fact that five of its members were military officers.[2] This was the first time in Australia that so many men, possessed of varied and extensive experience in colonial military affairs, had met together; and their opinions, as embodied in the report of the Military Committee, must therefore carry great weight. These officers brought to bear upon the subject an intimate knowledge of what was wanted, and a practical acquaintance with Colonial resources. Accordingly it is not too much to say they formed the most efficient local committee that up to that time ever had under its consideration the subject of Australasian defence.

[1] Held in Sydney in 1881.
[2] Sir Peter (then Colonel) Scratchley, K.C.M.G., R.E., Consulting Military Engineer to the Governments of New South Wales, Victoria, Queensland, South Australia, Tasmania, and New Zealand; Colonel Anderson, C.M.G., Commanding Local Forces of Victoria; Colonel Downes, R.A., Commanding Local Forces of South Australia; Colonel Richardson, Commanding Local Forces of New South Wales; and Colonel Roberts, Commanding Artillery Forces of New South Wales.

The Commission was appointed to inquire into the working of the laws, regulations, and arrangements made for the establishment and maintenance of the military forces of New South Wales, including the system of examination for appointments and promotion therein, and to suggest improvements with a view to economy in expenditure and efficiency in organisation, and generally to report upon the whole subject of the military defences of the Colony. A sub-Committee, composed of the military members, was formed in order to collect information and submit their opinions on the purely military questions involved in the inquiry. In addition to this, Admiral Wilson, then commanding the Australian squadron, gave evidence, and laid before the Commission suggestions respecting the naval defences which, in his opinion, should be adopted in order to complete the defence organisation of New South Wales. Thus the report and proceedings of the Commission may be said to embody all points connected with the naval and military defences of New South Wales.

The Commission accepted as a basis for their deliberations the scheme of land defence recommended by Sir William Jervois and Sir Peter Scratchley for New South Wales; but the question of naval defence, although not included in the instructions issued to the Commission, was entertained because it was found impossible to discuss the military defences without taking into account the naval measures required to complete the defence organisation of the Colony. The Commission in their report confined themselves to the naval measures for harbour defence; but at the same time full information regarding the naval defences for the protection of commerce will be found in the evidence received from Admiral Wilson [1] and Sir Peter Scratchley.

Although the defence organisation of New South Wales is necessarily on a much larger scale than that of the other Australasian Colonies, with the exception of Victoria and New Zealand, Sir Peter Scratchley considered that the general system of defence best suited for New South Wales would be found equally applicable to the other Colonies, modifications being admitted to suit local circumstances and requirements. The proposed measures contained in the different schemes of defence for the various Colonies set forth in these pages are based on the same principles, and composed more or less of the same elements; consequently the changes and improvements recommended in the defence organisation of New South Wales must, to a great extent, be suitable to the other Colonies. The following conclusions and recommendations were looked upon by Sir Peter as having an important bearing upon any military reorganisation scheme that might be adopted:—

CONCLUSIONS AND RECOMMENDATIONS OF NEW SOUTH WALES COMMISSION.[2]

(1) The necessity for maintaining a sufficient force of Permanent Artillery was advocated:—

In time of peace the care and guarding of the guns, maga-

---

[1] See chapter on *Naval Defence*, p. 58.
[2] For Sir Peter Scratchley's opinion on these conclusions and recommendations see chapter on *Local Forces* (β).

zines, and appliances demand the presence at all times of a skilled and disciplined body of men; and at the outbreak of hostilities, however efficient and numerous the reserve or Volunteer force may be, a large percentage of thoroughly competent and highly drilled soldiers is necessary for the working of each gun. In a matter of this kind an error on the side of false economy might be fatal. Nature has favoured the construction of some very formidable batteries at a moderate cost, but it must never be forgotten that the artillery placed in position will not answer the purpose intended unless handled with the utmost skill and precision attainable. Universal experience has shown that this skill and precision can be secured only by careful and continued drill as a business, and not by occasional exercise, differing very little from a pastime. The fully instructed artilleryman is in reality an artisan of a high order, and time, habit, and systematic teaching are necessary to make him thoroughly competent.

(2) The formation of a reserve of trained men was strongly urged :—

As the members of the permanent force retire from actual service on the termination of their engagements, being then well disciplined and instructed artillerymen, it is of the utmost importance that means should be adopted to secure their services for a further period of five years in case of emergency. The Commission therefore recommend the formation of a reserve force, to be composed of those who have passed through the regular force, and of such other equally fit and approved artillerymen as may present themselves for enrolment, to a number not exceeding 560 men. A considerable period must elapse before this limit can be reached, but this reserve force would be a constantly growing body, and would be as efficient as the permanent force. It is thought that, by a retaining fee of 6l., and a payment of 10s. for each of twelve daylight drills, coupled with the prospect of employment in the railway or some other department of the public service, the ranks of this reserve force would fill up with reasonable rapidity.

(3) The retention of the existing paid Volunteer force as a *Volunteer Militia*, with the then rates of pay (12*l.* per annum for privates),[1] was recommended, and an opinion expressed that the number of daylight drills should be increased to thirty per annum, exclusive of the continuous training of six days in each year; also that more stringent regulations be adopted to insure discipline; and that the *Militia* should be enrolled for one year, with leave to retire at any time, on giving one month's notice, complying with the regulations, and submitting to a penalty of two pounds.[2]

(4) The formation of a purely Volunteer force, to be affiliated to and trained with the *Volunteer Militia*, was suggested, but the expenditure on this force was confined to the provision of instruction, arms, and ammunition.

(5) The reorganisation of the paid Volunteer Naval Brigade was advised, so as to establish it as a Naval Reserve for service afloat in armed steamers, gunboats, torpedo launches, and boats for patrol and observation.

(6) The recommendations of the Military Committee with regard to the appointment, promotion, and education of officers, were adopted in certain particulars.[3]

(7) The recommendation of the Military Committee was endorsed as to the appointment of an Imperial

---

[1] The 12*l.* per annum paid as follows:—20 half-day drills, at 5*s.*—5*l.*: 6 days' continuous training in camp, 3*l.*; the balance, 4*l.*, as a bonus at end of year if the man fulfils all conditions.

[2] A majority of the Commissioners were in favour of maintaining the Militia on a less expensive footing.

[3] See *Appendix* A.

officer as inspecting officer of the Australian local forces, and military adviser to the several Governments.[1]

The duties of this officer should be to conduct periodical inspections of the local forces and the military defences and establishments of the Australian Colonies, and advise the Governments on all subjects connected with the maintenance of the local defences. In time of peace this officer would not exercise any executive command, but in time of war, should there be combined or federal arrangements for defence, he would assume supreme direction. The Committee, in making this recommendation, desire not to lessen the authority or full responsibility of the local commandants, but rather to strengthen their position.

(8) Certain suggestions of the Military Committee on sundry subjects relating to the organisation and equipment of the local forces were approved.[2]

The completion of the defence works in this Colony was somewhat delayed in consequence of the money vote proving insufficient. However, in 1883 a supplementary vote of 70,000*l.* was included in the military estimate of that year, and the work was carried on in accordance with the recommendations. Since then great progress has been made, and all the guns are now in position, so that in the event of war the batteries would be ready to repel attacks on Port Jackson, Botany Bay, and Newcastle. The barracks at South and Middle Heads are completed, and the entrench-

[1] This appointment to be held from three to five years, subject to renewal.
[2] See *Appendix* A.

ments recommended are finished. A system of submarine mines now guards the entrance to Port Jackson, while great progress has been made in the torpedo defences at Newcastle and Botany Bay. The military forces have been reduced in strength to some extent, and further alterations are contemplated. Practically, however, the original recommendations have been carried out, and the force is increasing in efficiency. The purchase of gun-boats is still under consideration.

In 1881 H.M.S. 'Wolverene,' a screw corvette, was presented to the Colony, and is still retained as a training-ship for the Naval Brigade. This force has lately been reorganised so as to be available for service afloat in accordance with the recommendations of the *New South Wales Commission*. In a private memorandum made by Sir Peter Scratchley in 1884 I find against the entry 'Naval Brigade likely to be organised and " Wolverene " (colonial ship) maintained for training purposes,' these words, 'This is the fatal blot in New South Wales. Should follow Victoria.'

CHAPTER VIII.

VICTORIA.

A GLANCE at the chart of Australia shows at once that an attack upon Victoria by a foreign Power can only be made along the seaboard, which forms the southern boundary of the Colony. The coast extends from Cape Howe to the south-east extremity of South Australia at the mouth of the Glenelg River, a distance of nearly six hundred miles, all more or less inaccessible, a considerable portion being iron-bound with high cliffs. Even in places where there are low sandy hills and beaches the sea breaks more or less heavily throughout the year, and a landing is almost impracticable.

Port Phillip, situated near the centre of the coast, is the only harbour of importance. It is an estuary about thirty miles long and twenty broad, having an extensive bay on the eastern shore; while a branch estuary, averaging five miles in width, extends westwards for a distance of fifteen miles. The extreme breadth of Port Phillip from east to west, inclusive of the branch estuary, is about thirty-five miles, and the total area about seven hundred square miles. At the western extremity is the town of Geelong, a shipping port for wool and produce from the westward. At the extreme north lies Hobson's Bay, about three miles in length by one and a half in depth, near the shores of which is situated the city of Melbourne, with its numerous suburbs, extending from Williamstown on the western, to Emerald Hill and Sandridge on the northern, and St. Kilda and Brighton on the eastern side.

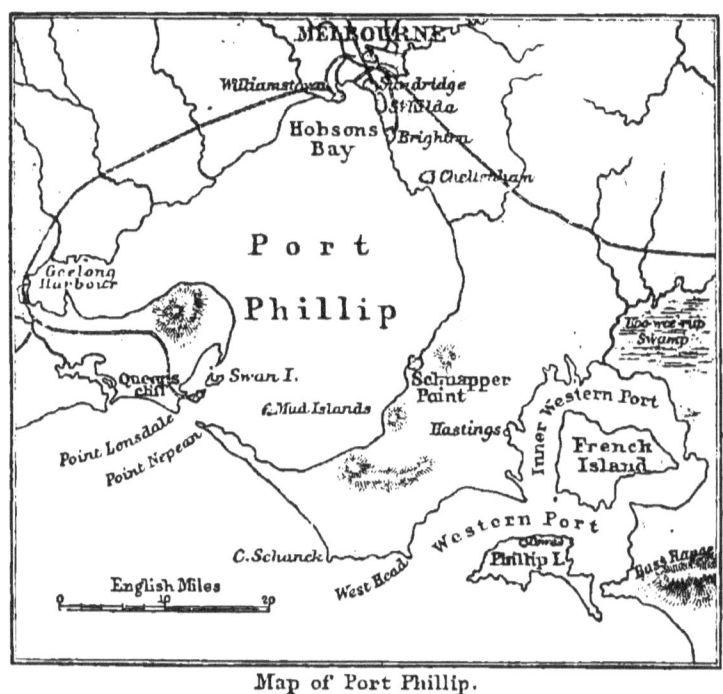

Map of Port Phillip.

The entrance to Port Phillip (about 4,000 yards wide) is between the two headlands, Point Nepean and Port Lonsdale. Facing the channel (about 3,500 yards from Point Nepean, and about 4,500 from Point Lonsdale) is Queenscliff. Owing to the existence of rocks and shoals on either side of the entrance, the navigable passage (called 'The Rip') is little more than 1,600

VICTORIA.

yards wide, and the tide runs through with great velocity. A vessel after navigating 'The Rip' and turning to the eastward would, after passing the line between Point Nepean and Queenscliff, find herself in an open deep-water harbour, about three miles long

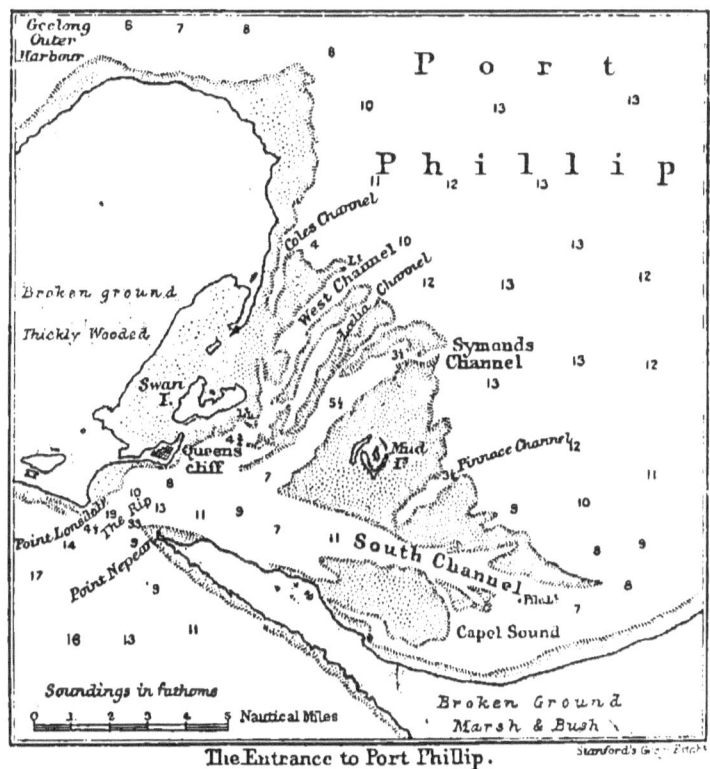

The Entrance to Port Phillip.

and one and a half broad. Thence the route to the inner waters of Port Phillip is by one of two channels, through shoals which for a distance of from six to ten miles render navigation difficult. The distance from 'The Rip' to Hobson's Bay by the 'West Channel' is about thirty, and by the 'South Channel' about forty miles. Besides these passages, there are Cole's, Lœlia, Symonds', and Pinnace Channels; but owing to difficulty in navigation these are seldom used.

Close to Port Phillip, on its eastern side, is Western Port, a good land-locked harbour, capable of accommodating ships of any size. About one hundred and ten miles south-east of the entrance to Port Phillip is Wilson's Promontory, the southernmost point of Australia. Near the extremity of this promontory on its eastern side is Waterloo Bay, and on its west side Waratah Bay, while to the eastward are Corner Inlet and Port Albert. Between the latter and Cape Howe there are no harbours. To the west of Port Phillip are the small harbours of Warrnambool, Belfast, and Portland.

The following extracts, taken from the Preliminary Report[1] on the Defences of Victoria, which was prepared by Sir William Jervois in conjunction with Sir Peter Scratchley, show the lines upon which the scheme of defence for the city of Melbourne was based :—

DEFENCE OF MELBOURNE.

(i.) *Considered with regard to an Enemy entering Port Phillip and occupying Hobson's Bay.*

The conditions under which the question has been considered on former occasions are in one important respect very different from those which exist at the present time. . . . Now there need be no fear that torpedoes will not be in their places when required, and will not be effective should an attempt be made to force the entrance to the harbour. . . . It must, however, be

[1] Made in 1877.

borne in mind, notwithstanding the greatly increased efficiency of torpedoes, that batteries of artillery are still essential to bear on attacking ships, under whose fire the submarine mines might otherwise be removed. The questions then arise, whether there are any positions where torpedoes can be applied in such manner as effectually to prevent the passage of an enemy's vessels to the inner waters of Port Phillip estuary ; and, if so, whether, having regard to questions of construction and expense, it be possible to erect batteries which shall absolutely protect torpedoes in such positions from being removed. Although it would be impracticable to adopt at the headlands a system of defence of which submarine mines would form part, the conditions are favourable for the application of torpedoes in the channels through the shoals within the entrance. . . . Forts can be constructed with facility, on sites well adapted for the protection and working of the torpedoes, where the width both of the West Channel and of the South Channel is about 1,400 yards. Thus, by a combination of forts and torpedoes at the channels through the shoals, the passage of an enemy's squadron to the inner waters of Port Phillip can be absolutely prevented.

In order to prevent the possibility of an enemy passing at night, the channel and approaches to it may be so illuminated by the magneto-electric light as to prevent any vessel attempting to remove the obstructions without being seen from the forts.

The forts defending the channels through the shoals will necessarily be too far distant from the anchorage between the shoals and the headlands to prevent an enemy's ships occupying that outer harbour, and so closing Port Phillip both against the ingress and egress of trading or other vessels. A battery of powerful guns should therefore be placed at Queenscliff, and another at Point Nepean, to bear upon hostile ships approaching the outer channel, as well as to cross-fire upon them in their passage through the channel, and, in conjunction with the 'Cerberus,' to prevent an enemy occupying the outer anchorage if he succeeded in reaching it. The 'Cerberus' will also aid in the defence of the passages through the shoals.

It has often been suggested that a fort should also be placed at Point Lonsdale; and no doubt such a work would be of advantage as affording a cross-fire with the guns on Point Nepean in the passage of a vessel through 'The Rip.' I think, however, that this additional work would be an unnecessary expense. It would not oblige a ship to pass any nearer to Point Nepean, and the narrowest part of the channel is not between Point Lonsdale and Point Nepean, but between the latter point and Queenscliff. An enemy, knowing that access to Hobson's Bay and Melbourne was absolutely barred by the defences at the shoals, would not risk the running of the gauntlet between the fire of the 'Cerberus' and the two outer works.

I should mention that I have fully considered whether, instead of defending Port Phillip by forts and torpedoes in conjunction with the 'Cerberus,' it would be better, as has been proposed on a previous occasion, to provide an ironclad vessel, in addition to the 'Cerberus,' in lieu of the forts. I am decidedly of opinion that it would not be desirable to adopt this course. I have long been aware of the advantages of floating defences, and for upwards of twenty years I have been a strong advocate for their employment; but I think that the case under consideration is not one in which the floating should be substituted for the fixed element of defence. Indeed, in the proposal to which I refer it is conceded that if it were adopted it would still be necessary to have land batteries for the defence of Hobson's Bay and Melbourne, and it is thereby admitted that the floating defences might not succeed in preventing an enemy obtaining access to the inner waters of Port Phillip. In considering whether it is desirable to employ floating batteries in lieu of forts it must be borne in mind that the vessel is liable to be sunk, not only by artillery fire, but by the action of offensive torpedoes or by ramming; she may be disabled by damage to her machinery, her screw, or her steering apparatus; she affords an unsteady gun carriage, and consequently the fire of her guns must, comparatively speaking, be more or less inaccurate. It may be added, as regards vessels of the 'Monitor' class, that in anything like rough weather they may be unable to fight their guns; again, the very advantage claimed for the vessel of being available for general service renders her liable to be absent when required at the particular spot where local defence is essential. As regards the relative expense of forts and ironclad ships, it must be observed that whilst the expense of the maintenance of fixed defences is insignificant, and the work once constructed is permanent, the cost of maintaining the vessel is considerable, and it is necessary to provide for her periodical renewal.

The question under consideration is the defence of Port Phillip and Melbourne, and if the artillery requisite for that defence can be mounted on fixed platforms, whence an effective fire can be brought to bear on the channels of approach, no object is gained by placing that artillery in a vessel afloat. There can be no object in substituting an unsteady platform, on which the amount of protection that can be afforded is limited by considerations inherent to floating structures, and which is liable to be taken away or to be sunk, for a fixed and perfectly steady platform, which can be fully protected either against its fire being silenced or from capture by an enemy. Further, if floating defences were substituted for forts, it would still be necessary to erect stations from whence the torpedoes could be worked, whereas the fort at once not only provides such stations, but perfectly fulfils the conditions required for the artillery defence.

The 'Cerberus' not being a sea-going vessel, an additional ironclad would no doubt be valuable for the protection of commerce at sea; but the provision of such a ship is a question that rests upon a different basis to that of the purely local defence of Port Phillip and the wealthy places upon its shores. It would be desirable that this principle of defence should be adopted for the defence of Australian commerce generally, and for the general protection of harbours on the Australian coast for which local defences cannot be provided. This question, however, may probably be better dealt with by arrangement with the Imperial Government, the Colonies undertaking to share the extra expense in proportion to their respective populations.

(ii.) *With regard to an Enemy occupying Western Port.*

It will be observed that, by adopting the plan of preventing an enemy from entering Port Phillip, the power is afforded of acting upon his flank or rear in the event of his attempting an attack upon Melbourne from Western Port. Bearing this in mind—considering, moreover, the distance he would have to march, his want of transport (for, of course, all horses and other means of transport would be removed from the neighbourhood directly an enemy appeared in Western Port)—in short, taking into account the whole conditions of the case, it does not appear at all likely that the operation would be attempted. If attempted, the amount of field force which the Colony can command would be amply sufficient to deal with any number of men—probably not more than 1,000 or 1,200—at all likely to be available for landing from a hostile squadron. It will be desirable to have a torpedo vessel to disturb an enemy if anchored in Western Port; and for this purpose an arrangement might be made by which the mail-boat that runs between Hastings and Cowes should be a specially swift vessel adapted for this purpose. Beyond this, and the maintenance of a sufficient field force, I think it unnecessary to make any special provision to meet an attack from that quarter.

It is sometimes stated that an enemy might land a force on the coast to the southward of Geelong, and thence make a raid upon that place. It appears to me that it is very unlikely that he would throw a force on shore on an open beach, where, even if he succeeded in obtaining a footing, he must calculate on a change of wind or weather cutting him off from his boats. In any case, whatever probability there may be of such an operation being attempted, it may be easily disposed of by a portion of the field force being despatched from Melbourne by railway to Geelong.

VICTORIA.

Defences of Victoria.—Original Scheme, codified by Sir Peter Scratchley.

LAND DEFENCES.

Heads.

Enclosed work on Point Nepean	To be armed with one 10-inch and six 80-pr. rifled guns
Batteries and keep at Queenscliff	To be armed with one 10-inch (new pattern), three 9-inch, and four 80-pr. rifled guns; batteries to be enclosed and keep provided

West Channel.

Enclosed work, keep, and torpedo depôt on Swan Island	To be armed with two 10-inch (new pattern), three 9-inch, and three 80-pr. rifled guns. Keep and torpedo depôt for submarine mines to be provided inside the work

South Channel.

Fort on Shoal	To be armed with five 10-inch and two 6-inch rifled guns (all B.L. chambered)

TORPEDO DEFENCES.

West Channel South Channel	Lines of observation and contact mines with light booms to be laid across the channels. Torpedo defences to be in charge of military authorities

MILITARY FORCES.

Regular Artillery Corps . . .	Required for manning the batteries and defences, 200 Regular Artillery and 400 Auxiliary Artillery
Coast and Volunteer Auxiliary Artillery	Ditto
Torpedo Corps	For defence of channels, 100 officers and men
Field force to repel landings	2,000 officers and men, Cavalry, Artillery, Engineers, Infantry

NAVAL DEFENCES.

'Cerberus,' turret-ship, 4 10-in. M.L.R. guns	In *peace time* to be maintained with a reduced crew at cost of 10,000*l*.; Naval Brigade being kept up to complete crew to war footing when required
Swift gun-vessel	To take the place of 'Victoria' and 'Nelson,' and to be manned by Naval Brigade

OUTPORTS.

WARRNAMBOOL, BELFAST, AND PORTLAND.

Battery and small artillery force at each port	Each battery to be armed with five 80-pr. rifled guns, acquiring 100 Volunteer Artillery at each place, with small detachments of Regular Artillery in time of war

This system of defence was adopted, but owing to the absence of necessary authority from the Government during 1877–8 and 1878–9, and the improvements in the manufacture and modes of mounting ordnance, which necessitated certain modifications in the original scheme, as well as to the insufficiency of the amounts voted during the years 1879–82, much delay took place in carrying out the works. In March 1882 so considerable a misconception appeared to exist on the subject of the Land Defences in this Colony that Sir Peter Scratchley thought it desirable to lay before the Victorian Government a brief statement of the then state of affairs, together with recommendations as to the steps necessary to be taken in order to complete the modified scheme.

He considered that as it would take several years to construct the South Channel Fort, according to the original design proposed by Sir William Jervois, it would be unwise to commence such a large and important work until a loan had been authorised for the purpose; accordingly it became necessary to consider what steps should be taken in the meantime to prevent hostile vessels passing up the South Channel. It was originally intended that the 'Cerberus' and a swift gun-vessel, together with torpedo-boats, should guard this channel pending the completion of the fort; but as these were not forthcoming, and the submarine defences for the channels had not been organised, a general impression existed in military circles that it would be unwise to leave to the 'Cerberus' alone the defence of this important channel. It was therefore proposed to provide additional floating defences, in the shape of gun-boats and fast torpedo-boats. This proposal, Sir Peter considered, should be adopted, provided that the gun-boats and torpedo-boats were of the latest designs, and that the gun-boats were armed with the most recent type of breechloading guns. At the same time he strongly advocated the necessity of some *fixed* defence for the South Channel, which would also serve the purpose of a *point d'appui* for the submarine mines.

Sir Peter Scratchley desired especially to call the attention of Victorians to the subject of Torpedo Defences for their channels. He intended these should form part and parcel of the fixed defences on shore, controlled by a special corps, organised for the purpose, under the military commander. Indeed, he considered that without the organisation of a Military Torpedo

Corps the batteries alone would not prevent an enemy's vessels passing up the channels. 'Torpedo defences,' he said, 'cannot be extemporised, for the simple reason that suitable explosives and electrical cables cannot be procured in the Colony, and, in the event of war, could not be obtained from England. The delay in the formation of a Military Torpedo Corps is becoming very serious. Success will depend entirely upon the efficiency of such a corps. This efficiency can only be attained by constant drill and practice.' Much experience and knowledge could, no doubt, have been gained by a moderate expenditure on experiments under the direction of competent officers, but no funds were available for the purpose.

Writing on this subject in connection with this colony he observed, 'The present[1] arrangements cannot be relied upon, as they are not in the hands of trained men; and, so far as I can ascertain, they are of an elementary and haphazard character, and not established on any well-considered plan. To rely upon such arrangements must, in my opinion, inevitably lead to disaster and an utter collapse of a most important portion of the defences, second only in value to the artillery on shore and afloat.'

He carefully considered with Major Ellery all matters connected with the reorganisation of the Military Torpedo Corps required for the defence of Port Phillip, and thoroughly agreed with that officer's memorandum and suggestions.[2]

---

[1] In 1882.
[2] These will be found set out at length in *Appendix* A.

Two years ago a considerable discussion took place in London on the subject of a change in the accepted modes of defending channels by submarine mines, and Sir Peter Scratchley discussed the question, so far as it concerned Port Phillip, with the War Office authorities, with the result that it was arranged that the plans for the defence of Port Phillip channels should be reconsidered according to the newest ideas. This was done, and it was found that, in spite of changes and improvements, the plan of defence generally, as settled by him with Major Ellery, practically remained the same. The conclusion come to was that the system adopted, both at Melbourne and Sydney, was the right one, provided that there were a sufficient number of permanently enrolled men, recruited from the Royal Engineers, to form a permanent section, comprising instructors, storekeepers, electrical mechanicians, and storemen. A permanently enrolled corps of submarine miners was looked upon as unnecessary, and altogether beyond the requirements of the defences.

As to the appointment by the Imperial Government for five years of a Royal Engineer officer to command the Torpedo Corps as well as the Engineer Corps of the Victorian military forces, Sir Peter Scratchley considered that once the submarine defences had been organised there would not be sufficient work for such an officer. It would probably take him about a year to organise, and for the remainder of his engagement he would have very little work to do, unless it was desired to employ him on other duties. The general supervision of the permanent defence works in progress naturally suggested itself as the extra employment; but here a difficulty arose in that submarine mining and telegraphy were taken up as specialities by officers of Royal Engineers; and, although such officers in his opinion were quite competent to deal with ordinary field engineering, they possessed little, if any, practical experience of permanent fortifications; while, so far as the mere supervision of the works was concerned, this duty could, as heretofore, be most satisfactorily performed by officers of the Public Works Department of Victoria. What appeared to Sir Peter to be a practical as well as a preferable arrangement was to appoint an Inspector of Submarine Mining for all the Colonies,[1] and to limit his engagement to three years as in the Royal Navy. 'This officer could proceed from one Colony to the other, organise in each the systems of submarine defence, and then remain to exercise a general supervision over the training of the Torpedo Corps established at each port.' The difficulty of appointing a retired officer is obvious. Submarine mining is a science as much as artillery, with this difference, that for years to come it will be eminently progressive; and no one residing in the Colonies for more than five years could, in Sir Peter's opinion, possibly keep himself thoroughly conversant with all the details of the work.

Any independent plan for torpedo defences which varied from that in connection with the defensive works, he considered, would vitiate the whole scheme, and

---

[1] Sir Peter considered great care should be exercised in the election, and that the Agent-General should have the right to veto any nomination by the Horse Guards.

render the expenditure thereon useless. This expression of opinion brings out forcibly the necessity of a *central* professional head, or responsible adviser, for the defence organisation of the colony, a necessity which Sir Peter was not slow to perceive. 'The theatre of operations for the defence of Port Phillip,' he said, 'will be altogether too circumscribed to require, or admit of, any independent action on the part of the naval and military commanders. If efficiency is desired, it can best be attained by establishing a central authority—well acquainted with the requirements and resources of both branches of the defence—to advise the Government, but not to interfere in any way with the executive duties of the commanders, nor to relieve them of their entire responsibility.'

A serious danger to the present system of Australasian defence is 'the omission of having everything carefully thought out and settled between the naval and military authorities, and approved by the Governments, *in time of peace*.' 'In this manner only,' said Sir Peter, 'will the Colonies be prepared to act with promptitude and decision—and without confusion—*in time of war*.' For example, in 1877 a comprehensive scheme of defence, comprising measures on shore and afloat, for repelling the attack of a hostile squadron on Port Phillip was submitted to the Victorian Government; but, although the scheme was approved at the time, up to 1882 a portion only was executed, and several of the most important recommendations were entirely disregarded or ignored, notwithstanding repeated appeals for further consideration.

The question of communication between the batteries at Port Phillip Heads, he considered, required much careful attention. In his opinion direct communication should be established by telegraph wires and signalling apparatus between Swan Island, Queenscliff, Queenscliff Neck, and Point Lonsdale, between Point Nepean and Queenscliff, and between Point Nepean and the South Channel Fort. A cable should be laid on the outbreak of war between the South Channel Fort and the mainland, and on Point Nepean by air line; and also between Swan Island and the South Channel Fort. Good and reliable intercommunication distinct from other telegraphs he looked upon as essential; while 'the question of communication between the naval and military forces should also be considered.'

The necessity for screening the batteries at the Heads from the enemy's view; the importance of establishing plantations[1] of trees for giving a background to the batteries at Queenscliff and Swan Island, and for providing timber suitable for creating obstructions round the works; the arresting of the encroachment of sand on Swan Island, Point Nepean, and the neck of land between Queenscliff and Point Lonsdale—were, in his opinion, all matters of great importance.

Lastly, Sir Peter Scratchley trusted nothing would be allowed to stand in the way of completing the

---

[1] The care of the plantations and vegetation at the batteries, Sir Peter Scratchley considered, should be vested in the permanent artillery force, and not left to the Public Works Department alone; while artillery working parties should be employed under the general guidance of the works superintendent at the Heads.

scheme of defence for Port Phillip in accordance with the original lines laid down by Sir William Jervois and himself.

Of late years great advance has been made with the defensive arrangements of this colony. The scheme originally recommended, although reorganised, has practically been adopted by the Victorian Parliament, who, in 1884, passed an Act especially appropriating 110,000*l.* per annum for five years to defray the expenses connected with the naval and military defences. The 'reorganisation scheme,' although hardly coinciding with the original recommendations, carries out in spirit Sir Peter Scratchley's suggestions.

The Heads and West Channel are now well defended, while the question of the South Channel fort[1] is being considered, with the object of reducing its cost and at the same time producing an efficient armament.

With regard to the naval defences, General Scratchley, writing in 1883, said, 'very large expenditure is being incurred, and I am very doubtful whether the Government are not drifting into difficulties with reference to the arrangements for maintaining these defences in an efficient state. As there is practically no independent outside inspection of these defences, there is no security for their being in proper order.' All this, however, is now rectified, and proper arrangements have been made.

The recommendation of a swift gun-vessel has been

[1] Sir Peter designed a fort which he estimated to cost 80,000*l.* inclusive of armament. This was a great reduction on the original plan.

executed by the provision of two gun-boats, but unfortunately these boats are *not swift*.

Little progress, however, beyond the establishment of Volunteer Artillery Corps, has been made in the defence of the outposts Warrnambool, Belfast, and Portland. Still, I have good authority for saying it is intended to carry out the original suggestions at some future date.

The condition of the naval defences of Victoria in 1885 was as follows:—

- (*a*) One turret-ship, the 'Cerberus.'
- (*b*) Two gun-boats, the 'Victoria' and the 'Albert.'
- (*c*) One frigate, the 'Nelson,' old type cut down.
- (*d*) One first-class torpedo-boat, the 'Childers.'
- (*e*) Two second-class torpedo-boats.
- (*f*) Four Harbour Trust dredgers, armed with old guns.

CHAPTER IX.
SOUTH AUSTRALIA.

THIS province is the central colony of Australia, and its territory extends from north to south of the entire continent. Hence the epithet 'South' appears somewhat inappropriate. The southern coast-line extends in a south-easterly direction, from the Western Australian boundary to the western extremity of Victoria, and, including the shores of Spencer's Gulf and St. Vincent's Gulf, is upwards of 1,500 miles in extent.

The entrance to Spencer's Gulf is forty miles broad, and, except where protected by the Gambier Islands, which are in the middle of the passage, is open to the Southern Ocean. St. Vincent's Gulf is separated from Spencer's Gulf by the Yorke Peninsula.[1] To the southward is Kangaroo Island, which forms a natural breakwater to the gulf, ninety miles in length and averaging about twenty in breadth. The approach to the gulf from the westward is by Investigator Strait,[2] between the Yorke Peninsula and Kangaroo Island. The approach from the eastward is by the Backstairs Passage,[3] between Kangaroo Island and the southern point of the

---

[1] A promontory, about 100 miles long and averaging about 25 broad, extends in a northerly direction for about 100 miles.
[2] About 50 miles long and 25 broad.   [3] About 7 miles broad.

gulf at Cape Jervis. There are lighthouses at Cape Borda, the north-west point of Kangaroo Island, on the Althorpe Islands, off the Yorke Peninsula, at Cape Willoughby, the eastern point of Kangaroo Island, and at Cape Jervis.

Adelaide, the capital and seat of government, is situated about seven miles south-east of Port Adelaide, which is nine miles from the entrance of a navigable inlet running for the most part parallel with the shore, from which it is separated by a low flat peninsula called Lefevre's Peninsula, about seven miles long and one wide. A railway connects the port with the city, and another,[1] about six miles long, joins Adelaide to Glenelg, a considerable watering-place on the coast, nine miles to the southward of Port Adelaide. About a mile to the westward of the port, at a place on the shore named 'The Semaphore,' is a long wooden pier, which affords communication from the outer anchorage without going up the inlet; there is also a pier at Glenelg, where the Peninsular and Oriental Steam Navigation Company's steamers land and receive their mails. To the southward, between Glenelg and Cape Jervis, are Brighton, Ports Noarlunga, Willunga, Myponga, Normanville, and Rapid Bay; while Clinton, Ardrossan, Stansbury, and Edithburgh serve as outlets for the produce of the country on the western side of the gulf.

On the shores of Spencer's Gulf, the first place to be noticed is Port Augusta,[2] which, though at present

---

[1] A private undertaking.

[2] For about twenty miles to the north of the point which may be said to be the head of the gulf, there is a channel affording access for vessels of large size to this place, which is to be the terminus of a railway, about 200 miles

but a small place, is probably destined to become an important town. About fifty miles to the southward of Port Augusta, and three miles up a narrow channel, on the eastern shore of Spencer's Gulf, is Port Pirie. A considerable trade is carried on here, and the country in the vicinity is very rich. Thirty miles south of Port Pirie lies Port Broughton, a small shipping place; while thirty miles further down the shore is Wallaroo, the seaport of rich copper mines. Moonta, a few miles inland and further to the southward, is another rich mining district. These towns are connected by railway with the head of St. Vincent's Gulf, and thence by lines, either existing or projected, with Adelaide. Port Franklin, on the western side, is a good though shallow harbour, in the neighbourhood of which the country is stated to be excellent. Near the entrance to the gulf is the magnificent harbour of Port Lincoln, but, owing to the lack of good agricultural land in its immediate neighbourhood, and the unsuccessful working of the copper mines in the vicinity, the port is but little used.

Encounter Bay lies to the eastward of Gulf St. Vincent, and possesses the harbours of Port Victor and Port Elliot. The latter is an insignificant anchorage, but the former is capable of being made an admirable harbour for the accommodation of large ships—indeed, Victor Harbour cannot fail to be the main shipping port for produce coming down the Murray River and the other rivers which flow into it from the neighbouring colonies. Further on, to the south-eastward, are the small

in length, the construction of which will greatly facilitate the transport of stock and produce from the interior.

harbours and townships of Kingston, Robe Town, Rivoli Bay, Greytown, and Port MacDonnell, of more or less importance as shipping ports for wool and produce.

Along the coast between Spencer's Gulf and the boundary of Western Australia, are Coffin's Bay, Waterloo Bay, Venus Bay, Streaky Bay, Smoky Bay, and Fowler's Bay. Some of these afford good harbours.

Sir Peter Scratchley's duties with regard to the defences of South Australia were restricted to the preparation of designs for the batteries for the protection of Adelaide. One of these batteries was completed some years ago, and the second is now in progress. The purchase of a swift gun-vessel for the general protection of the coast was decided upon by the Government of the Colony in 1882, and a 14-knot cruiser has since been purchased. 'The defence organisation,' said Sir Peter, writing in 1884, 'is in a highly satisfactory state.' What that organisation is, and the steps that led to its adoption, will perhaps be more clearly understood from a perusal of Sir William Jervois's defence recommendations, taken from his memorandum on the defences of South Australia :—[1]

One mode of attack which an enemy might adopt against South Australia would be to cruise off the entrances to the gulfs, with a view of capturing vessels laden with copper, wool, or other produce, in their passage from Adelaide, Wallaroo, and other ports. As regards Wallaroo, it should be noticed that large supplies of coal are kept there for the service of the mining districts in the neighbourhood, and an enemy would thus be enabled to supply his steamships with fuel for carrying on his operations.

[1] Made in 1877.

Another mode which he might adopt for carrying on hostilities would be to attack Adelaide itself. Having coaled at Wallaroo, he would probably steam up St. Vincent's Gulf; or, if he had sufficiently economised his coal during his passage to Australia, he might proceed up to Adelaide without previously replenishing his supply of fuel. In the absence of any means of defence, an enemy might take up a position within shelling distance of the port, and threaten a bombardment, or actually fire into the place. He might also capture the ships in harbour, and land a force, under cover of his guns, with a view of marching into Adelaide and demanding a heavy contribution.

It should be observed that Adelaide is much more open to attack, whether by sea or by a force landed for the purpose, than either Brisbane, Sydney, or Melbourne. Brisbane is situated on a narrow river many miles from the sea; Port Jackson can only be entered by a narrow passage, which can be perfectly defended; Melbourne can be thoroughly defended by torpedoes, and by forts on the shoals within the entrance to Port Phillip; and all three capitals of Queensland, New South Wales, and Victoria are more or less difficult of approach by an enemy who might desire to attack them by land. On the other hand, the coast in the vicinity of Adelaide is a low, open, sandy beach, on any point of which an enemy could land, and from whence an approach to the city is clear and open, with abundance of good roads; whilst Port Adelaide is entirely exposed to attack from seaward. The defence of the capital of South Australia is therefore more dependent on naval means than any of the capitals of the other Australian Colonies. Taking all the circumstances of the case into consideration, I have no doubt that the best

DEFENCE OF ADELAIDE

and its port, as well as of the commerce of South Australia, would be to provide a vessel of war superior in power to any hostile cruisers that would be likely to appear in these seas. Such a vessel, taking up her position in the bay on the north side of Kangaroo Island—where there is excellent anchorage, where she could be communicated with by telegraph from Cape Borda, from Sydney or Melbourne, from Adelaide and other places, and whence she would be in a position to move either westward through Investigator Straits, eastward through the Backstairs Passage, or up St. Vincent's or Spencer's Gulfs, as occasion may require—would be able to afford an active and effective defence against attacks to which this Colony is most likely to be exposed.

It is sometimes argued that the Imperial Naval Squadron would look after any hostile vessels in Australian waters; but when it is considered that that squadron, small as it is, and only composed of wooden vessels, is charged with visiting the islands in the South Seas, with the defence of Fiji Islands, of New Zealand, of Tasmania, and of all the Australian Colonies, the chance is but small of its being available for the special defence of any one Colony or any particular portion of the coast.

Proposals have been made at different times to provide small gunboats for the defence of Adelaide; and no doubt such vessels, in conjunction with other means, would be useful for this purpose. They are, however, wanting in the essential element of being superior to the vessel or vessels which would be likely to attack the commerce of the Colony, or its chief city and port.

I would recommend that an ironclad war-vessel, somewhat similar to one built about a year ago in England for the Portuguese Government, should be provided for the service of South Australia. This is a three-masted sea-going vessel, intended to aid in the defence of the Tagus and Lisbon, and capable of cruising to the Azores and the other Portuguese Colonies. It appears to me that the conditions which she was designed to fulfil are just those which are required for this Colony. The displacement tonnage of this vessel is about 2,500 tons; her length about 220 feet; her breadth 40 feet; her depth 25 feet. She is not a turret-ship, but has a fixed battery, protected by armour ten inches thick, which projects beyond the sides, and is so arranged that the guns—two in number, *i.e.* one on either side—can fire fore and aft as well as broadside. Each of these guns is about eighteen tons in weight. There is also a gun at the stern, of about six or seven tons weight, and from these three guns an all-round fire can be obtained. The vessel also carries four small pieces of artillery, for purposes for which the heavy and more powerful ordnance are not required. She is further constructed as a ram—the bow being specially strengthened for this object—and the armour-belt, which is nine inches thick, is carried down to the extreme point of the ram, about eight feet below the water-line. She has a raised forecastle, designed for protection against heavy seas, and she has a poop covering the stern gun. Her draught is about nineteen feet, and about seventeen feet forward. She is constructed with numerous water-tight compartments. The nominal horse-power of the engines is 450, and the speed of the vessel on her trial trip was at the rate of about thirteen knots an hour. The vessel ordered for South Australia should, in addition to her battery and ramming power, be fitted for propelling the Whitehead torpedo.

A vessel of this description would probably be less costly than one like the 'Cerberus,' and would be also capable of going to sea, whilst the 'Cerberus' is essentially a harbour-defence vessel.

Before finally deciding, however, on the nature of war-vessel to be obtained for the defence of South Australia, it is most desirable that a communication should be made to Her Majesty's Government, with a view of obtaining the opinion of the Admiralty as to the precise description of ship they would recommend, and in order to ascertain the expense which it would be necessary for the Colony to incur for providing such vessel, as also for manning and maintaining her.

It is, indeed, most desirable that the drawings for the vessel, the contract for building her, and the supervision of the work, should be undertaken by the Admiralty, provided Her Majesty's Government can make arrangements for meeting the wishes of the South Australian Government in this respect.

It will be unnecessary to have a full complement of officers and men on board the vessel except during war. In peace time there should be a commander in charge, two lieutenants, two engineers, two gunners, one paymaster, twenty-five petty officers, seamen, and stokers, and about twenty boys. The additional crew during war—except extra engineers and stokers, who would have to be specially engaged—could be supplied by seamen, organised as a Naval Reserve, properly trained during peace time, and receiving an annual payment for their services.

As regards the defence of the capital of the Colony and its port, it is desirable to guard against the chance of the war-vessel not being on the spot at the required moment, and of some little time elapsing before she could arrive at the scene of attack. It should, moreover, be observed that local defences at the capital would render the war-vessel more readily available for general defence. With this view I think it desirable—

SCHEME OF DEFENCE.

(*a*) That a battery for three heavy guns of eighteen tons weight should be constructed on the sandhills near the Semaphore, and another for two twelve-ton guns (already in the Colony) should be placed about three miles to the north of it.

(*b*) That the military road, already in course of construction, should be extended so as to afford ready communication behind the sandhills for field guns and infantry from LeFevre's Peninsula to Marino.

(*c*) That a few electro-contact torpedoes should be provided, to be placed across the Port Creek.

(*d*) That a force necessary for manning the defences and opposing a landing should be maintained.

	Officers and Men.
For Land Defence—	
Permanent Artillery	80
Volunteer Artillery	100
Volunteer Cavalry	60
Volunteer Infantry	700
Total	940

This number is irrespective of the small permanent Naval Force, about 50 strong, and the Naval Reserve, about 150 strong, which will be required for the proposed war-vessel.

CHAPTER X.

QUEENSLAND.

THE coast of Queensland extends in a north-westerly direction from Point Danger on the frontier of New South Wales to Cape York. At this point it turns nearly westward for about thirty-two miles, and then, running almost due south, forms the Cape York Peninsula; when, again turning westward, it forms with the Northern Territory of South Australia the coast line of the Gulf of Carpentaria. The seaboard, without following its windings, is about 1,900 miles in length.

Its general character is bold and rocky. From Cape York to the South Australian frontier, however, it is for the most part fronted with mangroves, mud flats, and shallows, from which the shoal water extends for a considerable distance into the gulf. The only town on this part of the coast is Normanton, the outlet for the Cloncurry gold and copper mines, and for the Etheridge goldfield; but fourteen ports and towns of more or less importance lie along or near the eastern coast.

After considering in detail the geographical position of Queensland, its harbours, rivers, and towns, the resources of the country, the distribution of population, and the measures which had already been taken for its defence, Sir William Jervois and Sir Peter Scratchley in 1877 arrived at the following conclusions :—

- That Brisbane, as the capital, required special consideration.
- That some local means of defence should be provided on the rivers Fitzroy and Mary, by which Rockhampton and Maryborough are approached.
- That at Townsville, Cooktown, and other places, when sufficiently increased in importance, some local protection should be afforded.
- That the protection of the coast generally must at present depend on naval means.

DEFENCE OF BRISBANE.

It was first thought that the defence of Brisbane could be attained by protecting Moreton Bay and so providing for the security of the capital and its outer anchorage at the same time. However, on examining the conditions of the case, this appeared unadvisable, as even under favourable circumstances the cost of defending Moreton Bay on these principles would be about 350,000*l.*; while to man works entirely isolated and far distant from any population, it would be necessary to incur the additional expense of maintaining a permanent force of artillery. It was finally decided that the best way to prevent an enemy entering and anchoring in Moreton Bay was by naval means, and that the defence of Brisbane against naval attack must be in the river by which the town is approached ; but, the river being shallow, it was only necessary to provide against the passage of *unarmoured* gun-vessels.

Brisbane

In considering the possibility of an enemy attempting to attack Brisbane by land, it was remarked:

At Redcliffe Point and Cleveland Point there are places at which a landing could be effected, and from whence there are roads affording access to Brisbane. These are, however, respectively, about twenty-eight and twenty-three miles distant from the town, and it does not appear likely that an attack would be made from thence. A small hostile force could, however, if unopposed, land, at high water, in Bramble Bay or Waterloo Bay, whence there are roads, each only about fourteen miles in length, by which Brisbane could be reached.

To oppose a landing, a gun-boat [1] of light draught was recommended.

Taking up a position in the boat channel at the mouth of the river, she would be very favourably placed for acting either to the north or south, and for directing her fire also against the enemy's ships if desired. Lying in shoal water at a considerable distance from hostile vessels in the bay, she might damage them without the probability of being hit.

A field force, consisting of a battery of field artillery, a company of engineers, and a body of infantry, was considered necessary either to co-operate with the floating defence in preventing a landing, or to oppose an advance on the town should an enemy succeed in obtaining a footing on shore.

There are several places favourable for resistance on the roads by which an enemy could move; and the services of the company of engineers and others would be turned to good account in forming earthworks, felling trees, making wire entanglements, and creating other obstacles, which would so impede a body of men in their advance that a small force would be able to prevent their progress.

---

[1] To draw not more than five feet of water, have a speed of not less than ten knots, and carry one eighty-pounder M.L.R. gun.

Defences of Queensland.—Original Scheme, codified by Sir Peter Scratchley.

LAND DEFENCES.

Brisbane, at Lytton.—Enclosed work with defensible stockade on Signal Hill	To be armed with two 6-inch (new pattern) and two 64-pr. rifled guns. Stockaded enclosure on Signal Hill with barracks

TORPEDO DEFENCES.

Brisbane River, at Lytton . .	Observation and electro-contact mines across river
Mary River (Maryborough) . .	Electro-contact mines across river
Fitzroy River (Rockhampton) .	Electro-contact mines across river

MILITARY FORCES.

Volunteer Garrison Artillery .	For battery at Lytton, 80 officers and men
Torpedo corps	For Brisbane, Maryborough, and Rockhampton, 90 officers and men
Field forces to repel landings .	Field Artillery, Engineers, and Infantry, for Brisbane, Maryborough, and Rockhampton, 1,080 officers and men

NAVAL DEFENCES.

Brisbane.—Gunboat and one or more torpedo-boats	For defence of Moreton Bay, to prevent landings
Maryborough.—Gun barge and torpedo-boats	For defence of river
Rockhampton.—Gun barge and torpedo-boats	For defence of river
Naval Brigades at the above-named places	To man naval defences, 110 officers and men

The object of this scheme was to bar the passage up the river to Brisbane, and thus force the enemy either to remain in Moreton Bay or attempt a landing, when he would be opposed by the gun-boat and the field force. Notwithstanding a certain opposition to the scheme at first, which, no doubt, arose mainly from its being misunderstood, the Legislature at length determined to carry out the greater portion of the recommendations, and voted a sum of 22,000*l*. on account of capital expenditure. It was decided to provide the battery at Lytton, and its armament, guns for Rockhampton and Maryborough, rifles for the infantry and artillery, rifle ranges, and drill-sheds, and also to sanction the annual expenditure for the proper maintenance and training of the Volunteers.

As to the idea that the defence of the Colony could be provided by a land force alone, unassisted or unsupported by any defensive works, Sir Peter Scratchley said: 'It is fortunate, indeed, that the defence of Brisbane has not fallen into the hands of people advocating these views, for, of all ideas ventilated on the defence question, there are none so mischievous or so utterly opposed to common sense and to recognised principles of war. Let any one take up a map of the country between Brisbane and Moreton Bay; let him imagine the battery and torpedoes at Lytton barring the river; let him suppose this battery to be supported by a defensible post on Signal Hill, within 1,200 yards of it: and he will inevitably come to the conclusion that no enemy would attempt an advance upon Brisbane, on either side of the river, without first capturing these defences—a task requiring time and appliances specially brought with the expedition—or without leaving a force to hold them in check. To conduct either of these operations with any chance of success, an enemy would have to land a force at least double that proposed for the defence of Brisbane.'

Remarking on the strength and composition of the military forces recommended, he observed, 'the chances of a landing are remote, provided certain precautionary measures are adopted; nor is it at all likely that an enemy would attempt extended operations on land, as, besides being exceedingly hazardous, they would require very elaborate preparations. He is more likely to attempt raids by sea. The field force recommended for Brisbane[1] acting on the defensive, fighting only in well-selected positions, knowing the country thoroughly, with its flank secured by the Lytton defences, would certainly be able to defeat a superior force. There is no reason, however, why a reserve should not be formed of Volunteers who have performed efficient service for a term of years. These men could be invited to attend the annual encampments, but no expenditure need be incurred beyond the provision of a very inexpensive uniform. In time of war no doubt they would join the ranks with alacrity. The formation of a reserve for the Volunteer force would be attended with the great advantage that in time of war an increase of strength would be obtained without additional cost in time of peace.'

He was opposed to the creation of a number of small corps (the evil effects of which system were brought very forcibly to his notice when inspecting the Volunteer force in New Zealand),[2] and recommended that the torpedo defences should be entrusted to the Queensland Volunteer Engineers.[3] 'It is fatal,' he said,

---
[1] 880 strong, including the up-country corps.   [2] See p. 237.
[3] This proposition was accepted by the Queensland Government.

'to military efficiency to have a number of small corps; economical management cannot be attained, nor can discipline be maintained as in larger bodies. This is found to be the case with regular troops; how much more, therefore, will it be so with Volunteers? For these reasons it has been found necessary, wherever Volunteer forces are maintained, to consolidate small corps into regiments and battalions.' He advised the division of the Queensland Volunteer Engineers into two divisions—one to be trained as submarine miners, the other as sappers and signallers, the general direction of the duties of the corps being entrusted to the officer commanding.

'When a permanent artillery corps is established, as in the other Australian Colonies,' he said, ' the duty of maintaining the battery at Lytton, and of any other permanent works of defence in connection therewith, can be undertaken by it; consequently it is only necessary to maintain a small body of engineers to form part of the field force, which has been provided with the object of meeting the contingency of a landing by the enemy for the purposes of turning the defensive position at Lytton and marching upon Brisbane by either bank of the river. Such an arrangement is in accordance with the plan of defence which is approaching completion. The battery and keep at Lytton are to be enclosed and rendered self-defensible and independent of the support of the field force, which will be set free to devote its entire attention to resisting the landing of the enemy, and will be relieved of all anxiety as to the garrisons of these works being able to hold their own.'

Considering that in the field much of the heavy work will have to be done by military and civil labour, under the direction of the engineer corps, Sir Peter considered it of paramount importance that as many of the men as possible should be trained to become the directors of the unskilled labour provided. With regard to the signalling duties, he thought the best course would be to train a few men of the Sapper division to acquire a thorough knowledge of the army system of signalling by flags during the day and by lamps during the night. When these men became thoroughly proficient they should be detailed to instruct such men in the artillery and infantry as were willing to learn, as, in his opinion, it was essential that all arms of the force should be able to communicate with each other in the field by visual signals. Signallers will also be required in connection with the submarine mining operations to communicate between the shore and boats.[1]

In this colony the defensive measures on land are practically complete so far as the protection of Brisbane is concerned. The battery at Lytton is armed and ready, and the works recommended at Signal Hill. The submarine mines are completed, and the reorganisation of the military forces, as approved by Parliament, is now in progress of formation. With regard to the naval defences, two ten-knot gun-boats have been provided for the defence of Brisbane; writing in 1883 Sir Peter Scratchley said, 'the Government have decided to defer

[1] For Sir Peter Scratchley's remarks on field fortification, see p. 50.

the provision of local defences for the rivers at Maryborough and Rockhampton, and intend using the second gun-boat for the general defence of the coast. Local companies of infantry are, however, retained at these places.'

CHAPTER XI.

WESTERN AUSTRALIA.

THE commanding geographical position of Western Australia cannot fail to attract attention whenever the subject of Australasian Defence is being considered, while King George Sound,[1] the first and last port of call in Australia for steamers carrying the mails between that continent, Europe, the East, and Great Britain, is a strategical position important alike to the Australasian Colonies and the mother-country.

The entrance[2] to the Sound is five miles wide, and divided into three channels by the two islands Breaksea and Michaelmas. The North channel is little used, as it is not considered quite safe; but the Middle[3] and Main[4] channels are perfectly secure for vessels of any size, while the latter is equally available during day and night and in all weathers. Sir Peter Scratchley considered that, in time of war, a look-out station should be established on Grove Hill, to the west of the entrance, from which point an enemy's ship advancing from the westward, close in to the shore,[5] could be easily detected.

[1] By sea the Sound is about 360 miles from Fremantle, the port of Perth; but overland, by a good road, the distance to the capital is only 256 miles.

[2] It should be noted that the heads, north and south of the entrance, together with the two islands across it, are quite inaccessible, being from 200 to 500 feet high, with very precipitous sides.

[3] 1,300 yards wide. [4] 4,000 yards wide.

[5] Here the water is very deep

The Sound is about four and a half miles wide and six long, measured from Breaksea Island to the entrance of Princess Royal Harbour, which is landlocked and affords a perfectly safe anchorage for large vessels at all times. The prevailing winds are N.W. to S.W. during the winter months (May to September), and S.E.

King George Sound.

to E., but generally E., in the summer (October to April); the force, however, of the easterly winds is broken by the two islands across the entrance. Good anchorage and holding ground are to be found everywhere, and more especially in Frenchman Bay;[1] but there are no landing-places outside.

[1] South of the entrance to Princess Royal Harbour.

The entrance to Princess Royal Harbour[1] is narrowed by shoals, and navigation is rendered somewhat difficult by the set of the tide. On the south side of the entrance is Point Possession, a bold promontory, somewhat in the shape of a flattened dish-cover, and connected with the mainland by a narrow and sandy isthmus. On the north side is Point King, on which stands a lighthouse possessing a light that can be seen from almost every part of the Sound; while inside the harbour a projecting point faces the entrance and completely commands the channel.

Unfortunately a great part of the harbour,[2] which is about three miles long by two broad, is shoal-water, owing to the drifting of sand from the surrounding hills—a matter of grave importance, and one which will require attention when King George Sound becomes a naval coaling station, and Albany[3] (a well-placed town situated on the north shore of Princess Royal Harbour) a centre of commercial activity.

The roadstead[4] off Fremantle is open to north-westerly winds, which often set in for periods extending from one to three weeks, and cause the sea to run very high. Several engineers have reported upon the proposal to construct a harbour at Fremantle, but all agree that this could only be done at great cost. Sir John Coode, indeed, was of opinion that a deep-water

[1] 600 yards across from shore to shore.
[2] The general character of the land around the harbour and Sound is of granite formation, very broken, irregular, and hilly, with intervening sandy valleys covered more or less thickly with scrub.
[3] Albany may be designated the 'Key of Australia,' and in the event of the Colonies federating will probably be chosen as a centre of organisation.
[4] Gage Roads.

channel from the sea could not be maintained in Swan River, and estimated the cost of a harbour outside Fremantle, in twenty-nine feet of water, at 638,000*l*.[1]

It has been stated that King George Sound is only of value for defence purposes to the Imperial navy and the Eastern Colonies of Australia. This view was not accepted by Sir Peter Scratchley, who considered that, without such a harbour, the future progress of Western Australia would be seriously retarded. A coal depôt at King George Sound, he thought, was required for steamers trading between the Eastern Colonies and Perth, and between the settlements on the west coast to the north and south of the capital; and, in his opinion, no other place existed in the south of Western Australia where coal could be securely kept for this purpose.

Notwithstanding the withdrawal of the depôt belonging to the Peninsular and Oriental Company, the prosperity of Albany does not appear to have been checked, although the dispersion of the large staff of employés and their families reduced the population for a time. The wisdom of this course is freely questioned, as notwithstanding the reduced consumption of coal consequent on the introduction of compound engines, there is great risk of steamers running short of fuel on the voyage out from Ceylon against adverse winds. For this reason alone, it would be a great mistake to look upon King George Sound as commercially unimportant, or simply as a place which it may or may not be desirable to occupy in time of war.

Yet until recently the Imperial authorities have

---

[1] Or 242,000*l*., according as a larger or smaller scheme was adopted.

declined to recognise its importance in this respect. True the matter has been much considered and action advocated; but little more has been done than to declare the defence of King George Sound part and parcel of a general scheme of Australasian continental defence which has never been definitely settled.

From a defence point of view King George Sound is of paramount importance. Admiral Wilson places particular value on it because it is to windward of all the Colonies on the Australian Station:—

Commanding, as it does, the trade route from the westward, it is a position which would, as a matter of course, be held by a squadron in time of war. It is also essential to keeping up steam communication with Western Australia, as none of her Majesty's ships on this station could steam from Adelaide to Fremantle during the prevailing westerly winds without taking in coal at least once on the way.

Sir William Jervois, in remarking on the necessity of providing fortified coal depôts on the routes of British commerce, has also pointed out that the fine harbour of King George Sound occupies a most important position with reference to the defence of Australian commerce:—

Undefended, it may in time of war be occupied by hostile vessels, which, issuing therefrom, might cut off our steamers and merchant ships. On the other hand, if defended, it would become a most valuable naval post for vessels of war acting for defence.

These opinions Sir Peter Scratchley thoroughly endorsed. In fact it is only necessary to examine the chart of Southern Australia in order to perceive, at a glance, that King George Sound is most favourably placed as a base for operating against an expedition that might be despatched from Europe, America, or the East against Australia. Albany, too, is in telegraphic communication with Perth and Adelaide, and through the latter place with the Eastern Colonies, New Zealand, Tasmania, the East, and Europe.

Similar views are entertained by some of the Australian Governments, and at the Intercolonial Conference, held at Sydney in January 1881, Mr. W. Morgan, then Premier of South Australia, moved that the time had arrived

> when joint action should be taken for the more efficient naval defence of the Australian Colonies and New Zealand, and for the protection of the large number of valuable vessels now engaged in the Australian carrying trade. . . . Any scheme of naval defence should also include the naval defence of the harbours of the capitals of the different Colonies, and the fortification of King George Sound or some other port in Western Australia, and the maintenance of a sufficient force for holding the same.[1]

Although the motion was defeated, it is not to be supposed that the views brought forward by Mr. Morgan are not shared by a large number of leading men in Australia. Public opinion in the Colonies, as in the mother-country, is not always easy to move in defence matters. Every day, however, statesmen are becoming more alive to the necessity of adopting all reasonable precautions for making her Majesty's dominions absolutely secure against foreign aggression. The Austra-

---
[1] For a fuller account of the debate on this resolution, see *Appendix A*.

lasian Governments have given practical proof of their determination in this respect by carrying out the recommended schemes of land defences. True the progress in the construction of these defensive works has been slow, but there is now a reasonable prospect of seeing the principal ports of all the Colonies well protected; while the question of Colonial naval defences, auxiliary to the Imperial navy, is already ripe for discussion.

'No doubt,' said Sir Peter Scratchley, 'if the defence of King George Sound were entirely undertaken in time of war by the Imperial navy or by Imperial troops, the maintenance of a garrison to man the defences would be costly and embarrassing; it would, however, be infinitely more so if the place were left unprotected, and thus became the only weak point in the Australian system of defence.'[1]

The Government at Perth is as much interested in the defence of the Sound as the Government at Hobart is in the defence of Launceston, and it has been reasonably observed that the duty which has been accepted by the other Australasian Colonies of providing an efficient defence for their ports should be undertaken by Western Australia. 'Were this done,' said Sir Peter, 'and the Imperial Government to sanction the carrying out of the scheme of defence, such a course would have a marked and most favourable effect upon the proceedings of the Eastern Colonies. In that event, they would probably be prepared to include Western Australia in their general scheme of naval protection without ex-

[1] See p. 72.

pecting any contribution from it beyond that of its local defence.'

This Colony stands in a totally different position from the rest of Australia. Whilst its territory is enormous, its population is very small and scattered in unimportant settlements at long distances apart. Yet its revenue is good, and the prospects of future progress are highly promising. On the other hand, in the Eastern Colonies, wherever protection against foreign aggression is required, population and resources for defences are to be found. 'In Western Australia,' Sir Peter Scratchley said, 'Perth, Fremantle, and Albany are the only places requiring protection; at Albany the population is so small that we must look elsewhere for the men required to garrison such defences as may be provided. Yet the place is of vital importance for the general defence of Australia.'

'The city of Perth and the port of Fremantle are not likely to be objects of serious attack, as they cannot be looked upon as valuable prizes to an enemy.' It has, however, been urged that an enemy, finding the Sound in a position to resist his attack with success, might direct his attention to the capital, and endeavour to enforce the surrender of Princess Royal Harbour by firing into Fremantle and landing a force to advance upon Perth.

Operations of this character, Sir Peter Scratchley considered, should be met by naval means—i.e. the combined action of the Imperial navy and the auxiliary Colonial naval defences—supplemented by moderate land defences. 'Although Fremantle may be exposed to bombardment from the sea, Perth is perfectly secure in that respect. On the other hand, hostile vessels could not take up a position off Fremantle which was not commanded by guns on shore, and, as there is no inner port for friendly ships, the enemy's fire could only be directed on the town.' This is a risk which, in his opinion, could not be avoided, in the event of the naval defences not being available to prevent the operation.

A disembarkation having for its object an advance upon Perth, he considered, could be opposed with success by a moderate force on land, especially if it were entrenched. The risk of being forced to retire by the resistance offered, the liability to attack by torpedo-boats, the chances of the British ships appearing on the scene, the probability of bad weather cutting off communication with the shore, in which case the party landed might have to be abandoned, are all contingencies which, in his opinion, would render it very doubtful whether a naval commander would undertake such an operation when the object to be gained is so small.

Although he deemed it would be very unwise to overlook the possibility of such attacks being made, he thought that undue weight should not be given to the point, which certainly does not diminish the necessity and importance of fortifying the Sound. 'It would suffice,' he said, ' to provide two guns of position at Fremantle, and a small field force for the purpose of resisting a landing and covering the approaches to Perth, with one or more torpedo-boats to harass the enemy's ships ; but local defences must be provided at King George Sound capable of meeting the attack of an enemy's squadron ; for however desirable it may be to keep the enemy outside the Sound, on account of the magnificent shelter it affords for vessels, this could not be effected by means of fixed defences alone ; or, in fact, by fixed and floating defences combined, except at a very great cost ; while Princess Royal Harbour, being landlocked and capable of accommodating a large number of ships drawing twenty-three feet of water in all weathers and at all times, must be sufficiently defended.'

To meet an attack on King George Sound, Sir Peter Scratchley advised a combination of fixed and floating defences. He recommended guns in suitable works at the Heads, submarine mines at the entrance, harbour defence gunboats, and several torpedo-boats. The guns on shore and submarine mines in the channel, he considered, would effectually close the entrance of the harbour ; while the gunboats would co-operate with the land defences in resisting a landing, and, with the torpedo-boats, go a long way towards preventing the occupation of the Sound by hostile vessels. An infantry force with field guns, he thought, would be required to resist the enemy as he was landing, and to arrest his advance on the town. At the same time he was fully aware that the maintenance of local forces presented great difficulty, and, for that reason, was impressed with the necessity of providing floating defences to act against the enemy as he was landing.

Sir Peter Scratchley fully recognised the advantage of *floating* defences,[1] where they would afford the necessary protection in a more economical manner and yet

---

[1] See footnote to Chapter on Naval Defences, p. 69.

be as effective as *fixed* defences, but entirely dissented from the opinion that the defence of the Sound would be sufficiently provided for by an extemporised battery, a gunboat, and a few torpedo-boats. At the Sound extemporised defences, he considered, 'could only be established by the Imperial army and navy, as the men, stores, or appliances for the purpose are not on the spot.'

The annual expenditure on maintenance would, in his opinion, be insignificant in the case of coast batteries, as they could be added to from time to time so as to increase their defensive power, and the works would be practically indestructible, whilst gunboats, although they could be hauled up out of the water, would necessarily require periodical renewal; besides, were gunboats alone provided at the Sound, he considered it very probable that an enemy would endeavour to destroy them by torpedo-boats sent in for the purpose at night.

The relative importance of the measures for the defence of Princess Royal Harbour, Sir Peter placed in the following order:—

> Guns in batteries on shore.
> Torpedo-boats.
> Gunboats.
> Submarine mines in the channel.

The guns, he considered, would, besides commanding the interior of the harbour and its approach from the Sound, practically close the entrance, and render a landing outside very difficult. The torpedo-boats would co-operate in the defence of the entrance by attacking ships as they were passing in; or by attacking the enemy's vessels whilst engaged in landing a force; and they would also be available in the event of the guns on shore being silenced, besides rendering the blockade of the port by the occupation of the Sound a much more hazardous undertaking.

He thought that the torpedo-boats might, at first, be improvised torpedo launches, which, in time of peace, could be utilised for harbour service both at Albany and Fremantle. Torpedo-boats of great speed he believed absolutely necessary for European warfare, but did not think them of importance for Colonial defence; in fact, he would rather have made up by quantity for inferiority in quality, two or three boats of moderate speed being, in his opinion, more formidable than one boat of great speed and power. 'The former,' he said,[1] ' can be readily found in most of the Colonial ports, whilst the others, being practically useless in peace time, are out of the question on account of their cost, at any rate for the present, at such a place as King George Sound.'

These measures, he considered, would meet all probable attacks on the harbour itself, and it would only be necessary to provide, in conjunction with the Eastern Colonies, external naval defences for the protection of commerce.

The gunboats [2] would be invaluable for preventing

---

[1] In 1882.

[2] The gunboat, Sir Peter Scratchley considered, should be of the 'Staunch' class, of low speed, and shallow draught, and armed with a gun capable of piercing such a thickness of armour as could be carried by ships sent out to attack the Australasian Colonies.

an occupation of the Sound and for co-operating generally in the defence, especially if an armoured vessel were to form part of the attacking squadron. Submarine mines, however desirable, he thought scarcely applicable to the defence of Princess Royal Harbour; as it would be extremely difficult to organise and maintain them. At the same time, he advised a few mines in the channel, in order to produce the moral effect resulting from their employment.

The occupation of Mounts Melville and Clarence has been recommended in order to guard the coal depôt and stores against attack by land. Such a defensive position Sir Peter considered too retired to serve this purpose, as a landing on the south side would lead to no result, whilst ' a landing on Middleton Beach would be best resisted by the construction of a semi-permanent work, to be held by a small field force, and so placed as to command both the beach and road leading to Albany.'

The suggestion that the Imperial garrison at Ceylon should furnish a contingent for Albany, and the recommendations by Admiral Wilson that marines, provided by the Australian squadron, should form the garrison for the extemporised battery, and a paid naval reserve should be raised for the floating defences, are thus commented upon by Sir Peter Scratchley: 'If Western Australia were to depend upon Imperial assistance, circumstances might arise which would render it impossible either to send men from Ceylon, or for the Commander of the Australian squadron to spare a sufficient force of marines, especially on the outbreak of war, the time of greatest danger to King George Sound. No doubt, either of these arrangements would be the best in a military sense ; but there is an element of uncertainty connected with them which it would be extremely unwise to admit in establishing a system of defence.'

It has also been proposed that the Eastern Colonies of Australia should combine to supply a contingent of the defending force. This proposal found no favour with General Scratchley, who, knowing it is no easy matter to induce these Colonies to maintain sufficient forces for their own protection, was opposed to increasing the difficulty by asking them to undertake the responsibility at a time when they might be heavily pressed to provide for local defences.

There is, too, a reasonable prospect of Albany, and, in fact, the Colony generally, increasing in importance, and therefore in population; accordingly no reason exists why the defence organisation of Western Australia should not be self-supporting and self-reliant. In Sir Peter's opinion, the total strength required for the defence of Perth and King George Sound was 770 [1] officers and men. Although this force could be raised within the Colony, he thought it was a matter for consideration whether, for a few years at least, a money contribution towards the cost of maintaining these forces should not be made to the Government of

---

[1] This total, however, provides the maximum number which he considered necessary. Writing on the subject in 1882, he said, 'I think that the present requirements will be met by 350 at Perth and 300 at Albany.' It should be noticed that a large expenditure on barrack accommodation is not necessary for Sir Peter's scheme of defence.

Western Australia by the Imperial authorities or the Eastern Colonies.

He believed, too, that by adopting an organisation differing from that of an unpaid Volunteer force, it would be practicable to form corps at Perth and Fremantle from which, in time of war, men could be transferred to Albany when required. The organisation he proposed was that of a *Volunteer Militia*, similar to that in New South Wales [1] and South Australia. He considered too that a detachment of mounted men should be raised to perform, in time of war, the duties of orderlies, scouts, and escorts; but until the defence of Perth and Albany had been provided for, it appeared to him unwise to expend money upon the maintenance of country corps, unless required for police purposes.

The remuneration of Volunteers by land grants, which had been tried in the Eastern Colonies, though without success,[2] he considered would be well adapted to Western Australia; but there appeared to him another source from which men could be drawn, viz. a pensioner force somewhat similar to that which was in existence at Perth up to 1880.[3] Writing on this point in 1882, he said: 'Considerations of expense would doubtless prevent the re-establishment of this force on its original footing; and no doubt there are very few

[1] See recommendation of New South Wales Commission on this point, p. 156.
[2] 'The cause of this,' said Sir Peter Scratchley, 'is to be found in the fact that although these grants were given as a reward for a certain term of military service, no attempt whatever was made to enforce a high standard of efficiency.'
[3] When 133 N.C.O.s and men were serving.

of the old pensioners remaining who would be fitted for further military service. If any were available they might be induced to join a paid *Volunteer Militia*. Others might be willing to remove to Albany, provided that the Government gave them free grants of land *conditional* on their joining the militia for a term of five years. If some arrangement were devised whereby these men, besides receiving the payment for attendance at drill, could at once enter into possession of the land,[1] an immediate inducement would be given to them to settle on it and build cottages for themselves and their families. Time-expired men from the Imperial army, carefully selected for the purpose, might be enrolled for service at Perth and Albany, on the understanding that they would receive a small rate of pay for a term of years in addition to grants of land. The men might be encouraged to seek employment after their arrival within a certain distance of the places named, and, if successful, transferred to the ranks of the *Volunteer Militia* on the same conditions as the old pensioners.

'Besides the artillery corps, a naval brigade, fifty strong, would be required for the gunboat and torpedo-boats, which would have to be recruited from that portion of the population which is engaged in maritime pursuits. This brigade should be organised on the same system as the land forces.'

Considering the scarcity of labour in Albany and the importance of keeping down the money expendi-

---

[1] Somewhat on the plan adopted with free selectors in the Australian Colonies, who pay for their land by yearly instalments.

ture, Sir Peter Scratchley advised the employment of prisoners in the construction of the defence works. These prisoners [1] might be housed close to Point Possession, and being cut off from communication with Albany, except by water, could be easily guarded. Such an arrangement, too, would be economical, although the time required to construct the works might, perhaps, be greater. Good lime is to be had in the vicinity, but though bricks are made near Albany, they are scarcely suitable for defence works. The stone from the excavations for the battery would, however, do for the concrete and masonry; while cement, timber, bricks, and all ironwork and fittings could be procured from Perth. Water could be readily stored on the site.

A railway is now in course of construction, which when completed will join Albany and York [2]—a rising township situated in the centre of an agricultural district—and open up a large quantity of good land still the property of the Government. When this railway is finished, Albany, being the only natural outlet for the produce of the country to be traversed by the line, will at once become the most important place in Western Australia.

An offer has also been made to the Western Australian Government by an English syndicate, to construct a railway on the land-grant system from York to Eucla.[3] The proposal is being favourably entertained. In the event of the work being undertaken some arrangement will probably be made with the South Australian

---

[1] The cost of keeping and clothing a prisoner is about 1s. 8d. per diem.
[2] 60 miles east of Perth.   [3] 700 miles due west.

Government to extend the line from Eucla to Port Augusta. In this event direct communication will be established between Perth and Brisbane *viâ* Adelaide, Melbourne, and Sydney.

I was much struck, when at Albany two years ago, with the amount of land commanding the harbour and its approaches that appeared unoccupied. On remarking this to Sir Peter Scratchley at the time, he told me that when last at King George Sound he had advised the Government to make considerable reservation of land near the harbour for naval and military defence purposes. Fortunately for Western Australia, his suggestion was adopted, and the land referred to, greatly risen in value both on account of its position and other advantages, was the very land Sir Peter Scratchley had advised the Government to reserve.

CHAPTER XII.

TASMANIA.

TASMANIA, an island nearly equal in size to Ireland, lies near the south-eastern extremity of the Australian Continent, between 40° 41' and 43° 39' south latitude, and between 144° 30' and 148° 30' east longitude. Bass's Straits, which average about 150 miles in width, separate the island from Victoria. Between its north-east point and the mainland of the continent is the Flinders Group, and about midway between its north-west point and the mainland lies King's Island.

To the westward, between South-east Cape and Cape Grim, are the bar harbours of Port Macquarie and Port Davey, and the mouths of the rivers Pieman and Arthur. The coast on this side is dangerous, owing to the heavy rolling sea. On the northern coast, which is comparatively sheltered, are the ports Duck Bay, Circular Head, Boat Harbour, Table Cape, Port Frederick, and Port Sorell. The principal harbour, however, on this side, is Port Dalrymple, at the entrance of the river Tamar, forty miles from the mouth of which lies Launceston, the second place of importance in the Colony. On the eastern coast, which consists of perpendicular cliffs, with long intervals of low shore, are

George's Bay, Oyster Bay, and Spring Bay, while many deep bays and harbours affording safe anchorages for ships of any size are to be found on the south-eastern part of the coast. The best known are Port Arthur, Storm Bay, Frederick Henry Bay, Norfolk Bay, D'Entrecasteaux Channel, Port Espérance, South Port, Recherché Bay, and the Derwent, upon which river Hobart Town, the capital of the Colony, is situated.

Tasmania occupies an important position with reference to the general defence of the Australasian Colonies. Being within three days' steaming distance from Adelaide, one from Melbourne, two and a half from Sydney, and four from New Zealand, it would be no difficult task for an enemy, occupying any of the fine harbours it possesses, to harass the commerce of those Colonies. A hostile occupation of the Tasmanian harbours can only be prevented by naval means, for the provision and maintenance of which the Colony has not sufficient resources; therefore, their defence against such occupation must be considered in connection with that of the coast and harbours of the adjacent Colonies.

In 1878 Sir William Jervois prepared a memorandum on the subject of Tasmanian defences in conjunction with Sir Peter Scratchley. This memorandum deals with the principles upon which, in their judgment, the defences of Tasmania should be based; but the recommendations were restricted to such measures as were requisite for protection against attack by a cruiser or privateer, and as were within the means of Tasmania to afford. I give some extracts concerning the defence of Hobart and Launceston :—

TASMANIA.

DEFENCE OF HOBART.

It would be out of the question to provide local defences to prevent the occupation by an enemy of the numerous harbours upon the coast of Tasmania. It is, however, practicable to protect Hobart Town against the attack of an unarmoured vessel of war, which, eluding our naval squadron, and in the absence of

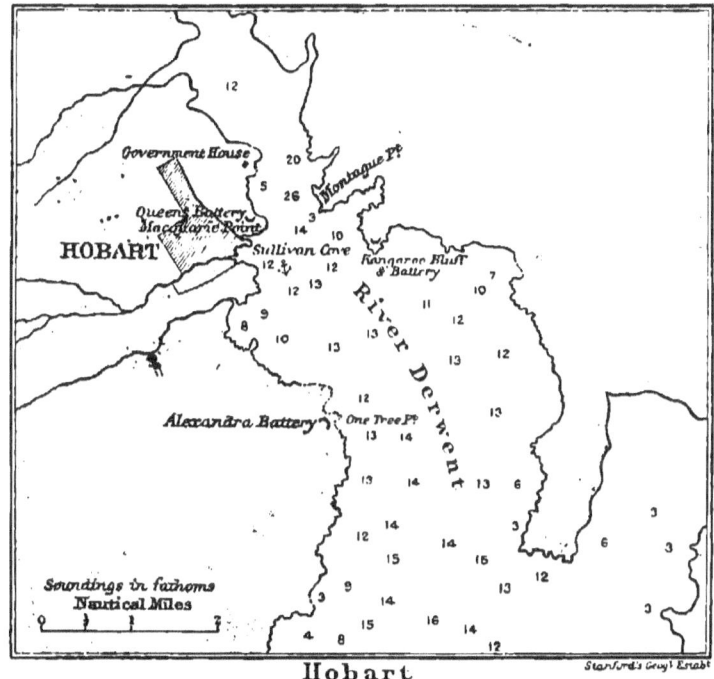

Hobart

sufficient defences, might, under threat of bombardment, or after actually firing into the place, levy a heavy contribution upon the Colony.

The width of the Derwent, below Hobart Town, being from 4,000 to 5,000 yards, the depth of water being sufficient for vessels of any size, and the passage perfectly clear, it would be out of the question, by means of land batteries, to prevent an enemy's vessel steaming rapidly up the river and occupying a position whence she might throw shells into the city. If, however, batteries be established which would bring an effective fire to bear upon her when she lay opposite the town, and if a line of obstructions be placed in such a manner as to prevent her running up the river beyond the town and out of fire from the batteries, she could neither remain in such a position nor get to any other point whence she could effect a bombardment. She would then be obliged to retire. It is on this principle that the defence of Hobart Town should be based.

DEFENCE OF LAUNCESTON.

The only other town in the Colony besides Hobart Town which can be considered liable to attack, with a view to levying a contribution, is Launceston. This town is in the northern part of Tasmania, and forty miles distant from the mouth of the Tamar River. It is 130 miles from Hobart Town, and the two places are connected by a railway.

The best plan of defence for the Tamar River would be to establish a small strong work at its mouth, near the lighthouse, and to place some torpedoes in connection with it across the entrance passage. This would at once protect Port Dalrymple, George Town (a small place three or four miles from the entrance), and the town of Launceston itself. There is, however, no population near the mouth of the river from which a force could be drawn to man a fort there; and altogether the project is beyond the present resources of the Colony to undertake. Any provision for the defence of Launceston must be near the town itself.

The passage up the Tamar is tortuous and difficult, and only vessels of light draught can navigate the river. It appears at most only necessary to provide for the protection of Launceston against the attack of a small gun-vessel. Considering the small size, and the limited number of the crew of a vessel that could navigate the Tamar, it is scarcely probable that any body of men would be landed on either shore of the river to attack Launceston. It is, however, desirable, in order to protect the battery against assault, that, besides the artillery required to man the guns, a small volunteer force of infantry should be organised and maintained in the place.

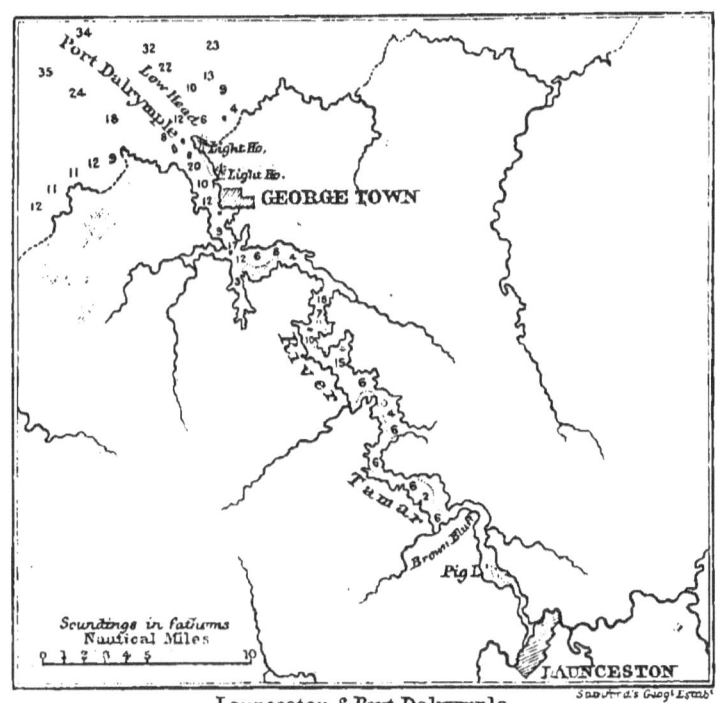

Launceston & Port Dalrymple.

Sir Peter Scratchley found it desirable to introduce several modifications[1] in the proposed recommendations in consequence of changes and improvements which had been made since 1878 in the construction of ordnance and the mode of mounting guns in coast batteries. In consequence of the increasing importance of Launceston it was decided to defer the construction of the battery on Pig Island for the defence of the

[1] These modifications received Sir William Jervois's concurrence.

river Tamar; and Sir Peter recommended that, on the outbreak of war, a defensive position should be established at Brown Bluff, about nine miles from Launceston, on the left bank of the river, so as to bar the advance of an enemy by water or land. Movable defences were proposed to be established at Brown Bluff. It was considered that, if a battery were required for the defence of the river, it should be placed close to the entrance, in order to prevent an enemy's vessels from entering the Tamar. Under the then [1] circumstances of the Colony the cost of such a work was too great to warrant its construction; nor would it have been possible, without great expense, to have provided for its garrison.

The general effect of the changes at Hobart was to largely increase the defensive power of the batteries; in fact, to render them capable of repelling the attack of an ironclad when auxiliary floating defences were added. Sir Peter recommended that Alexandra Battery and Kangaroo Bluff should be completed, and that Queen's Battery, then in good order, should be mainly used to guard the torpedo defences, the organisation of which was at that time being vigorously carried on in accordance with his suggestions. The works were designed on a more extensive and substantial scale than was originally contemplated, so that it should be practicable at any time, without much alteration of the several batteries, to add guns or to replace the smaller guns by more powerful ordnance.

These changes, of course, increased the cost of the

[1] 1882.

scheme; and it became necessary to ask Parliament for a further grant of money; a proceeding entirely justified, said Sir Peter, on the ground that, having in view the improvements in ordnance already mentioned, it would have been a serious mistake not to have introduced them in the coast batteries at Hobart, more especially as the same course had been adopted in all the Australian Colonies, where considerable modifications had been made in the original schemes of defence.

For the purpose of comparison I give (1) the Original Scheme of Defence as codified by Sir Peter Scratchley, and (2) his Modified Scheme:—

Original Scheme of Defence codified.

LAND DEFENCES.

HOBART.

Queen's Battery.—Reconstruction, improvement, and repair.	To be armed with two 70-pr. rifled guns, three S.B. 8-inch shell guns, and two S.B. 32-prs.
Kangaroo Bluff.—Enclosed work with barrack.	To be armed with 8-inch (new pattern) and two 80-pr. (converted) rifled guns.
One Tree Point, Alexandra Battery.—Enclosed work, with keep.	To be armed with two 6-inch (new type), two 7-inch, and one 70-pr. rifled guns; enclosure and accommodation for garrison.

LAUNCESTON.

Pig Island River Tamar.—Enclosed work.	To be armed with two 64-pr. rifled guns, stockaded enclosure, and accommodation for garrison.

TORPEDO DEFENCES.

Hobart	Observation and electro-contact mines at mouth of river Derwent.
River Tamar (Launceston) . . .	Electro-contact mines across river.

MILITARY FORCES.

Regular Artillery detachment	20 officers and men.	
Volunteer (Auxiliary) Garrison Artillery . .	130	,, ,,
Torpedo detachment	30	,, ,,
Volunteer field force to repel landings at Hobart and Launceston	450	,, ,,
Total	630	

Scheme modified by Sir Peter Scratchley.

LAND DEFENCES.
HOBART.

Queen's Battery.—Reconstruction, improvement, and repair. — To be armed with two medium rifled guns, five 8-inch S.B. shell guns.

Alexandra Battery.—Enclosed work, with keep. — To be armed with two 7-inch and three 70-pr. rifled guns.

Kangaroo Bluff.—Enclosed work, with cover for men. — To be armed with two 8-inch (new pattern chambered) and two medium rifled guns.

LAUNCESTON.

River Tamar.—Defensive position on the left bank near Brown Bluff. | To be armed with two 20-pr. B.L. rifled guns.

TORPEDO DEFENCES.

Hobart . . . . — Mines at mouth of river Derwent with advanced group in front of Sullivan's Cove.

River Tamar (Launceston) . . . — Mines across river at Brown Bluff.

MILITARY FORCES.

Garrison Artillery for Hobart	200
Torpedo detachments for Hobart and Launceston . .	50
Field forces to repel landings at Hobart and Launceston .	600
	850

In 1882 Sir Peter Scratchley inspected the Volunteer force of Tasmania, and arrived at the following unfavourable conclusions :—

(1) The Volunteer force was in an unsatisfactory condition.
(2) It was not sufficiently drilled.
(3) Its discipline was indifferent.

(4) There were elements of disorganisation in the force, which, unless checked, would prove fatal to its military efficiency.

(5) The force was not improving.

(6) It could not, as then organised, and in the absence of a regular or highly trained force, be entirely relied upon for defence purposes.

(7) Changes in organisation were imperatively necessary.

(8) It was practicable to introduce these changes, but they would involve an increase in the annual expenditure. He felt bound, however, to make an exception in many respects in favour of the Artillery branch of the force.

It was, therefore, obvious that changes would have to be introduced and the local forces reorganised. Sir Peter considered it unsafe to rely upon the force in its then condition for defence purposes, and, after carefully weighing the matter, came to the conclusion that an organisation similar to that of South Australia, modified to suit local circumstances, would be found best adapted to Tasmania.

Tasmania did not stand alone in respect to the unsatisfactory condition of its Volunteer force. In Victoria, Queensland, and New Zealand the Volunteers were reported to be inefficient from causes similar to those which existed in Tasmania, such as want of daylight drill, absence of power to enforce attendance at drill, insufficient control over the men, and indifferent discipline generally. Measures are, however, being taken in the Colonies named to remedy these defects.

Before introducing any change, Sir Peter considered it necessary to institute a careful inquiry into the whole question—in fact, to follow the course adopted by the Government of Queensland, where, on his reporting that the Volunteer force of that Colony was of little value for defence purposes, a military committee, composed of himself (as inspecting officer), the commandant, the officer commanding the Volunteer Artillery, and the officer commanding the First Regiment of Rifles, with the staff officer as secretary, was appointed to enquire 'into the working of the laws and regulations for the establishment and maintenance of the Volunteer force, including the appointment, promotion, and examination of officers, and the arrangements for the management of the force ; also to suggest improvements in organisation or otherwise, with a view to military efficiency and economy in expenditure.'[1]

A Commission was consequently appointed to inquire into the general condition of the local forces of Tasmania, and the subject was considered under the following heads :—

    i. Authorised and present establishment and distribution of force.
    ii. Laws and regulations. Corps rules.
    iii. Present condition of force.
    iv. Training of officers, non-commissioned officers, and men. Encampments, daylight drills, field-firing for infantry, gunnery instruction, submarine mining.
    v. Appointment, promotion, and education of officers and non-commissioned officers.
    vi. General staff and instructors. Inspecting officer.
    vii. Rifle companies and Volunteer reserve.

Prior to the meeting of the Commission a series of questions was addressed to the officers commanding the various regiments and corps of the local forces, as

---

[1] For a detailed report of this Committee see *Appendix* A.

well as to the staff officers. Returns were called for, and the commandant collected information on all points relating to the inquiry, and these reports, returns, and documents were condensed and circulated among the committee. The Commission came to the same conclusions that Sir Peter had done on his inspection, and deemed it imperative that a change should be made in the organisation.

Since Sir Peter Scratchley made the above suggestions the land defences of Tasmania have progressed rapidly. The improvements at Queen's Battery were finished some time ago, and although operations at Hobart were discontinued for a time in 1883, as the vote for works and armaments had been expended, the Tasmanian Parliament soon sanctioned a supplementary vote, which enabled the work at Kangaroo Bluff to be resumed and completed. The recommendations for One Tree Point and Alexandra Battery have also been carried out; but the construction of a battery on the river Tamar has been deferred, although it is intended at some future time to proceed with this work. Meanwhile it has been decided to provide movable defences in its place.

The military forces have been reorganised, and the necessary funds for that purpose voted by Parliament, so that they ought soon to be in a state of efficiency.

The plan of defence now being carried out is intended to protect Hobart and Launceston against unarmoured cruisers or privateers. The entrance to the Derwent is guarded by a system of submarine mines, and the Tamar is similarly protected.

CHAPTER XIII.

NEW ZEALAND.

THE Colony of New Zealand comprises three islands, two of considerable extent, and Stewart's Island, situated in the extreme south, small and unimportant. In the larger islands are numerous bays and inlets constituting fine natural harbours.

In the North Island, which embraces a coast line of nearly 1,250 miles, the only ports[1] of importance are Auckland, in the north, and Wellington (Port Nicholson), in the south. On the west coast, the harbours at Hokianga, Kaipara, and Manukau afford good anchorage and accommodation, while the small harbours of Waikato, Whangaroa, and Kawhia, and a few open roadsteads,[2] serve as places of refuge for ships in case of need. On the east coast the ports are Russell, the Thames, and Tauranga, while good roadsteads exist at Gisborne and Napier.

In the South or Middle Island the extent of coast is about 1,130 miles. Lyttelton and Otago[3] are the principal harbours, both on the east coast. Further south the Bluff holds an important position, being the last and first port of call for vessels trading between

---

[1] 600 miles apart. [2] Such as New Plymouth.
[3] About 190 miles apart.

New Zealand, Tasmania, and the southern ports of Australia. The minor harbours are Akaroa, Nelson, and Picton, but there are several roadsteads, such as Timaru and Oamaru, on the east; and Hokitika, Greymouth, and Westport, on the west coast, where breakwaters shelter vessels in all weathers. The Sounds along the south-western portion of the coast are numerous, and the water is deep, but being surrounded by high and precipitous mountains, without any settlements on their shores, they are of little practical value.

New Zealand stands in a somewhat different position from the Australian Colonies. In Australia there are few harbours of importance which are not the centres of large populations, consequently the resources in men and appliances for defence are to be found where they are most wanted. In New Zealand, on the contrary, the population is scattered over a wide area, and there are several large harbours requiring protection. Many settlements on the coast are exposed to attack, but these, Sir Peter Scratchley considered, could not be included in a general scheme of defence without great expense.

Owing to the very extensive seaboard and the principal harbours being situated at great distances apart, the Colony can scarcely be properly defended by naval means alone. Even the possession of a ship in one or more of the harbours, or a small squadron for general defence, could not be relied upon as a sufficient protection for individual ports scattered over a length of coast from north to south of over 1,000 miles. For instance, supposing an attack were made upon Auckland, when the ship or squadron was at Lyttelton, two or three days must inevitably elapse before the protecting ship could reach Auckland, during which time much mischief might be done; while if the squadron happened to be at sea, instead of in port, an extra day or even more might elapse. Or again, a feint by a single ship on one port might be made, to draw the squadron away from the real point of attack. These reasons made it obvious to Sir Peter that the principle upon which the defence of New Zealand should be based was to place each of the principal harbours in a position to repel attack from one or two hostile cruisers, and at the same time afford points of refuge and support to such of her Majesty's ships as would, in time of war, be detached to co-operate in the general defence of Australia and New Zealand.

Sir Peter Scratchley gave much time and attention to considering the nature of attack to which New Zealand was likely to be exposed, and the measure of defence that should be adopted for the protection of the Colony in the event of the mother-country being at war with a foreign Power.

The only places that appeared to him of sufficient importance to require local protection were Auckland, Wellington, Christchurch, Dunedin, and Invercargill. ' An enemy might possibly occupy one of the minor harbours, such as Russell, Tauranga, Nelson, Picton, or Akaroa, with a view to an attack upon one of the large ports, or as a means whereby to capture passing vessels, or might lie off such roadsteads as Gisborne, Napier, Timaru, or Oamaru, for the purpose of levying contributions ;' but such operations, he considered, could be counteracted either by naval means or local protection for each place. To provide against these contingencies, however, a large expenditure would have to be incurred; accordingly he directed his attention more particularly to the measures necessary for the defence of the five principal harbours, Auckland, Wellington, Lyttelton, Chalmers, and the Bluff.

'The towns situated on these harbours can only be approached by sea through channels that afford, more or less, natural facilities for *fixed* defences.' These defences, he advised, should consist of land batteries rendered self-defensible and independent of external support, in combination with offensive and defensive torpedoes; and the best mode of providing against attacks made by bodies of men landed for the purpose of turning them would be to maintain local troops capable of meeting the enemy in the field. It has been suggested that floating defences might with advantage be adopted in preference, or as auxiliaries, to the batteries on shore; but Sir Peter Scratchley thought nothing would be gained by the substitution.[1]

The plan of defence he considered best adapted for the harbours of New Zealand was similar in design to that recommended for the harbours of the Australian Colonies.[2] Had, however, the question been merely the defending of one harbour, he would probably have inclined to the adoption of defensive torpedoes. Wel-

---

[1] For further particulars on this point, see p. 69.

[2] Batteries armed with heavy rifled ordnance, together with submarine mines in the channels, and torpedo-boats for attacking the enemy's vessels. For the protection of the principal cities near the seaboard, from attacks by bodies of men landed from the enemy's ships, the maintenance of local forces capable of operating in the field.

lington is the seat of Government and the headquarters of the telegraph system of the Colony, consequently he saw less difficulty existed in establishing there a reliable organisation for the purpose. But after carefully weighing all points, and bearing in mind that other harbours equal in importance to Wellington required consideration, he came to the conclusion that it would not be practicable to maintain in a state of efficiency complete systems of submarine defences at each place, except by a very great expenditure of money. He estimated that it would require 20,000*l*.[1] for the establishment of complete systems of defensive mines at Auckland, Wellington, Lyttelton, and Port Chalmers. A Torpedo corps, too, would have to be raised; buildings for the reception of the stores erected; and a small staff maintained at each place to look after the equipments; while at the outbreak of war, the mines having been laid by the Torpedo corps, men would have to be permanently stationed on the spot to look after them. At the same time, holding as he did the opinion that no scheme of defence could be considered complete without submarine mines, he thought it would be advisable to establish the nucleus of a Torpedo corps at Wellington, and to arrange for the instruction of a certain number of employés in the Telegraph Department.

As guns alone will not prevent hostile vessels from forcing their way into a port, he considered that in the absence of submarine defences *offensive* torpedoes should be employed in order to support the batteries on shore,

---

[1] Inclusive of works, torpedo stores, and equipments, but exclusive of the cost of laying the mines in time of war.

and that the kind best suited for New Zealand harbours was the spar torpedo.[1] I may add that although he was well aware an attack upon an enemy's vessel with torpedo-boats would be attended with great danger, he was quite satisfied no difficulty would arise in obtaining volunteers for that purpose in the harbours of the Colony.

Let us now investigate the requirements considered necessary for the defence of the five principal harbours.

AUCKLAND.

This town is situated on the south shore of the harbour, at about 4,000 yards from the entrance.[2] Ships can approach this entrance by three channels, which join in two outside the Heads, where the navigable width is reduced by a shoal. Supposing no defences to exist, a vessel could either enter the harbour or lie off the entrance and bombard the town. In order, therefore, to secure the town and shipping from such attacks, Sir Peter Scratchley advised the erection of batteries at the Heads in conjunction with submarine mines in the channel, or in the place of the mines three torpedo-boats.

An enemy thus prevented from attacking Auckland by sea, might land a body of men at some convenient spot outside. Such an enterprise, he considered, would have to be met by a field force, and, if the attack were

---

[1] Which can be adapted for use from ordinary steam launches and pinnaces. For further information about the spar torpedo see p. 97.
[2] 2,000 yards wide.

from the north, the signal station on Mount Victoria would have to be occupied.

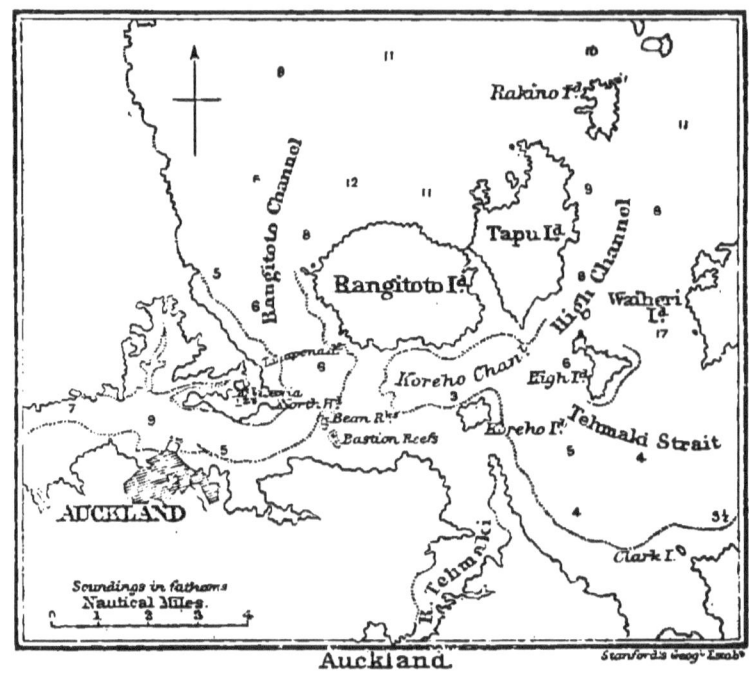

Auckland.

WELLINGTON,

the seat of government, is situated on the west shore of Port Nicholson, at a distance of seven miles from the entrance. This extensive inlet, about eight miles long and six broad, with deep water throughout, is generally free from obstruction. The entrance to Port Nicholson is through a channel about 2,000 yards wide and 5,000 long. Barrett's Reef inside the mouth divides the entrance into two channels. The main passage is 1,300 yards across and perfectly straight, while Chaffer's Channel is about 500 yards at its narrowest part. These passages, Sir Peter advised, should be guarded by torpedoes, the main one both against hostile

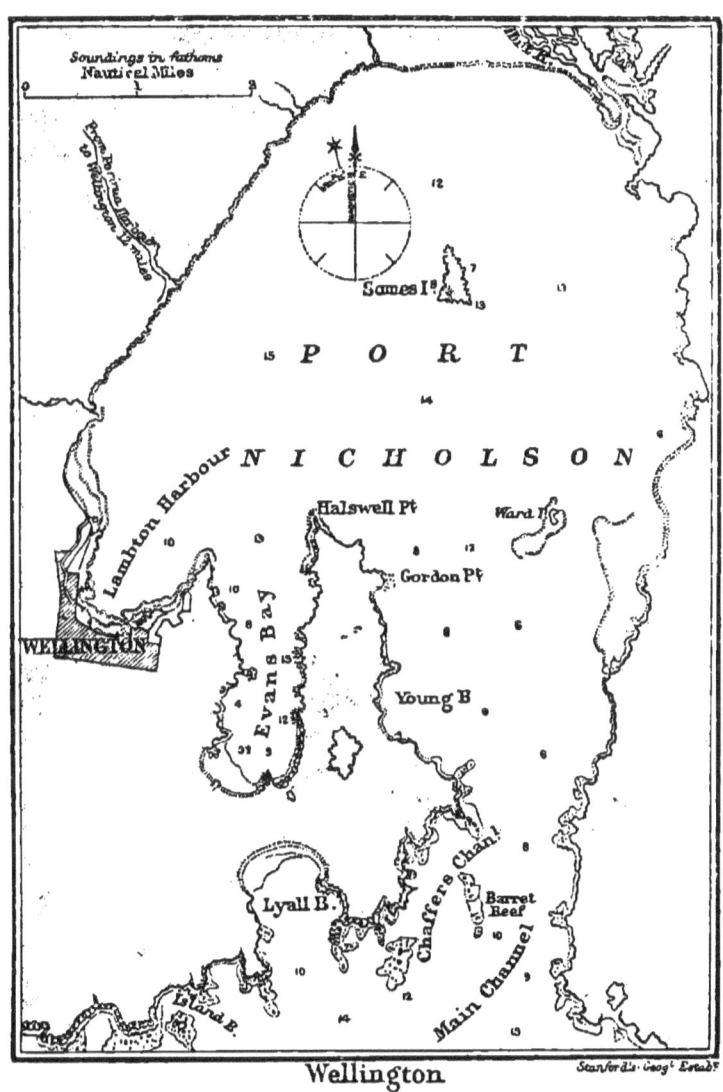

and friendly vessels, but Chaffer's Channel only against the enemy.

'Finding the Heads defended, the enemy might attempt to attack Wellington by landing at one of the adjacent bays.' This operation would be difficult, but a landing might possibly be effected at Island Bay,[1] from which a valley extends towards the city. At Lyall Bay, however, the sea generally breaks in all weathers. Two roads lead into Wellington from Lyall Bay ; one skirts the shore of Evans Bay and Lambton Harbour, the other passes over a high range of hills. It has been suggested that an enemy might land in Porirua Harbour ;[2] but, being a bar harbour, with an entrance not easy of navigation, Sir Peter looked upon such an undertaking as improbable.

The possibility of hostile vessels bombarding the city from outside the entrance to the port is a risk he thought might be safely disregarded, but in order to meet this mode of attack, suggested the employment of spar torpedo-boats.

LYTTELTON.

The town of Lyttelton[3] stands on the north side, about 8,000 yards from the entrance of the harbour, which is six miles in length and a little over 2,000 yards in width. The requirements for the protection of Lyttelton being nearly similar to those at Wellington, it was proposed to adopt the same defensive

---

[1] Situated about 6,000 yards to the west of the entrance and 4,000 yards from the southern portion of the city.
[2] Distant 12 miles from Wellington, with a fair coach ride all the way, which could, however, be easily obstructed.
[3] The port of Christchurch.

measures—viz. batteries on shore and torpedo-boats, to be afterwards supplemented by submarine mines.

'In the absence of any batteries,' said General Scratchley, 'for the defence of the harbour no landing could be effected within the Heads which could not be resisted with the local forces proposed for the place. It has been suggested, however, that if the battery were constructed on the southern side an enemy might enter Port Levy and send a small body of men across the range of hills [1] which separate the harbour from the port, with a view to capture the work and bombard the town and shipping. Such an operation is not at all likely, as it would be extremely difficult owing to the very rough nature of the country; and, as the battery would be well secured from assault, it could not be seized by any force likely to be landed.'

It has also been urged that the weak point of Lyttelton and Christchurch is that both places are open to attack from the direction of Sumner, a small settlement at the mouth of the river Avon, situated about eight miles from Christchurch. To the supporters of this theory Sir Peter replied, 'Unless the enemy possessed a force superior to that of the defenders, he would not attempt to land his men on an open beach where, even if he succeeded in obtaining a footing, his retreat might possibly be cut off by a change of wind or weather. Operations of this sort, therefore, are not likely to be undertaken if a small field force is maintained at Christchurch to counteract them.'

[1] Over 1,000 feet high.

CHALMERS.

The harbour of Otago is a narrow estuary, twelve miles long, running nearly parallel to the coast, from which it is separated at its upper end by a narrow neck of land, called Ocean Beach.[1] Dunedin is situated at the upper end of this estuary; and Port Chalmers, which is in railway communication with the city, lies about half-way between it and the sea. Although a considerable expenditure has been incurred in improving the channel leading up to Dunedin, the shiping lies at Port Chalmers. The channel has a bar across the entrance, and its navigation is somewhat difficult. Point Harrington, within the Heads, in Sir Peter's opinion, affords an admirable site for a battery.

It is extremely improbable that an enemy would be able to land on Ocean Beach, as the sea breaks upon it all the year round; while no favourable point is to be found for such an operation along the coast outside the harbour.

The bombardment of Dunedin from the open sea is a danger which should be well considered before the expenditure required for the defence of Port Chalmers is incurred. Sir Peter Scratchley considered the most effectual way of keeping the enemy's ships at such a distance from the shore as to render a bombardment impracticable would be to erect two batteries, one on Lawyer's Head to the east, the other on the west of the beach.

[1] 1,500 yards wide at its narrowest part.

BLUFF.

This harbour, situated at the south-east corner of the South Island, is the port of Invercargill, a city rising in importance. The harbour, which is capable of receiving vessels of large tonnage, is being improved, but the entrance is narrow and the navigation difficult. It would therefore be easy, said Sir Peter, by means of fixed defences, to keep an enemy beyond bombarding range of the wharves and shipping.

Although General Scratchley was of opinion that the Bluff is not at present of sufficient importance to justify so large an expenditure for its protection as that proposed for the defence of one of the large harbours of the Colony, yet it stands in a different category from Nelson, as its harbour is capacious, well sheltered, and not difficult to enter. Moreover, it is much exposed to attacks by sea and land, whilst the harbour at Nelson is small and not easy of access by sea. Invercargill is situated eighteen miles by railway from the Bluff, and the only approach to it by water is up the New River, which is not deep enough to admit vessels drawing over seven feet.

For the defence of Nelson, Timaru, Oamaru, and other places not large enough to require local defences, he proposed that small bodies of riflemen, provided with field artillery, should fulfil the double purpose of keeping hostile vessels at a distance from the shore with their guns, and also of resisting predatory attacks on land undertaken with the object of levying contributions.

It is sometimes advanced as a weak point in a scheme of defence by coast batteries that an enemy could pass them at night. At Wellington, Auckland, and Lyttelton Sir Peter considered this would perhaps be practicable, but at Port Chalmers and the Bluff there was much less likelihood of its occurring. At all events, he advised the provision of electric[1] lights at each port to illuminate the channels and approaches, and that the entrances should be patrolled by means of one or more torpedo-boats, which in time of war should always be kept ready for action.

As regards the men required to work the guns and defend the batteries, he thought the best plan, if expense had not to be considered, would be to maintain permanent artillerymen at each port, who, in time of war, would reside in the batteries. The necessity for permanent garrisons has been urged as a reason against guns being placed at a distance from the object to be protected. It is obvious, however, that, under any circumstances in time of war, wherever the batteries may be situated, men must reside in them to keep everything in order, and ready to open fire at the shortest notice. Consequently, in his opinion, the best arrangement would be one that provided a nucleus of permanently enrolled men placed in the batteries on the outbreak of war, supplemented by a sufficient force to complete the gun detachments and garrison the works at the time of attack. 'There

---

[1] Concentric.

already exists[1] in the colony the armed constabulary. The depôt for this force is at Wellington;' and, 'in order to render it in every way fitted to supply the permanent detachments for the batteries, it would only be necessary to appoint a qualified artillery instructor and provide the necessary appliances for drill. Every man after he had passed in infantry drill should be put through a course of gunnery instruction, including shot practice. The amount of knowledge required to work the ordnance in the several batteries will be small and easily acquired, as all the guns will be alike in character, and similarly worked and mounted.'

The auxiliary detachments which are to reinforce the permanent men, he considered, should be organised on a system analogous to the Naval Reserve[2] in Victoria, for service afloat and on shore. 'Where the number of men required at each place is small, it is important to avoid the creation of a number of small corps—an evil which, in the New Zealand Volunteer force,[3] has reached such serious dimensions as to be fatal to military efficiency.' He proposed, therefore, to establish at Auckland, Wellington, Lyttelton, and Port Chalmers, Naval Brigades which would furnish detachments for working the guns, garrisons for the batteries, and crews for the torpedo-boats. Thus the defence against attack by sea would be in the hands of one commander at each port.

The number of torpedo-boats suggested was twelve, three at each of the principal ports, Auckland,

---

[1] Sir Peter Scratchley made these remarks in 1882.
[2] See p. 127.   [3] See p. 191.

Wellington, Lyttelton, and Port Chalmers. At least three men, he considered, would be required for each boat: one to command, an engineer for the engines, and a man to work the spar torpedo. The sections of the naval brigades entrusted with the torpedo-boats he thought might number in peace-time ten men; but in time of war the crews would have to be permanently enrolled, and so increased as to have men in reserve to fill up vacancies, and ready for duty, day and night.

As to the constitution and strength of the field forces, Sir Peter Scratchley thought the idea of maintaining a nucleus of permanent infantry at each place could not be entertained until the country was more advanced; nor, indeed, was it quite clear to him that such a step was necessary. At the same time he thought it desirable to draw attention to a source from which a substitute could be drawn. 'If, while serving in the police, the military training of the men were kept up, it is obvious that a reserve would be created which, in time of war, would furnish a most valuable nucleus of trained men of the highest class for the volunteer field forces. But it would be possible to go further, and to throw open to the armed constabulary employment in all departments of the State, on condition that the non-commissioned officers and men agreed to serve in a Reserve for a term of years, and be liable to be called out in time of war. By such inducements a superior class of men would be attracted, who would be content to serve for small pay in consideration of the chances of obtaining permanent and well-paid appointments under the Government as a reward for efficient service and good conduct. At the same time the evils would be avoided which inevitably result from the maintenance of armed bodies of men in time of peace, with insufficient employment and indifferent prospects of advancement. Under such a system the defensive power of the country would be increased year by year, and there would be absolute security that a small, but thoroughly trained, force would be immediately available when it was wanted.'

In the absence of this reserve of trained men he considered a Volunteer force must be relied upon, of sufficient strength at each place to repel an attack by one or two cruisers landing from two to three hundred men. For this purpose he deemed it necessary that a field force should be maintained at Auckland, Wellington, Christchurch, and Dunedin; as in this manner a compact body of men would be provided at each of the principal harbours, with a definite sphere of action. The battery at the entrance to the port being secure from capture, owing to its being enclosed and self-defensible by its garrison, the field force would be free to act to the best advantage in repelling an attack by land.

The mounted detachment, Sir Peter thought, might well be designated 'Mounted Rifles,' a description of force, better suited to the work required from them than 'cavalry.' 'The officers and men should be good horsemen, expert in the use of the sword and rifle, and trained especially with the view of acting in time of war as scouts, escorts, and orderlies, while reconnoitring and the conveyance of accurate intelligence should be carefully practised.'

The Field Artillery, he considered, should be taught such movements as are likely to be required on service, and the men armed with carbines, and properly instructed in their use. Arrangements should also be made to establish a school for the instruction of the employés of the Telegraph Department in torpedo work. The object of this proposal was to create a corps whose duty would be to study the subject and carry out experiments, to watch what was going on in England and elsewhere in torpedo matters, and collect information concerning the harbours of the colony.

A general impression seemed to prevail that, in time of war, the Volunteer corps would afford valuable reserves from which to draw the necessary forces for defence, and that their organisation into fighting bodies could be safely left to the time when the emergency arose. 'On this point,' Sir Peter observed, ' to oppose with success the sudden attacks that an enemy would probably make upon the shores of New Zealand, the armed forces of the Colony should be ready on the spot, commanded and administered in peace and war upon one and the same system. If the object is to foster the military spirit of the country it is probable that it could be done equally as well, and probably better, by adopting a less costly organisation. The military forces of New Zealand have done good service in the field, reflecting the greatest credit on both the officers and men engaged; and the Volunteers have shown patriotic spirit and devotion in giving their time, and in many cases their money, to the service of the State; but I fear that their energies will be misdirected and wasted unless a better organisation is adopted. The principle of making a distinction between forces maintained so as to be immediately available for defence against foreign aggression, and others which are established for the encouragement of rifle-shooting and other reasons, has already been recognised in South Australia.[1] I believe that an organisation of a similar character would be well adapted to certain districts of New Zealand.'

The defences of New Zealand are not so far advanced as those of the Australian Colonies. 'In this colony the defence affairs,' said Sir Peter Scratchley in 1883, 'are in an unsatisfactory state.' When I was in New Zealand in 1885 (during the time of the Russian war scare), great anxiety existed among the colonists generally with regard to the defence of their coasts, while hurried preparations were being made for the expected appearance of Russian cruisers. Sir Peter, who was at that time in Sydney completing his arrangements with the mother colony before proceeding to New Guinea, wrote me a letter (dated March 28, 1885) in which he made the following pointed reference to these islands: 'The Colonies, *excepting New Zealand*, are fairly well prepared.'

It is but fair, however, to remark that previous to

---

[1] For information concerning the South Australian organisation see chapter on *Local Forces* and *Appendix* A.

1883 the Government decided to purchase four torpedo-boats of the second class (one for each of the four principal harbours) in accordance with his recommendations; and early in 1884 an officer of the Royal Engineers was appointed to carry out his scheme for the construction of batteries at Auckland, Wellington, Lyttelton, and Port Chalmers.

CHAPTER XIV.

TORRES STRAIT.

TORRES STRAIT is about seventy miles across from land to land, and separates New Guinea from Queensland. To the west the sea is open, and the only dangers to ships approaching from that direction are the Proudfoot Shoal and Cook's Reefs; but on the east lies the northern end of the Great Barrier Reefs; indeed, the whole strait is more or less obstructed by islands and reefs, rendering navigation very dangerous.

Although there are many channels and passages through the reefs of Torres Strait, Prince of Wales Channel, a little north of Thursday Island, is the safest and most expeditious. It is about ten miles long by one wide; and although the tide flows with considerable velocity[1] it so nearly follows the direction of the channel that navigation is not difficult.

Further south lies Endeavour Strait, another passage between the group of islands and the mainland; but though the most extensive of the western channels, and quite practicable with due precaution, it abounds in numerous and dangerous sunken patches. Prince of Wales Channel can be well observed from a signal station within a short distance of Thursday Island; but to

[1] Three to five knots.

watch Endeavour Strait Sir Peter Scratchley considered additional look-out stations would have to be established in time of war. The other channels in the north are not used, although it is possible to navigate them. In a report to the Queensland Government Mr. Chester states

that there is probably a deep passage between Talbot Island and New Guinea which, if properly surveyed and marked, would be available for the largest vessels. If so, a man-of-war, by sending her steam launch ahead to sound, could in moderate weather avoid Torres Strait—i.e. Prince of Wales Channel—altogether. In war-time an enemy's ship might thus elude observation, and before her presence was known intercept every vessel passing through the North-East Channel.

A vessel coming from the westward, after passing through one of these channels, would have the choice of two routes if proceeding to the southward: the inner route, which lies within the Great Barrier Reefs, along the eastern shore of Australia; the outer route, outside the Great Barrier Reefs.[1]

The inner route is chiefly used by the steamers[2] which run between Singapore, China, and the east coast of Australia, and by the steamers that carry on the coasting trade of Queensland.

The Great Barrier Reefs extend south from New Guinea for a distance of about 1,300 miles, as far as

---

[1] To get outside these reefs the vessel can proceed through two openings—the Great North-East Channel, near the coast of New Guinea, and Raine Island Entrance, 170 miles south and about 100 miles from Cape York. The latter is not, however, recommended, as it is very difficult to navigate.

[2] Steamers are now rapidly taking the place of sailing ships for the carrying trade of Australia.

Port Curtis, in Queensland, and thus protect about fivesixths of the eastern coast of the Colony. These reefs, Sir Peter considered, will be found to have an important bearing on the naval defence of Queensland. Their direction is generally parallel to the coast, and at one part, near Cape Melville, they approach within ten miles of the shore. Besides the Great North-East Channel and Raine Island Entrance, several openings are quite practicable, although seldom used—Cape Melville Entrance, the Lizard Entrance, Trinity Opening (near Cairns), and the Flinders Passage.[1] The latter is nearly opposite and about seventy miles distant from Townsville,[2] a rising place in Queensland, situated close to the sea, and likely to become an important port. Further south the Capricorn and Curtis Channels lead into Keppel Bay (Rockhampton).

The principal islands in Torres Strait are, Prince of Wales, Friday, Horn, Goode, Hammond, Wednesday, and Thursday Islands to the north. They vary much in size. The largest of the group is Prince of Wales Island, eleven miles long by ten broad. Horn Island, nearly rectangular, is fifteen miles in circumference. Friday Island is only two miles long by three-quarters of a mile wide. Goode Island, still smaller, is a signal station, from which all vessels approaching and passing through Prince of Wales Channel from the east and west can be observed. Hammond Island, hilly and precipitous, is about three and a half miles long, and two broad; at the north end it is 495 feet high, and

---

[1] About 250, 300, 440, and 620 miles respectively south of Cape York.
[2] See Chapter on *Naval Defence*, p. 71.

Torres Strait and Thursday Island.

commands a view of the whole of Torres Strait. Wednesday Island, of irregular shape, is at the eastern end of Prince of Wales Channel. Thursday Island is high and well wooded, rectangular in shape, and is one and a half miles long by half a mile wide.

The general character of these islands is the same. They are said to be composed of porphyry, syenite, and silicious schists; are thickly wooded throughout; more or less hilly, many of the hills being very steep and lofty, with intervening valleys ending, in some places, in mangrove swamps, with fine trees which are suitable for piles. Sir Peter Scratchley, writing from Torres Strait in 1881, said: 'There is no great depth of soil, and the surface is generally covered with disintegrated rock, boulders being found here and there. Where the surface has been cleared of trees and scrub, which is very thick and difficult to penetrate in parts, grass grows in tufts, and to a great height during the rainy season— January to March. During this season plenty of good water is to be found on the surface, but it does not penetrate the soil. There are also numerous permanent springs. It is believed that cattle and sheep might be kept on Prince of Wales Island; also that plantains, cocoanuts, and other tropical fruit might be grown if water were stored for irrigation. Natives are only to be found on this island, and their number is supposed to be about 100 to 150 men, women, and children. They subsist on fish and yams. They are not of a warlike nature, and are willing to work during the northwest monsoon, when they cannot fish. The natives from the mainland do not frequent any of the islands.'

Normanby Sound is enclosed by Goode and Friday Islands at its western entrance, by Hammond and Prince of Wales Islands in the middle, and terminates at its eastern end in Ellis Channel, which lies between Thursday and Horn Islands. There are several approaches to the Sound, the deepest and widest of which is from the west. Small vessels may enter from the east into Ellis Channel by way of Flinders Passage, and from the north-east through Aplin Pass between Thursday and Hammond Islands; the latter channel is, however, very narrow and difficult to navigate. The other approaches from the north and south are nothing better than boat channels, being full of obstructions. The tides through these various channels are strong,[1] very irregular, and uncertain,[2] often rising higher and running stronger at neaps than at springs. The anchorage, extensive and commodious, with good holding ground throughout, is well sheltered by the islands, and safe in all weathers and seasons. The only dangers in the deep waters of Normanby Sound are the Ghibber Rock, the reefs off Wai Weir Island, the reef off Thursday Island, the Pinnacle and Hovell Rocks, all of which lie in the course of a ship entering from the westward; but, being well defined by beacons, they are not dangerous, provided the tides are understood. At the same time it would be dangerous to pass through Prince of Wales Channel or enter Normanby Sound during night or thick weather. The latter, how-

---

[1] From three to six knots.
[2] The extreme range observed is eleven feet six inches at neap tides; the lowest is four feet six inches.

ever, only prevails during the heavy rains of the northwest monsoon; at other times during this season the atmosphere is very clear, the smoke of steamers being discerned from the signal station on Goode Island at a distance of fifty miles. On the other hand, in southeast winds, although fogs and mists are unknown, there is almost always a constant haze, which renders it difficult to see to a greater distance than fifteen to twenty miles.

CHAPTER XV.

THURSDAY ISLAND.

THURSDAY ISLAND is little more than an isolated post, but occupies a commanding position on the northern route of Australian commerce, and there is little doubt that in time of war it will have to be occupied in order to afford security to merchant vessels.

The island belongs to the Colony of Queensland, and lies in the midst of a group situated in the southern portion of Torres Strait, about twenty miles to the north-west of Cape York, the most northerly point of the Australian continent.

In 1878 the boundary of Queensland was extended so as to include the whole of the Strait, up to a short distance from the southern coast of New Guinea, and all the islands within this boundary were annexed.[1] About the same time the Government settlement at Somerset, a place on the mainland, within five miles south-east of Cape York, was removed to the island. This step was taken because the trade route through Torres Strait was growing in importance, and a port was required, which, in addition to being a harbour of refuge and port of call, would be a harbour suited for

---

[1] Under the authority of Letters Patent, dated October 10, 1878, and an Act of the Queensland Parliament (43 Vict. No. 1).

general traffic, and at the same time the headquarters of the pearl-shell fishery.

Indeed the increasing value of Thursday Island is mainly due to the fact that it lies in the trade route between China, Japan, and the Eastern Colonies;[1] besides, it is highly probable that, in the course of a few years, nearly all the trade between Queensland, the East, and Europe, will be diverted northward, instead of passing *viâ* Melbourne. In this event the exports of gold, copper, tin, coal, wool, hides, tallow, frozen and preserved meats, from the settlements possessing outlets on the eastern coast of Queensland, would be forwarded *viâ* Torres Strait. It is very evident, then, that to Queensland the possession of Torres Strait is commercially of vital importance : an importance which will go on increasing with the prosperity of the Colony.

The island at the same time stands in a different category from other places in Australia which it is proposed to defend. It is situated at a great distance from any large settlement, and, although in course of time outlets for the export of coal, minerals, sugar, and other produce may be established along the shores of Northern Queensland, Thursday Island must continue to be simply an advanced post for the general defence of Australia, and a port of call and harbour of refuge for commercial purposes.

---

[1] The distances from Thursday Island to the undermentioned places should be noted :—Saigon, 3,000 miles ; Singapore, 2,500 ; Ceylon, 4,000 ; Batavia (Java), 2,200 ; Port Darwin, 750 ; Point Parker—the terminus on the Gulf of Carpentaria for the proposed Transcontinental Railway of Queensland—450 ; Brisbane, 1,400 ; Sydney, 1,880 ; and New Caledonia, 1,550.

The protection of Thursday Island, in time of war, Sir Peter Scratchley considered, would no doubt be costly and embarrassing if entirely undertaken by the Imperial Government; but, at the same time, he looked upon the defence of Thursday Island as part and parcel of the general scheme of Australasian defence by land and sea. Whether the burden of defending the island should be shared between the mother-country and her Australasian Colonies is a very important question, and one which cannot fail to attract attention whenever the subject of Colonial defence is discussed.

He considered it was an absolute necessity, in any scheme of naval defence that may be desired for the Australasian Colonies, to secure a fortified coal depôt in the north of Australia, and writing upon this point a few years ago remarked: 'Were this connecting link with the East left undefended in time of war, an enterprising enemy could, on its outbreak, take possession of Torres Strait, with a view to ulterior operations against Australian commerce, and once the enemy was established it would be a very difficult task to dislodge him.'

In such an isolated position as Thursday Island, where there is never likely to be a resident white population of any size, he thought it doubtful whether a large expenditure should be incurred on *fixed* defences, even if there were a guarantee that the officers and men for manning them would be available when required.

The difficulty of providing these forces afforded fair grounds for the opinion expressed by Admiral

Wilson to the effect that naval means, with extemporised defences, established on the outbreak of war, would be best suited to the case;' and although Sir Peter contended that this was going too far in favour of naval defences alone, he admitted that the large expenditure contemplated by the War Office rendered it imperatively necessary to look closely into both sides of the question.

Landings on Thursday Island, he said, 'could be effected with more or less ease almost anywhere, owing to the prevalence of smooth water and the general character of the shore of these islands; but naval means will suffice for their discomfiture, without it being necessary to provide land forces. Should the floating defences, however, not be provided, the danger of a landing being effected would be too serious to be disregarded.'

The sources from which the defending forces are to be drawn is a difficult problem to solve. The complete isolation of Thursday Island from any large settlement, and the improbability of its ever having a large resident population, clearly indicate that the forces required for defence must be sent there before the commencement of hostilities. On the other hand, Torres Strait being an important route for commerce, the transport of troops to Thursday Island would be very easy.

As to the question whether military and naval forces should be employed to garrison the battery and man the floating defences, General Scratchley was of opinion that 'if the Admiralty would undertake, in time of war, to set apart officers and men for these purposes, there could be no question that naval forces alone would be the best in every respect—marines for the battery, and seamen for the gun and torpedo-boats—as in that case the defence arrangements on shore and afloat would be under one direction. But to throw such a burden upon the Imperial navy would possibly be undesirable, while uncertainty might exist as to whether men could be spared.' Under the circumstances he considered it would be preferable to look elsewhere for the land force, and count upon the navy solely for service afloat.

He thought it possible to raise a corps on the spot to reinforce any men the Imperial Government might provide on the outbreak of war. 'A portion of the force might be recruited from the residents and people employed on the fisheries, provided there existed an organisation for the purpose. The officials and residents at Thursday Island would doubtless join a local force if it were established, but the number of white men on the spot is very small.' At the time of Sir Peter's visit the Government establishment comprised a magistrate, an officer of customs, a carpenter, a gaoler, five water police, a pilot, a signalman, and three seamen; there were also about ten white and a dozen coloured men employed in connection with the stores and the coal hulk for intercolonial steamers; while 700 men were engaged in the fisheries, pearl-shell and bêche-de-mer.[1] Mr. Chester, who formerly served in the Indian Navy, and has considered the subject,

---

[1] Thirty only were whites. The coloured men are Aboriginals, South Sea Islanders, Malays, with a few Lascars and Chinese, the latter being employed as carpenters, cooks, and servants.

believes that, owing to most of the men engaged in the fisheries being from the nature of their employment active and hardy, little difficulty would arise in forming, in the event of war, an irregular corps for service afloat and on shore.

As to reliance being placed on Queensland and the other Australian Colonies, Sir Peter did not think much difficulty would be experienced in obtaining recruits for a paid force; but they would not be of a superior class, owing to the general prosperity of the working classes in Australia. He also thought it was a matter for consideration whether the Australian Colonies should not combine to supply a contingent of the defending force, but inclined to the belief that the idea would not be favourably received, owing to the question being outside that of a joint naval defence for the protection of Australasian commerce. The fact must not be overlooked that the Australasian Colonies find it somewhat difficult to maintain sufficient forces for their own protection, and would therefore be naturally careful before adding to the difficulty by undertaking the burden and responsibility of providing a garrison for Thursday Island.

The rapid progress that Queensland is making is an important factor in the question, and it is reasonable to anticipate that its Government may in the future recognise the great strategical importance of Thursday Island to the Colony, and be prepared to assist towards its defence in time of war. It is not possible, however, to apply to Thursday Island the same argument that may be applied to the Australasian Colonies, viz. that its defence organisation should be self-supporting and self-reliant.

General Scratchley remarked 'that the necessity for establishing the defences of Thursday Island on the most economical scale as regards maintenance must be recognised, as defence preparations in the Australasian Colonies will for some time be looked upon as burdens which may at any time be thrown off, in the face of the remote prospect of their ever being called into play. At any rate, steps might be taken to establish a small corps from the white residents on Thursday Island, with an organisation capable of rapid expansion when war was imminent.' The organisation he advised was a paid *volunteer militia* (both officers and men); and he considered the establishment of this corps would be facilitated if seamen who had served in the Royal Navy were to be employed at Thursday Island by the Queensland Government. The probable annual expenditure required for the maintenance of these forces in time of peace cannot, of course, be estimated until it is known from what source the officers and men are to be procured.

With regard to the custody of the battery on Thursday Island, he thought the Government officials and residents might be made available for the purpose; but if the *floating* defences were to be kept on the spot, an addition would have to be made to the present Government establishment. 'The *floating* defences might, however, be kept at Cooktown, where it would be possible to organise a Naval Brigade which could be utilised in time of war.'

From a sanitary point of view, considering the geographical position of Thursday Island, the settlement is well situated. It is exposed to the south-east winds, which blow steadily during nine months of the year, and, although the land close to the sea is only a few feet above high-water mark, it rises everywhere to the range of hills at the back of the settlement. The place is considered to be healthy. The south-east winds moderate the temperature to a great extent, and the unpleasant part of the year is during the north-west monsoon (January to March), when the rainfall is heavy.

Notwithstanding the favourable impression Sir Peter Scratchley formed of the healthiness of the locality, he considered it would be most undesirable to quarter white soldiers, without employment, on Thursday Island in time of peace; although in time of war there would be little difficulty in keeping them in good health by adopting ordinary precautions.

NEW GUINEA.

NEW GUINEA

CHAPTER XVI.

THE POLITICAL SITUATION.[1]

NEW GUINEA, or Papua, is the largest and perhaps the most important island in the Western Pacific. It lies immediately south of the equator and north-east of Australia, and is under the control of three European Powers in the following estimated proportions :—

	Square miles
Western New Guinea (Holland)	112,350
Kaiser Wilhelm Land (Germany)	68,390
British Protectorate (Great Britain)	86,800
Total area	267,540

The Bismarck Archipelago consists of the Admiralty group, New Britain, New Ireland, Long, and Rooke Islands, and several smaller dependencies. These islands are still imperfectly known.

The Louisiade Archipelago is included in the British protectorate, and embraces the islands of Adèle, Roussel, and St. Aignan, and the groups Rénard, De Boyne, Bonvouloir, D'Entrecasteaux, and Trobriande. Roussel and St. Aignan are the largest, the latter being about twenty-seven miles long. Many of the islands are thickly populated, and the natives, who are mostly

[1] Part of the subject-matter in this chapter appeared in 'Europe in the Pacific.' See *Nineteenth Century* Review, Nov. 1886.

T

cannibals, are less to be trusted than those on the mainland.

The discovery of New Guinea is due to the Portuguese. Don Jorge de Meneses landed there in 1526, and called the island Papua, which some authorities translate 'black,' while others construe it 'curled hair,' either of which meanings suits the native inhabitants. Thirty years later De Retes, a Spanish mariner, sailed along the northern coast, and rechristened the island Nueva Guinea, owing to its fancied resemblance to the Guinea coast on the west of Africa. In 1606 Torres sailed through the strait which now bears his name, and Dampier, in 1699, made further discoveries along the coast. Captain Cook visited the place in 1770. The Dutch navigators in the early part of the seventeenth century explored the south-western shores of New Guinea as far east as the Torres Straits, while Le Maire, Schouten, and Abel Tasman (1613-43) traced the northern shores from about the 144° meridian to the westward. The Great Geelvink Bay was explored in 1705. In 1820 and 1828 more explorations were made, and a settlement founded. In 1835 the Dutch sent out another expedition, which was followed in 1858 by a third to Humboldt Bay. None of these endeavours to colonise the place was, however, very successful.

Lord Carnarvon in 1875 endeavoured to obtain some definite information as to the title, or alleged title, of the Dutch to the western portion of New Guinea, and to trace out the precise boundaries of the territory held by them. No specific information, however, on these points was forthcoming, beyond the fact that

they claimed to extend from the west coast to 141°
of longitude east of Greenwich. The assumption is
that their title depends upon right of discovery and
exploration.

Twenty-three years ago a company was started in

Sydney to colonise that part not taken by Holland;
but the idea was abandoned when the promoters of the
scheme found they could not form a British colony
without the express consent of the Imperial authorities.
Since that date the coast-line of New Guinea has been

to some extent explored by various Europeans who have visited its shores, while of late years missionary enterprise has done much towards making the island inhabitable, and Sir Peter Scratchley was ever ready to acknowledge the valuable help afforded him in his work by the influence possessed over the natives by the Rev. W. G. Lawes and the Rev. James Chalmers.

Comparatively little is known concerning German New Guinea, and, although recent White-Books give some information about the interior of Kaiser Wilhelm Land, the greater part of that territory remains unexplored. Owing, however, to the energy of Sir Peter Scratchley, who personally visited eighteen districts, twenty-seven islands, thirty-four inland and sixty coast villages, some definite and reliable information respecting the British territory has been acquired.

I do not propose to deal with either the British or German occupation of New Guinea at any great length, but it may be interesting to give a short account of the way Germany obtained a footing in what may be regarded as the Ireland of Australia, and a hold on the Western Pacific.

The question may be discussed from three points of view—Imperial, German, and Colonial. This I will do as briefly as possible, and leave my readers to draw their own conclusions. The Imperial authorities, after much delay and a good deal of outside pressure from the Colonies, decided not to annex New Guinea, but to declare a Protectorate up to a certain point in the island. On Sept. 9, 1884, her Majesty's Government announced to the German authorities that it was intended to establish a Protectorate over the coast and contiguous islands, excepting that part between 145° of longitude and the eastern Dutch boundary: whereupon Baron von Plessen made certain representations in London, the outcome of which was that another note was sent to Berlin on October 9 stating that as an act of courtesy we would, pending negotiations with Prince Bismarck, limit the immediate declaration of the Protectorate to the south coast and islands. It was understood that this was done without prejudice to any territorial question beyond that limit, and it was expressly stated that, in the opinion of her Majesty's Government, any question as to districts lying beyond the limit actually taken should be dealt with diplomatically rather than be referred to a South Sea Committee, as suggested by Baron von Plessen. Germany, however, saw no reason for entering into the negotiations suggested by England, or waiting for the diplomatic discussion of Baron von Plessen's representations, and proceeded to annex a portion of the territory in question.

This action on the part of a friendly Power naturally caused some amount of irritation at the Foreign Office, and did not tend to allay the anxiety which was rapidly springing up at the Colonial Office in consequence of the alarming nature of the telegrams from Australia. Much correspondence ensued on all sides, and on December 24, 1884, an interview took place between Prince Bismarck and Mr. Meade in Berlin, when the matter was personally introduced to the German Chancellor. Six months later (June 18, 1885) it was officially announced in London that an arrangement had been agreed upon between the two Governments. Under this a point was selected on the north-east coast, where the eighth parallel of south latitude cuts the sea-shore, as the coast boundary; while inland, the English and German territories were defined by a line of demarcation, which, starting from the coast in the neighbourhood of Mitre Rock, on the eighth parallel of south latitude, and following that parallel to the point where it is cut by the 147th degree of east longitude, goes straight in a north-westerly direction to the point where the sixth parallel of south latitude cuts the 144th degree of east longitude, and is continued to the point of intersection of the fifth parallel of south latitude and of the 141st degree of east longitude. The British possessions lie to the south, and the German to the north, of the boundary line.

By this arrangement nearly 78,000 [1] square miles of territory passed under German control, which might have formed part of the British Empire without any additional expense to the British taxpayer, had the mother-country but listened to the voice of the Australasian colonies.

From the German point of view the matter stood thus:—

Prince Bismarck's explanation to Mr. Meade, who at the interview in question expressed some surprise at Germany annexing land which she had proposed should form the subject of special negotiation, was that the correspondence alluded to above was quite new to him,

---

[1] This calculation includes the area of the islands that passed to Germany.

neither had he any recollection of having seen it. He considered his country free to take the north shore, as we had limited our Protectorate to the south side. The case for Germany, however, is more plainly put by M. de Kusserow, who, being thoroughly conversant with the matter in dispute, may be considered as accurately expressing the opinion of his Government when he explained to Mr. Meade:

That Germany looked upon our second note as a final withdrawal from any claim to go to the northward of the limit we then fixed, and that the question to be diplomatically discussed was not whether we should ultimately go farther up the coast, but merely how far inland towards the interior from the south coast.

That in May or August, 1884, Count Münster was ordered to tell us that a German expedition was going to the north coast of New Guinea, and that they were apprehensive of the jealousy of the Australian colonies, who had actually recommended that everything in that quarter of the globe not already British territory should be at once annexed.

That Count Münster was desired to leave an *aide mémoire* with Lord Granville,[1] so that the intentions of Germany might be clearly made known.

[1] *The Right Hon. the Earl Granville, K.G., to Sir E. Malet, K.C.B.*
Foreign Office, December 29, 1884.
Sir,—From Mr. Meade's memorandum of his recent conversation with Dr. Busch and Mr. von Kesserow, of the German Foreign Office, enclosed in your despatch, confidential, of the 24th instant, it appears that they stated that in July or August of this year Count Münster was ordered to inform her Majesty's Government that a German expedition was going to the north coast of New Guinea, and that later his Excellency was desired to leave an *aide mémoire* with me on the subject.

I have to acquaint your Excellency that no *aide mémoire* on the subject

That when a question was asked in Parliament as to our limits inland, the reply was that it would depend on local requirements, and could be decided later, and this was the question which was left open for diplomatic treatment.

That the trading association should be recognised under the protection of the German flag, if the association was established at any point between the Dutch limit (141° of longitude) and East Cape, which is our limit on the southern coast.

Summing up these reasons, it is apparent that Germany considered the matter settled by the second note, and the only question that remained open was how far the limits of our Protectorate should extend so as not to clash with those of Germany on the opposite coast.

The third and perhaps most important side of the question is the Colonial. On April 4, 1883, Mr. Chester, on behalf of her Majesty and the Government of Queensland, took possession of all that part of New Guinea and its adjacent islands lying between the 141st and 155th meridian of east longitude. This fact was reported to the Imperial authorities, and the other Colonies urged the necessity of the territory being

of these islands in the South Pacific has been given to me by Count Münster.

He communicated to me, on August 8, the substance of one which he had received from Berlin, and you will find it recorded, together with the terms of my reply, in my despatch to the late Lord Ampthill of August 9.

I submitted the draft of this despatch to Count Münster, who agreed with me that it contained a correct report of our conversation upon the occasion in question.

I am, &c.
(Signed)   GRANVILLE.

taken under British rule. In spite, however, of the unanimous feeling expressed by Australia in the matter, the annexation was annulled.

Some soreness naturally resulted from this shortsighted policy on the part of her Majesty's advisers; but when, on July 2, 1883, Lord Derby publicly announced in the House of Lords that it would be regarded as 'an unfriendly act if any country attempted to make a settlement on the coast of New Guinea,' confidence was again restored in the Colonies; and when this expression was followed, on May 9, 1884, by the assurance that 'her Majesty's Government are confident that no foreign Power contemplates interference in New Guinea,' Australia felt secure. Still the Colonial Governments continued to urge the necessity of annexation, and ultimately agreed to pay a subsidy of 15,000*l.* towards the expenses of a New Guinea Protectorate. On September 9 the announcement stated above was sent to the German Government, and on November 17, General Scratchley received his instructions to proceed, as her Majesty's Special Commissioner, to assume jurisdiction over the southern shore of New Guinea and the country adjacent thereto ' from the 141st meridian of east longitude eastward as far as East Cape, including the islands adjacent thereto and in Goshen Straits, and southward of these straits as far south and east as to include Kosman Island.' These instructions also stated clearly that he was to act as Deputy Commissioner to portions of New Guinea outside the Protectorate—a fact that goes far to prove that either Lord Derby misled the Colonies or Prince Bismarck misled Lord Derby.

Sir Peter pointed out the absolute absurdity of such a partial protectorate; but, buoyed up with the hope of his powers being extended, and the understanding that no foreign Power had any design on New Guinea, he left England on November 20, 1884, for Australia. At Albany the news reached him of the German annexation, and, before he had been many days in Australia, further information was received that negotiations were going on between Great Britain and Germany for dividing between the two countries the unappropriated portion of New Guinea. Public opinion ran very high in the Colonies against the Home Government when they found their confidence had been misplaced, and this feeling of irritation was intensified upon discovering that they were to be asked to increase the subsidy, when half the territory for which they had agreed to pay was already in the possession of a foreign Power. It is not that the Australians dislike the Germans as colonists, but they object to them as next-door neighbours in the Pacific. With the example of South Africa before their eyes, the danger of border disputes is ever present to their minds, and it would be idle to attempt to disguise the fact that, in the unhappy event of a European war, Kaiser Wilhelm Land, from its size and position, may prove the basis of awkward complications in that part of the world. The Germans, too, have a peculiar interest in New Guinea, seeing that their other neighbours are so nearly allied to them in speech and habits.

CHAPTER XVII.

EARLY DIFFICULTIES.

GENERAL SCRATCHLEY arrived at Melbourne on January 4, 1885, and met with a very favourable reception. There existed, however, a deep feeling of irritation, and indeed disgust, at the manner in which the Imperial Government had dealt with the question of annexation in the Western Pacific. Indignation ran high against Lord Derby as the responsible Minister. Victorians felt he had taken advantage of the apparent want of union amongst the several Colonial Governments to do as little as he possibly could in the matter while the attempt to constitute the question an Australian one, when the colonies had always desired to recognise it as affecting the whole Empire, was unanimously condemned. The primary intention of those who felt most strongly on the subject was to prevent the Pacific being converted into an asylum for the habitual criminals of France. Provided this objection were removed, the whole question might have been re-opened on the basis of meeting equitable claims on the part of other foreign nations. But the chief contention at the time was that through the hesitating policy of the Imperial Government the Germans were in a way invited to annex a portion of New Guinea. The Australians felt that they had been put off from time to time by evasive answers, and their well-intentioned desire to strengthen the hands of the Imperial Government had been deliberately set aside. The most reasonable men agreed that the whole affair had been muddled from beginning to end. Even those who were favourable to the Germans considered that the mother-country, in allowing a possibly hostile nation to gain a footing in New Guinea, had not sufficiently considered the future welfare of the Australasian Colonies.

General Scratchley was much impeded in his preparations for reaching New Guinea, by reason of the fact that the Imperial authorities failed to provide the steamer, which, in his instructions, ' it was proposed to place at his disposal, for the duties of the Protectorate,' in order that he might more easily ' make the acquaintance of the country, its harbours and general features.' New South Wales, seeing the difficulty of obtaining a suitable vessel, and anxious that her Majesty's representative should arrive in a fitting manner, placed H.M.S. *Wolverene* at his disposal for six months. This offer was accepted, and after some little delay the acceptance was sanctioned by the authorities at home. The suggestion had come from Mr. Bede Dalley, the same statesman who took upon himself the responsibility of offering aid to the mother-country during the late war in Egypt.

Scarcely was the matter settled when rumours of impending war between England and Russia were telegraphed out to the Colonies. Matters began to look serious, and Sir Peter felt it his duty to hand over the *Wolverene* to the New South Wales Government for defence purposes. The war scare caused the Colonies to look more carefully to their defences, and application was made to Sir Peter for advice. This was readily given, and for a period of three weeks, during which the panic was at its height, General Scratchley devoted his time to the question of securing the Colonies against the expected appearance of Russian cruisers.

As soon as the prospects of peace became more certain, the preparations for proceeding to New Guinea were resumed. The *Wolverene* being no longer available, tenders were accordingly invited for a suitable steamer. Twenty answers were received, but the prices asked by the majority were so exorbitant that the choice was necessarily limited. After considerable trouble and deliberation, the tender of the Australasian Steam Navigation Company for the ss. *Governor Blackall* was accepted, and in July the vessel was laid up in Sydney to be refitted and prepared for the New Guinea work. Meantime, at the request of the Queensland and New Zealand Governments, Sir Peter visited those Colonies for the purpose of discussing the subject of his mission.

While in Queensland General Scratchley consulted Sir Samuel Griffith, Q.C., upon his authority and status as Special Commissioner. This eminent colonial lawyer gave it as his opinion that—

> General Scratchley has at present no legal jurisdiction and authority of any kind, except such as he can exercise as a Deputy Commissioner for the Western Pacific ; and in particular that he has no power to make any regulations having the force of law, or to impose or collect any taxes or license fees upon ex-

ports or imports, or otherwise to exercise any legislative or judicial functions in the Protectorate.

Hence another and altogether unforeseen difficulty arose, which, while the matter remained in doubt, required the exercise of much tact in the early administration of affairs in the Protectorate.

Perhaps, however, the most difficult and delicate question to settle was the financial one, and much animated discussion took place upon the memorandum issued to the Colonial Governments, in which Sir Peter opened up the question of future payment. The answers one and all showed that much dissatisfaction existed upon the subject. That of New South Wales was chiefly founded upon the resolutions passed at the Australian Convention held in Sydney in 1883, at which Conference all the Colonies were represented. It was as follows:—

This Government paid its first year's contribution, 4,084*l*. 14*s*. 4*d*., on May 22 last.

This Government has always understood that the Imperial Government was to pay a portion of the expense. At the Convention it was generally understood that the Imperial contribution would not be less than half, for it was clearly pointed out that the strategic importance of securing the southern shores of New Guinea was as much if not more an Imperial than a Colonial advantage, for the ships navigating Torres Straits were, both in number and in tonnage, representative far more of British than of Colonial capital. The Convention did not consider that it would be courteous to dictate what portion the Imperial Government should pay, but preferred leaving it to the Imperial Government to state what portion, in its opinion, the Colonies ought to bear; and thus it was that the fifth resolution was adopted, by which the various

Governments represented 'undertook to submit and recommend to their various Legislatures measures of permanent appropriation for defraying, in proportion to population, *such share* of the cost incurred as her Majesty's Government, having regard to the relative importance of Imperial and Australasian interests, may deem fair and reasonable.' To cast the whole cost upon the Australasian Colonies would be to ignore the resolution of the Convention, unless the Imperial Government were prepared to advance the doctrine that Imperial interests are not concerned in this matter.

Under these circumstances, all that this Government can do is to recommend to Parliament that a permanent appropriation shall be made of its share according to population, to the extent of 15,000*l*. for the whole of the Colonies, so soon as the Imperial Government shall have intimated the extent to which it is prepared to bear the common burden.

(Signed)   ALEX. STUART.

The answer from Victoria was perhaps the most bitter. Mr. Service did not hesitate to express the great disappointment felt by his Government and people at the meagre result of the efforts to secure the whole of Eastern New Guinea for the British Crown; 'but for good or for evil,' said the Victorian Premier, 'the matter, with all the incidents which led up to it, now passes into history.' He agreed however to ask the Parliament of Victoria to continue the contribution, but only until the Imperial Government had time to decide what portion of the cost should be borne by the Imperial Exchequer. Indeed, the vein of sarcasm running throughout his reply was very telling, and in refusing to ask his country to grant any increased expenditure Mr. Service ably paraphrased Lord Derby's instructions to Sir Peter Scratchley, by giving as his reason 'the limited area of territory annexed, and the lack of information as to the intentions of her Majesty's Government.' These were no mere idle words put together for effect, but the expression of a matured opinion from one of Australia's ablest statesmen. I had discussed the New Guinea question with Mr. Service long before Sir Peter issued his memorandum, and his reply only embodies what he said to me on that occasion. Tasmania promised to continue her contributions, but stated that for the future she would be guided by the course Victoria took in the matter. Sir Samuel Griffith, on behalf of Queensland, to which colony the future of New Guinea is naturally of the greatest importance, sent an exhaustive reply, in which, after dealing minutely with the question of cost, he practically adopted Sir Peter's programme, and, on behalf of his Government, promised to continue the contribution. At the same time he remarked in a decided manner upon the dilatory way in which the Imperial authorities had acted.

New Zealand made many useful suggestions, and Mr. Stout, the Premier, agreed to submit to his Parliament the following resolutions:—

That, in the opinion of this House, the portion of New Guinea annexed to the Empire should, for the present, be created a Crown colony, with the view of its ultimately being annexed to Queensland, or created a constitutional colony.

That aid should be given by the Imperial Government to the new possessions by placing at the disposal of the Governor a war vessel for his use.

That, for a term of three years from the 1st day of June, 1886, this colony will undertake to pay its share of 15,000*l.* a year proportionately to population, on the condition that the other colonies of Australia join in the contribution on the same terms.

Western Australia paid nothing. South Australia withdrew altogether, and Fiji, being unable to provide more than 100*l*., was exempted from any contribution. Thus the financial difficulty was patched over for a time, but it could hardly be said to be finally settled. Sir Peter Scratchley wrote the following opinion on the subject:—

'The ignorance of the intentions of the Colonial Office as to the future creates difficulties in the Colonial Governments coming to an agreement with the Imperial Government on the subject of the cost of governing British New Guinea.

'Until full information is given on all points, there is little prospect of a permanent settlement of the question, and the policy of the Australian Colonies will continue to be of a hand-to-mouth character.

'The object should be to get the several Governments to propose Acts of special appropriation to their local Parliaments, in order to permanently secure the contributions to be granted yearly to her Majesty. An Act has been passed in Queensland, and, although that Government declines to increase its contribution, there is little fear of the Act being repealed. It is doubtful whether the other Governments will do more than vote the contribution yearly.[1] If so, every year there will be discussions, more or less unpleasant, in the local

[1] It was also suggested that the payment should be made half yearly, and that the financial year should begin on January 1, instead of June 1.

Parliaments; and it will be difficult for the Imperial officer in charge to look ahead and establish an economical administration.'

Sir Peter Scratchley felt much embarrassment owing to the differences of opinion which existed between the Imperial authorities and the Colonial Governments; since, under the only arrangement then in contemplation, it was not intended that New Guinea should form any part of the Anglo-Australian political system. On this subject I give Sir Peter's opinion in his own words :—

'A Crown Colony, with the simplest machinery for its government, will probably be the best. The judicial powers of the Governor should be such as to enable him to deal summarily with minor offences, and to remit, say to the Queensland Courts, offences of a more serious nature. Everything will, at first, be necessarily of a tentative character.

'What proportion of the expense of the cost of government will be borne by the Imperial Government? This is of paramount importance. If the whole of the expense is to be borne by the Colonies, the Imperial Government will practically have no control, and I foresee that a deadlock must eventually arise between the Imperial officer and the Australasian Governments.

'The exercise of tact, patience, and diplomacy will keep matters going for the first two or three years; but the deadlock will ultimately occur, as he will be dealing with half a dozen Governments, all holding more or less divergent views.'

Some idea may thus be formed of the preliminary difficulties that delayed Sir Peter Scratchley in Australia and surrounded his mission at its commencement. We may now turn to what was actually done.

CHAPTER XVIII.

ENGLAND'S NEW COLONY.

SIR PETER SCRATCHLEY completed his business arrangements with the Australian Colonies in the early part of August 1885, and on the 13th of that month left Sydney in the *Governor Blackall* to take possession of her Majesty's newly acquired territory in New Guinea. The *Governor Blackall*, which during the next few months was to serve as a floating government-house for Sir Peter and his staff,[1] slipped her moorings in Farm Cove shortly after seven o'clock in the morning, and under easy steam made her way down the harbour, followed by a steam-launch in which were Lady Scratchley and several friends who had come to bid him farewell. The Harbour Heads were cleared soon after eight o'clock, and the ship's course shaped for Brisbane, which was reached the following morning.

Here Mr. Romilly joined the expedition, and a passage was given to Mr. H. O. Forbes, who, owing to the loss of the greater part of his outfit by the sinking of a barge at Batavia, had been for some time detained

[1] Sir Peter Scratchley's staff consisted of Mr. Hugh Hastings Romilly, C.M.G., who had been appointed Deputy Commissioner; Mr. G. Seymour Fort, private secretary; Mr. George Ranken Askwith, assistant secretary; and Mr. Doyle Glanville, surgeon; besides a photographer and photographer's assistant.

in Queensland. Business transactions caused a delay of a few days, but soon another start was made, and the *Governor Blackall* proceeded on her way *via* Townsville and Cooktown to Port Moresby, where she arrived on Friday, August 28.

Before proceeding inland, Sir Peter Scratchley had much work to do at Port Moresby in settling the lines upon which the country should be governed. Every step required the greatest care. Preconceived opinions, based upon Australian or English ideas, often proved erroneous; while many statements, made by persons professing a knowledge of the country, turned out to be false, or concocted for selfish purposes. Port Moresby was fixed upon as the seat of government. Arrangements were made for the registration of coasting vessels; port and customs dues; the establishment of a mail service; and a supply of fresh water for ships. Questions regarding revenue, its source, permanence, and increase, required consideration, and amongst other matters which engaged Sir Peter's attention were the rivalry between the Protestant Mission and the Roman Catholic missionaries at Yule Island; the establishment of officials along the coast; arrangements for the supply of coal and provisions; the site of the Deputy Commissioner's[1] house; the settlement of land claims; and the alleged murder of white men by natives.

A considerable area of land, comprising the best sites in the harbour and nearly the whole of the sea-frontage, was purchased from the natives. In obtain-

[1] Mr. Musgrave was appointed resident Deputy Commissioner.

ing the assent of the claimants for this land to part with their property *in perpetuo*, and thus securing a sound title for the Government, the assistance rendered by the Protestant Mission was invaluable. A portion of the land thus obtained was set aside for Government buildings, part was marked out as a site for a future township, and the rest held as a native reserve. Boevagi, the chief of the village, was formally recognised as head of the district, and instructed to refer all complaints, whether of a tribal nature or against white men, to the High Commissioner. Twenty-five chiefs were invited on board the *Governor Blackall*, and gifts made them. They were told to regard white men as their friends, whose presence would be to their advantage, to look up to Boevagi as their Head, and to refer to him all cases requiring arbitration.[1]

In addition to the land purchased at Port Moresby, a large tract was acquired at South Cape. These were the only purchases of land made.

LAND CLAIMS.

Previous to Sir Peter Scratchley's arrival in New Guinea, several Europeans had gone through the form

[1] When New Guinea was formally annexed to the Crown, Boevagi, being the most influential man in his own district, was presented by Commodore Erskine with an ebony stick having a florin let into the head, as a mark of authority, and was also invested with a cast-off commodore's coat, cockedhat, and trousers. Either no boots were given him or they had been lost. As he did not consider himself properly dressed without boots, he threw out strong hints to Sir Peter Scratchley that he should like a pair, but unfortunately no one had any to spare. He came on board looking very quiet and gentle, and sat down beside Sir Peter, who addressed him through an interpreter and made him a present of some red cloth, tobacco, and a tomahawk.

of purchasing land from natives. Two classes of claimants had to be dealt with: those who based their claims on purchases made prior to the proclamation of the Protectorate; and those who claimed a prescriptive right to lease lands, on the ground of occupancy or original exploration.

Of the first class, a claim to about 700 acres of land at Port Moresby, alleged to have been purchased in 1878, and a claim to 15,000 acres of land in the Kabadi district in 1880, were the most important. Under paragraph 6 in Commodore Erskine's Proclamation of November 1884,[1] these claims had no recognised legal basis. Each case was, however, thoroughly investigated by Sir Peter Scratchley.

The first was a purchase made in July 1878 by the master of a trading vessel, who assigned his rights. His assignee claimed about 500 acres of headland, and two plots of about 100 acres each, which were comprised in the land purchased as a native reserve. The purchase-money was alleged to be 600*l*.; but, after careful inquiry, it was proved to Sir Peter's satisfaction that not more than 8*l*. in value was actually given. The claim was consequently refused.

In the case of the 15,000 acres in the Kabadi district, as the land was fertile, the area extensive, and the claim possessed an official history, a special expedition was made for the purpose of investigation, with the result that this claim was also refused.

His eyes glistened at this access of wealth, and he stood gazing in undisguised delight at the reflection of his own figure in a long mirror. On leaving he shook hands all round, and said 'Good morning' very politely.

[1] See *Appendix* B.

All applications for leases[1] based on the grounds of occupancy or original exploration were temporarily shelved or refused until the sites had been visited by Sir Peter Scratchley or one of his officers. Applications for concessions of land were recorded from :—

(a) A firm in Australia, on behalf of a German Company, for the purpose of establishing trading stations, which was referred to the Imperial Government;

(b) The New Guinea Land and Emigration Company in London, which was rejected;

(c) A New Guinea trader, who desired to start a company for the development of native industries.— The correspondence in reference to this application was never completed.

Permission to occupy Government land, for the purpose of erecting a house and store, was granted to certain traders at Port Moresby and at South Cape. Mr. H. O. Forbes, who established a station at Sogeri, about fifty miles inland from Port Moresby, was authorised to purchase land from the natives in that district. A land register, on the same plan as that adopted in Fiji, was begun, with the object of giving those persons who expended money in the purchase of land, or in working and cultivating it, a prior right as against subsequent claimants.

To prevent the indiscriminate influx of adventurers and speculators, no person was allowed to go to New Guinea without a permit. Several permits to trade were granted to private companies and individuals, subject to the observance of certain conditions.[2] The customs officers at Townsville and Cooktown were

---

[1] See *Appendix* B.   [2] See *Appendix* B.

authorised by the Queensland Government to prevent any vessel without a permit from clearing from either of the above-named ports.

Although it was a prominent feature in Sir Peter Scratchley's policy to encourage exploration when conducted upon a proper footing and under recognised leaders, he rejected every application for a permit to explore, where he was of opinion that the attempt would not only result in ruin to the applicant, but might cause a breach in the relations with the natives, which it would possibly take years to heal. The following remarks on this question appear in Sir Peter's note-book:—'All explorations must be methodical and systematic. No time must be fixed for the return of the exploring party, which should be composed of as few members as possible. No exploring party should act independently of the Government.' The most important explorations undertaken during Sir Peter Scratchley's administration were the expedition of the Australasian Geographical Society, under Captain Everill, and that by Mr. H. O. Forbes.

It may be mentioned that Sir Peter Scratchley was favourable to the formation in Australia of a New Guinea trading company, on a basis somewhat similar to the British North Borneo Company.

LAND TENURE.

The ownership of land in New Guinea appears to be divided amongst groups of individuals, who are more or less related by kin. The number of individuals in each group varies. In some cases it has dwindled down to one representative, in others it has indefinitely increased. Each member of a group is deemed to have a separate interest in the land, but no one member can dispose of the property without the consent of the whole, while each claims to receive a share of the profits when it is sold. The sense of individual proprietorship is very strong, and extends to particular trees, and even to the fruit upon them. If the land to be disposed of belongs to a family group, of which a district chief is also the patriarchal head, he would be the most prominent figure in the transaction; but if it is the property of a different family group to his own, his authority and power as district chief will weigh but little in the matter. It is exceptional to find a chief strong enough to negotiate independently for the disposal of land belonging even to his own group. It is still less common to meet with one who will negotiate with regard to land in which he has not himself a personal interest. These distinctions may appear vague to Europeans, but they are well defined and understood by the natives, as is illustrated by the following instances:—

In the case of the land purchased at Port Moresby[1] certain natives claimed payment, and, although they were only a part of their tribe, their right to receive the money was acquiesced in by the whole; and at South Cape, the independent right of one person (and he not a chief) to dispose of a large area of land was recognised by the rest of the tribe, no one else assert-

[1] *Ante*, p. 283.

ing any claim. No title-deeds were drawn up, nor did the seller attach his name to any document; but a statement was signed to the effect that the native (Pusa) had a sole right to the land, that he had parted with it voluntarily, and that he and the tribe were satisfied with the payment given.[1] On the other hand, in the case of some land adjoining, there were many owners in the tribe, each of whom, including the chief, required to receive payment. At Kabadi, a piece of land belonged to a family group, of which the district chief was not the patriarchal head, and although he objected, he could not stop the sale.

The general rule appears to be that on the death of the buyer the land reverts to the original vendor, or if the buyer resells the land, the price is taken by the original vendor. In cases of absolute sale, the whole family assert their rights by the individual members standing by a tussock of grass, which they twist up until a satisfaction is received by each. The multitudinous division causes innumerable small allotments. Koapena[2] alone seems to have broken the family system by insisting that all land must be bought from him. Sir Peter Scratchley thought it might be possible to establish recognised tribal chiefs through whom a title should accrue, but he determined that in no case should

---

[1] The following particulars of this transaction may be interesting :— About four square miles along the beach were bought for one axe, one adze, three tomahawks, three sheath-knives, one grass knife, twelve looking-glasses, one bundle of hoop-iron in small pieces, six long pipes, twelve short pipes, three wooden pipes, one piece of Turkey red cloth, one piece trade handkerchiefs, five pounds of tobacco, one gimlet.

[2] See *Sir Peter's Diary*, p. 334.

land be bought from natives without the intervention of the Government, to ensure fair play and prevent disputes.

NATIVE ORGANISATION.

The social and political organisation of the New Guinea natives is quite rudimentary; and, though they are far superior in physique to the Australian blacks, there is no such developed tribal system as formerly existed in Fiji, Java, and New Zealand.

In the west and north-west, from the Fly River to Hall Sound, the tribes are large. Farther south, villages are smaller but more numerous. Concerning the natives on the north-east coast little is known. Sir Peter Scratchley and his guard only carried arms on rare occasions, but no hostility was ever shown; and even at Mr. Forbes' station, the farthest settlement inland hitherto attempted by white men, the natives displayed a friendly spirit.

Much difficulty, however, was experienced in dealing with the natives, owing to the great variety of dialects that exist among them. Not only each district, but every village speaks a different dialect. The Motu is the most common, and extends from Port Moresby to Kapa Kapa.

The natives everywhere showed themselves ready to trade with Europeans, and eagerly exchanged, not only natural products, but even personal ornaments, relics, and house utensils, for tobacco, axes, and cloth. They have also a good deal of inland trading among themselves, the inland supplying the coast tribes with food products in exchange for fish, salt, &c. In the Port Moresby district expeditions[1] are annually made to the Gulf of Papua for the purpose of exchanging pottery, made at Port Moresby, for sago grown in the west. Tilling the ground is mainly done by women, the men, as a rule, being idle and incapable of systematic labour. The principal food consists of bananas, yams, sweet potatoes, taro, cocoa-nuts, sugar-cane, bread-fruit and other native fruits, and fish.

In order to render the natives more capable of self-government, Sir Peter Scratchley proposed to appoint a tribal chief in each district, who was not only to be trustee for the lands, and responsible for the conduct of the inhabitants in his district, but also an official vested with government authority. Under existing circumstances three rival chiefs are often found in a single village: the patriarchal chief, who is more or less connected by kin with all the village; the man who is chief by virtue of his individual prowess in war; and perhaps a sorcerer chief. It occasionally happens that the three attributes are centred in one man, as, for example, in the case of Koapena, chief of Aroma.[2] The remedy Sir Peter Scratchley suggested was a modified form of the Java system, making the Government-elected chief the recipient of a fixed annual payment, and responsible for the safety of foreigners, as well as for the maintenance of law and order within his district.

Sir Peter proposed to introduce the cultivation of

[1] For a detailed account, see *New Guinea Notes*, p. 364.
[2] See *New Guinea Notes*, p. 370.

rice and maize, by means of the official chief and native teachers, in order to give the natives an inducement to steady labour and systematic cultivation.

MISSIONARIES.

The London Missionary Society began work in New Guinea in 1871. The Mission is divided into three districts: Western, Central, and Eastern. The Western begins at the Baxter River, includes the Fly and the Katan Rivers, and ends at the Aird River. Its headquarters are at Murray Island. Here the native students are taught many industrial arts; and a schooner,[1] built by them for mission purposes under the direction of an English boat-builder, has been recently launched. The Central begins at the Aird River and ends at Orangerie Bay. The mission house for this district is at Port Moresby, where native teachers are also trained for the purpose of carrying on the mission work. The Eastern extends from Orangerie Bay eastward.

There are forty mission stations where South Sea Island and New Guinea teachers are employed in the work of the Society. These stations extend from East Cape to Maclatchie Point, as well as to the west of the Fly River. Nearly every mission station possesses its own mission teacher, who has a large house and garden, and also a whale-boat. Missionary labour in New Guinea has not only opened up communication with the natives along nearly the whole coast-line of

[1] The *Ellangowan*, mentioned in *Sir Peter's Diary*.

the protected territory, and far into the interior, but, what is more important, has inspired them with confidence in white men. Had the result been different, and the natives made hostile or suspicious, none but armed bodies of men could have ventured into the interior, nor could individuals have cruised along the coast in fair security. Under present conditions, a single white man, unarmed, can go fifty miles into the interior from any point between Port Moresby and Hula in perfect safety.

Much of this success is due to the native teachers, who have been pioneers to break down native superstition and distrust. Some idea of their courage and influence may be gathered from the following incidents:—

Some trading canoes of the Motu tribe, coming from westward to Port Moresby, were blown by a gale of wind past that port and wrecked on a reef at Aroma, with the people of which place they were at enmity. The latter at once prepared to attack and slaughter the shipwrecked Motuans. The native teacher, however, interposed at imminent risk to his life, and persuaded the Aroma warriors to return, thus saving the lives of nearly sixty Motuans. The courage of this act can only be realised by those who know what it is to check a large number of armed natives bent on slaughter and bloodshed, especially bloodshed which the force of custom has caused them to consider theirs by right. In recognition of his bravery Sir Peter Scratchley presented him with a silver watch engraved with the words, 'From the Great Queen Victoria.'

The native teacher at Dinner Island was also presented with a watch for his services on the occasion of Captain Friar's murder, having, at imminent risk to his own life, rescued the schooner belonging to the murdered man, and navigated her back to Dinner Island.

Experience shows that among primitive barbarians the teaching of different creeds is not infrequently the cause of disturbance. The efforts of the Roman Catholic Mission to establish themselves in places which the London Missionary Society had occupied for years, were, in Sir Peter Scratchley's opinion, to be discouraged upon political grounds, as he considered such efforts likely to produce trouble among the natives. When he heard, therefore, that certain Roman Catholic priests had established themselves at Yule Island, which had been previously occupied by the Protestant Mission, he wrote to the head of the Roman Catholic Mission at Thursday Island pointing out that the settlement of these priests on Yule Island was undesirable, and that other areas were available for their efforts. He further offered to take them in the *Governor Blackall* to the Louisiade Group, or any other island they might select.[1]

GENERAL FEATURES.

The climate of New Guinea is one of its greatest drawbacks. It is enervating for Europeans; and the fever, which is everywhere prevalent, is of a severe character. All early attempts at permanent settlement, especially on the coast, are likely to be attended with a high rate of mortality. It is probable, however,

---

[1] See *New Guinea Notes*, p. 300.

that as the country becomes settled and the soil worked, the pestilential character of the climate will be modified. In breaking up land for sugar plantations in the north of Queensland, every one, Kanakas [1] as well as Europeans, was attacked with fever—some fatally; on the same stations fever is now almost unknown. Cornwallis Island, Port Moresby, Dinner Island,[2] Killerton Island, and Teste Island, are perhaps the least unhealthy places on the coast of the British Protectorate. In the interior, although fever prevails, it is less severe than on the coast, while the atmosphere, especially on the highlands, is even bracing and invigorating.

The Gulf of Papua affords no safe anchorage for ships. Thick and muddy water obscures the reefs, and for miles from the shore the depth is frequently only two fathoms. From Redscar Head eastwards the south coast is skirted almost continuously by a reef,[3] which extends seawards to a distance of five or six miles. Its numerous indentations afford excellent harbours. On the south-west coast the most important harbours are Port Moresby, Orangerie Bay, Milport Bay, and South Cape. Navigation along the whole coast is troublesome, and no vessel can sail at night.

The whole of the Protected Territory, with the exception of the district around Port Moresby, is well watered. Of the rivers the largest is the Fly, which rises some hundreds of miles in the interior, and is supposed to have many tributaries. Owing to the action

---

[1] Kanakas are natives brought from the surrounding islands.
[2] Dinner Island was so named because Captain Moresby took a meal there. It is a small island about 25 miles E.S.E. from South Cape.
[3] See chapter on *Torres Strait*, p. 245.

of the south-east monsoon, which blows during the healthy season, the mouths of these rivers become silted up with sand and mud. This is especially the case in the Aird River, which it is only possible to enter during the north-west monsoon, the unhealthy season. On the south-east coast the rivers are numerous, but small when compared with those in the west. The north-east coast is well watered by several rivers of considerable size. In Dyke Acland Bay, where there is a vast tract of level country densely wooded, intervening between the coast and the distant highlands, the mouth of a very large river was seen. This river is not marked on any map.

In Milne Bay, two rivers were discovered and explored. The first (native name Davadava) flows into the north-east of the bay. It was explored for a distance of about six miles. The banks, covered with coarse vegetation, were steep and precipitous. This river is navigable for a small steamer. The other (native name Hadara) is a very large river, and apparently leads into the heart of the country. The land on either side is flat and the soil rich, the vegetation tropical and abundant, and the depth of water varies from twelve to sixteen feet.

A central range of mountains running north and south forms the backbone of the Protected Territory. The highest point in this range is supposed to be Mount Owen Stanley, 13,200 feet. Leading to the base of this central mountain-range on the west side, is a series of high ranges or spurs, having their sides densely covered with a forest of tropical growth, while valleys, full of rich deep soil, patches of open country covered with coarse grass, and craters evidently formed by recent volcanic action, are met with here and there. Many of the hillsides and valleys have been cleared, fenced, and cultivated by the natives. In some cases the ranges extend almost to the coast; in others, as at Kabadi, the intervening land is flat and open; while at others, again, such as Kapa Kapa and Hula, miles of gently undulating country, well watered, with patches of forest intervening, stretch far back into the interior. The character of the vegetation (especially on the coast), and in many cases of the soil also, is Australian; towards the interior, however, it becomes more tropical.

The plains about Port Moresby afford good hunting-ground for wallaby, and wild pigs are plentiful. The cuscus, an animal resembling the Australian native bear, and a species of tree kangaroo, are also to be found in the district. It is supposed that monkeys exist in the interior. Various kinds of birds, such as pigeons, ducks, cassowaries, and birds of paradise, are met with everywhere.

The mineral resources of British New Guinea are still a matter of conjecture. It is the opinion of Mr. H. O. Forbes, based upon geological observation, that gold will not be found to the westward, but may exist in the high country of the Milne Bay district, and on the north-east coast. Pebbles and small fragments brought down from the interior indicate that the formation there is similar to that of the New South Wales gold-fields. Plumbago was seen at various places along the south-west coast.

NATIVE INDUSTRIES.

Glowing accounts of the prospects of the timber trade in New Guinea have from time to time been published. It is true, cedar and 'malava' (a species of cedar) abound in the Manu Manu district, and on the banks of the Kemp-Welch, Edith, and other rivers, but it is not generally known that a very large proportion of this timber is so small as not to be of marketable value. Before the proclamation of the Protectorate large quantities of cedar had been cut by Australian firms, and permits were granted them to remove this timber. As, however, in many cases large numbers of young trees, too small for use, had been cut down in wanton waste, any further felling of timber was prohibited until the various sites had been visited by Sir Peter Scratchley or his representatives. A forester was also appointed to prevent trees being felled of less than a certain girth. The agent for an Australian company, who had for some years been engaged in cutting timber in New Guinea, stated that out of 10,000,000 superficial feet of cedar and malava felled, only about 500,000 superficial feet were of marketable value; that he did not think the future prospects of the cedar trade were hopeful, and that his firm would hardly cover the expenses they had incurred in the business. Besides the cedar and malava, however, indiarubber, 'massoi' (the bark of which has a medicinal value), sandalwood, ebony, hardwood, and 'tamonu' trees are abundant—

especially in the district around South Cape. Two or
three large firms are engaged in the trade, one of
which employs a number of Kanakas.

'Bêche-de-mer,' or the sea-slug, which is esteemed
by Chinese as an edible dainty, is found all along the
coast from Port Moresby to Aroma, including Constance Island, Milport Bay, Milne Bay, Slade Island,
Bentley Bay, and, it is believed, in some bays on
the north-east coast. The quantity to be obtained,
however, especially on the south-west coast, has materially decreased during the last few years. The
profits are small and precarious, and much hardship
has to be undergone in the fishery. In some districts
the natives, through superstition, dislike handling the
bêche-de-mer. The value of the article annually
exported from New Guinea has been estimated at
8,000*l.*; and it is possible that a considerable revenue
might be raised by a tax on the trade, but the expense of collecting it would be great. Sir Peter
Scratchley intended to establish a depôt for the industry at Teste Island, and appointed an inspector to
report the number of vessels engaged and the number
of tons exported. It is stated that ten schooners are
now employed, and the estimated quantity exported is
about 500 tons. The persons engaged in this pursuit
are, for the most part, small traders.

'Copra' is made by splitting cocoanuts and
drying them either artificially or in the sun. It is
largely used in Europe in the manufacture of oilcake and other cattle foods. The localities at present
suited for making copra are on the south-west coast

from Hula to Aroma, all along the shores of Milne Bay, at Bentley Bay, and along the north-east coast as far as Dampier Straits, and in many of the islands of the D'Entrecasteaux and Louisiade Groups. At each of these places cocoanuts grow in abundance. The trees, if planted in a certain manner, bear fruit in three years, and consequently the industry may be made very profitable. In order, however, to facilitate its development, it would be necessary to ensure a constant supply of nuts by establishing a chain of stations at various points, at which natives could be advantageously employed. At Milne Bay and the surrounding islands there would be considerable difficulty in drying the nuts in the sun owing to the dampness of the climate, and as 'sun-dried' is superior to 'smoke-dried' copra, it would, perhaps, be more profitable to bring the nuts to Port Moresby, to be dried there by the sun, than to treat them by artificial means.

The existing pearl fisheries are on the western extremity of the Territory, and occasionally large quantities of pearls have been collected there. Recently, however, a large find of pearl was made in the Louisiade Group, and it is not improbable that this industry may assume much greater proportions, especially among the islands on the east coast.

New Guinea is admirably adapted for the production of cinchona, coffee, rice, sugar, arrowroot, cotton, vanilla, and tobacco, all of which the natives might be taught to cultivate; while amongst the products indigenous to the soil, and capable of forming sources of revenue, in addition to those previously mentioned, may be enumerated nutmegs, ginger, pepper, spices of all kinds, sago, hemp, cocoanut fibre. saffron canes, and rattan.

In some portions of the interior it would be possible to graze sheep and cattle, which might supply a local market, but, on account of the difficulties of communication, the obstacles in the way of developing purely agricultural interests in the country would be great.

THE FUTURE OF NEW GUINEA.

In order to secure the systematic administration of the country, the machinery of government would have to be augmented. This would involve increased expenditure in building houses for Sub-Commissioners, providing accommodation for native police, and in other items, such as whale-boats, which may be treated as capital outlay, while the yearly charges would be increased by the salaries of additional Deputy-Commissioners and native police, and by the establishment of a regular mail service. It may, however, be reasonably anticipated that increased expenditure for administration would result in a corresponding development of natural sources of revenue.

It has been confidently anticipated by those who have seen the fertility of the Protected Territory, and its capacity for producing articles of tropical growth, that it may be made self-supporting. The following methods of raising revenue might be found practicable and economical :—

(1.) By granting licenses for bêche-de-mer and pearl-fishing boats. These should be registered, and the licensees required to report themselves at Port Moresby at least once a year.

(2.) By granting licenses for the erection of smoke-huts and copra stations.

(3.) By imposing export duties on cedar and malava, at a fixed rate per hundred superficial feet of timber; and *ad valorem* duties on sandal and black woods. With reference to this last suggested impost, I have been informed that one trader alone, if he had been assessed according to Queensland timber-dues, would have paid the Government about 2,000*l*. The Customs officers at Cooktown and Townsville might, with the consent of the Queensland Government, be empowered to act for the New Guinea Protectorate.

(4.) By funds arising from trading licenses, judicial fees, harbour dues, and leases of certain unoccupied lands.

(5.) By imposing import duties.

(6.) By levying contributions from the natives towards the expenses of government; but as these would be paid in kind, their value could hardly be estimated as a source of revenue at present.

The most prominent question with regard to New Guinea, from a commercial point of view, is whether it can be made a successful outlet for capital. The fact should not, however, be overlooked that the island was primarily annexed for political purposes, and its value to Australia in this respect, although, perhaps, diminished by a part of it having been ceded to Germany, is still great. Not only is the British portion nearest the Australian shores, but it possesses the best climate, the finest harbours and ports, the most fertile soil, and the largest rivers.

An important consideration is the responsibility which rests on the annexing Powers for the proper protection of the natives. Probably, in no country and at no period of history has there been a more favourable opportunity for successfully adjusting the mutual interests of white and coloured [1] races than in New Guinea. On moral as well as political grounds, it is essential that the natives should be protected, not only from aggression and usurpation on the part of Europeans, but also from physical degradation. Regulations with regard to the introduction of spirituous liquors should be strictly and rigidly enforced. The following statement with reference to this subject appears among Sir Peter Scratchley's notes:—'The only hope of

---

[1] Three separate types are met with in New Guinea, the Papuan, Malay, and Polynesian, which are much intermixed. The pure Papuan is only found within a small area in the interior and on some portions of the north-east. The Papuan type, however, prevails with modifications throughout almost the whole of the Protected Territory. In stature they are short and squat—low foreheads and prognathous; in character they are noisy and demonstrative, shy and suspicious, with a low estimate of human life, but not aggressively bloodthirsty. Their standard of comfort is low, and they show but little capacity for any higher organisation. The Malay element appears to predominate in the tribes to westward and in the tribes at Aroma and Cloudy Bay district. They are aggressive and bloodthirsty, and are gradually driving back other tribes; they show capacity for a higher organisation. The Polynesian element is most prominent at South Cape, although the Polynesian form of religion is entirely wanting; they have a tendency to be treacherous, and noisy and demonstrative, and the artistic faculty is strongly marked among them. Distinct types of Papuan, Malay, and Polynesian nationality are frequently to be seen in the same village.—G. SEYMOUR FORT.

making New Guinea pay is by the employment of natives, who can, by patience and care, be trained. If they disappear, others will have to be imported. Putting, therefore, the protection of the natives on the lowest ground, it will be seen that it will be cheaper to preserve and educate them. New Guinea must be governed for the natives and by the natives.'

The future of the country materially depends upon this vital question. If the natives are rendered hostile or corrupt, New Guinea will continue to be the hunting-ground of needy adventurers and speculators ; if, on the other hand, they learn confidence in their rulers, settlement in many parts is possible, and the Colony may become the regular source of supply of tropical products to the Australian market. It will, therefore, be seen that the duty of the Government and the interest of the capitalist coincide ; and if, in the scheme for the administration of the country, the efficient protection of the natives is provided for, the introduction of European capital should be attended with financial success.

CHAPTER XIX.

SIR PETER'S DIARY.

SIR PETER SCRATCHLEY'S Diary is a record of his daily life while in New Guinea. It was written simply for his wife's perusal, and possibly that of a few friends. Lady Scratchley has, however, yielded to Sir Arthur Gordon's suggestion, and placed it at my disposal.

The Diary has been edited in conjunction with Lady Scratchley and Mr. Philip Scratchley, and its contents will enable some idea to be formed, from Sir Peter's own words, of the early days in the New Guinea Protectorate.

Sunday, August 16, 1885.—Here I am sitting in my cabin on deck, after lunch, smoking a cigar, with a delightful breeze blowing through the windows, and a sensation that I should like to go to sleep—a sensation I shall very probably yield to before another fifteen minutes. It is a dead calm; with a bright, sunny, cloudless sky. We had a delightful night, quite calm; in fact, excepting a little tumbling about off Newcastle Light, we have had perfect weather, and I feel my journey has commenced most prosperously. Everything on board is comfortable, and I have every reason to be satisfied. We had a very nice service at a quarter to eleven o'clock; a large number of the men and all the officers attended. I read the prayers, Fort a chapter in the New Testament and the Psalms. We had a hymn (the 'Old Hundredth') which was very well sung. All the men joined in it as well as the responses. Under God's blessing we have made a good beginning. The moral effect will be good, and I think we shall continue in the same lines. Sailors are open to these influences, and I should like them all to look back upon this trip as a pleasant episode in their lives.

Thursday, August 27.—I invited Mr. Milman, magistrate at Cooktown, to dinner last night, and after dinner had a very interesting conversation with him about New Guinea. He was a member of the Royal Commission on the kidnapped natives from the New Guinea Islands, and visited New Guinea by order of the Queensland Government last year. It was owing to him that the iniquities of the schooner *Hopeful* were brought to light. In fact, the Commission was appointed in consequence of his investigations. A more hateful tale of brutality could not be written.

He gave me much useful information, and altogether impressed me as being a reliable, safe, and upright man. He is not popular, I hear. No doubt because he does his duty.

In the afternoon I was interviewed by several people. Mr. Burkitt, collector of customs—a sensible man; Captain Liljeblad (Russian-Finn), of the schooner *Ellangowan*, who tendered his services in any capacity; Mr. Power, agent of Aplin Brown and Gibbs; Mr. Bright, sub-inspector of police; Mr. Blair, agent to the London Mission, and Mr. Armit, of the 'Argus,' a man of some capacity. He called to offer his services. He has visited the coast of New Guinea, and resided some time at Hoopiron Bay in Moresby Island, the scene of the recent murder (? justifiable homicide) of Captain Friar of the *Lalla Rookh*.[1] He hoped that the blind, rough-and-ready punishment usually inflicted by a man-of-war would not be resorted to in this case. He gave Captain Friar a bad character as a bully and as treating the natives badly. He hinted at other irregularities as the probable cause of the murder, and gave the natives of Hoopiron Bay a good character, having lived amongst them for several weeks by him-

---

[1] Captain Friar, of the schooner *Lalla Rookh*, was murdered on July 28, 1885, under the following circumstances:—He anchored in Hoopiron Bay, Moresby Island, for three days; the natives appeared friendly, but on the second day a native interpreter, named Billy, warned Captain Friar that they were going to kill him. Captain Friar treated the warning with contempt. On the morning of the third day Billy again warned Friar, but, finding he would pay no attention, left the ship, professedly to go and buy pigs; the carpenter also went ashore to cut wood. In the meantime large numbers of natives crowded round the ship and came on board. Suddenly one of them seized Friar from behind, and one in front cut his throat. The carpenter, who was on shore, was killed in a similar manner. From the evidence given by a chief, named Bailala (see p. 344), it appears that some years previously two natives had been taken on board Captain Friar's vessel, and worked for him for some time, but that both had been drowned one night while attempting to escape. No payment had been made for their death. Further, that amongst the natives who had been recruited from Hoopiron Bay several had died, but that, when the *Victoria* returned the survivors, payment had been made for all who had died except one. There were, therefore, three families whose relations had died away from their homes, and for whom no payment had been made. These three families made it known to all the villages that they would murder the first white man who came to that part of the island. The *Governor Blackall*, with H.M. Ships *Diamond* and *Raven*, went in search of the murderers, but after two days vainly spent in endeavouring to find them, were obliged to return to Dinner Island, having only captured some canoes. The skulls, however, of Friar and his carpenter were given up. A month or so afterwards H.M.S. *Diamond* returned to the bay and burnt down all the villages.

self. He recommended the employment of a native teacher, 'Seegon' by name, of Teste Island, who suffers from skin disease.

Soap he declared would cure this disease. We will try remedy on 'Seegon' if he will submit.

After dinner several of the party went to the Chinese town in Cooktown. Cooktown was made by the Chinese. At one time there were some 15,000 Chinamen employed on the 'Palmer' gold-fields. Now there are only 700.

The village is thoroughly Australian in character, reputed to be healthy, and preferable as a residence to Townsville.

At 6 A.M. I woke and found we were twelve miles or so from the Barrier Reef. Sea perfectly calm, with a moderate S.E. wind. At 7.30 A.M. we passed through the Lizard Passage in reef. Captain Lake in the top, directing course. I watched proceedings from bridge.

We are now well on our way to Port Moresby, and may get there in afternoon of to-morrow. There is a fair S.E. breeze, the steamer is lively, rolling and tumbling about. It is pleasantly cool in my cabin. Thermometer, 2.30 P.M., 75°. The sea is very rarely smooth except during the N.W. monsoon.

Friday, August 28.—At 7 this morning we were 60 miles from Port Moresby. We are doing remarkably well, 10 to 10½ knots. with S.E. breeze on beam.

At 10 we sighted top of Mount Owen Stanley Range.[1]

---

[1] 'We first caught sight of New Guinea early in the morning of August 28, 1885. A dim mountain line appeared, high in the clouds, gradually growing more and more distinct. Every hour, as we approached, the

Expect to arrive before 3. I am beginning to think I shall enjoy the trip. I feel very well, my appetite is good. For example, this is one of my days: Sunrise; cup of cocoa—Van Houten's, the only decent kind. I make it myself with preserved milk. Then I walk up and down the very small deck for one and a half to two hours, pitching into Fort at intervals as a relaxation.

Before bath I sometimes eat a piece of melon or a banana. After bath Anthony brings up breakfast: cup of cocoa, two small pieces of dry toast, two eggs and curry, and sometimes fruit afterwards. After breakfast —cheroot, read, write, occasional snooze; read, write, cheroot. I lunch at 1.30 on deck: salad, vegetables, fruit, pint claret, no meat. Afterwards, cheroot, read, write. The afternoon passes in same way. Walk about for quarter of an hour before dinner, which takes place at 7 in saloon: soup, meat curry, sweets, pint of champagne very occasionally, pint of claret regularly; then I return to deck, coffee and cheroot, talk, retire to cabin at nine, read and to sleep.

outlines of the coast sharpened, until its whole character could be clearly seen. Around us, white-crested billows were tossing on a deep blue sea, while close inshore, and stretching out from the entrance to the harbour, wherever the unseen coral reef broke the force of the waves, calm water of vivid green contrasted sharply with the azure blue. Brown hills of varied heights, covered here and there with gum trees, rose abruptly from the water's edge, and above them towered the Astrolabe Mountains. In the course of the day the *Governor Blackall* dropped her anchor in the harbour opposite to Port Moresby. On a low hill immediately rising from the sea stood a row of small houses, some thatched, and some roofed, in Australian fashion, with galvanised iron. Seven white people at that time represented the British Empire in the capital of the country: Mr. Anthony Musgrave, Assistant Deputy-Commissioner; Mr. Lawes, a missionary, Mr. Lawes's son, Mr. Chalmers, and Mrs. Lawes, the only white woman in the island. Goldie, a storekeeper, and Hunter, who had married a native, completed the seven.'—G. R. ASKWITH.

This is my day, and will probably be the same for weeks to come, varied by a visit on shore.

It is astonishing in how small a space one can live in comfort on board ship. There is literally not room to swing a cat in my cabin. (Why a cat I could never make out. Why not a club, a dumb-bell, or a dog?) I have my surroundings, drawers for my clothes, drawers for my dressing things, drawers for my papers and plans; hooks and racks; book-case; photos of my family on walls.

I could not be comfortable, however, were it not that I have ample room below for my clothes. Anthony, my servant, is invaluable. He thoroughly understands his business, is punctual, very quiet, and looks cool.

At 3.30 we arrived in Port Moresby. It was very rough indeed outside; the captain as usual was in the tops, picking out his course. The passage through the reefs which fringe the shore is not difficult. The water over them is the most beautiful emerald green I ever saw. It is much broken, especially in rough weather. It is an oasis of green water in a sea of blue. Once past the reefs we get into calm water, although there was a stiff breeze blowing.

I confess a great disappointment at my first glimpse of Port Moresby. Coming up to the coast, the Astrolabe Range of mountains (5,000 to 6,000 feet) to the eastward is really grand. Owen Stanley Range (supposed to be 11,000 to 13,000 feet) was hid in the clouds.

Port Moresby is a large sheet of water, landlocked and surrounded by an amphitheatre of hills of more or less altitude. At present the country is much burnt up, as there has been no rain for several months.

The Mission Station is situated at the head of the harbour on low hills, with the native villages at their foot.

It is a barren country, but I can see it is a healthy place, as the S.E. trade wind blows steadily. There is a sheet of water.

Musgrave came up with Lawes junior after we had dropped anchor. Captain Pullen, H.M.S. *Lark*,[1] also called. Both stayed to dinner. Temperature—maximum 78°, minimum 76°. Wonderful!

Saturday, August 29.—I did not land yesterday; but this morning was up early as usual, and went on shore. Lawes and Chalmers met me, and we walked up to the Mission House to pay a visit to Mrs. Lawes, who was very pleased to see me. After a while, I took a walk with Lawes through the village, which was filled with naked native men, women, and children of all sizes, not unpleasing to look at, but chattering much like the Arabs, and, like them, listless and lazy. Here I met the chief, Boevagi,[2] who apologised for being without his trousers. (He had on a dirty shirt.) He left me somewhat suddenly, but after a time reappeared with a harlequin shirt, red felt hat, and pair of trousers, and we shook hands again. The naked natives were on the whole very well behaved. We saw old and young women making pots and pans, but the men were mostly engaged in their canoes preparing for their

---

[1] H.M.S. *Lark* had been engaged for some months surveying the coast.
[2] *Ante*, p. 282.

annual expedition to the westward, where they proceed in large numbers to trade with their pottery, which they barter for sago.[1]

I returned on board the steamer and had a bath and breakfast, rather pleased than otherwise with my capital. Chalmers goes with me round the German boundary.

Sunday, August 30.—Did not go on shore to-day, as I wished to establish the principle that the boats were not to be used on Sundays. Had usual inspection, then service, which was even more successful than before. The men sang three hymns by themselves, Nos. 160, 165, and 254 (Ancient and Modern), a most creditable selection. We have no music, but the voices are good, and every one joins, and the service is done remarkably well. I wrote, and commenced 'Robertson's Sermons.' I am beginning to like Port Moresby. It is very cool, and the land improves on acquaintance. Fort is most active and attentive; Askwith is writing a diary.

Monday, August 31.—Sent off letters. Boevagi called on me, and this time he had on Commodore Erskine's uniform. He is a nice old man, with not at all a bad face. None of the natives have bad faces, and they are vastly superior to the Australian blacks. I gave Boe his present—a fine axe, tobacco, and red cloth. He was nervous, and after a time I sent him off. Worked away at business.

Tuesday, September 1.—Twenty-four native chiefs came on board, and I gave them each a small axe and tobacco, and a pocket-handkerchief. They were a queer

[1] *Ante,* p. 289, and *New Guinea Notes,* p. 304.

lot, stark naked, of all ages, some merry looking, but none of them understanding in the least why they had come. Some shook hands with me, others did not even see me. I asked Lawes to make them a speech, which he did, and then I soon got rid of the chiefs.

In the afternoon I landed and had a walk with Musgrave, across the site where I think a Government House may be built, but *not by me*! On the other side of the hill there is a beautiful beach, along which we walked. It was delightfully cool, with the S.E. wind blowing on us. I like Musgrave. His duty will be to found the administration of what may become a big colony. Fort and Askwith went shooting, without result. In the evening Chalmers, Lawes, and young Lawes (now promoted to post-master, harbour-master, collector of customs, chief clerk), came to dinner. It poured with rain. Mr. Lawes is a wonderful man, able to rough it, and cheerful under all circumstances. They left at nine, at which hour I always retire.

Wednesday, September 2.—Did business all morning and afternoon. Musgrave came to lunch, and afterwards we landed to look at the site he has selected for his house, which I ordered when at Townsville. I approved of it, and after a stroll returned on board.

Thursday, September 3.—Business all day; I did not land. Musgrave came to lunch, and we arranged for his trip to Yule Island.[1] He is very cheerful about it, and undertakes to be back again on Monday. Weather very pleasant and cool. The S.E. wind always freshens in the afternoon, and at night it blows pretty hard.

[1] *Ante*, p. 292.

We do not feel it, however, on board, because the vessel lies head to wind, and the motion does not affect her. Askwith returned, and had shot a good many birds and a wallaby. Doctor is ill.

Friday, September 4.—Up at six as usual. S.E. breeze freshened about noon. Last night it blew a strong gale. The sea is rough for a small boat, but with the steam-launch, however unsatisfactory, we get on very well. We find it best to sit in a whale-boat and be towed.

To-day Anthony Musgrave has gone off in the *Ellangowan* mission schooner to see the Roman Catholic missionaries who are located at Yule Island without authority, or rather have located themselves there. His orders are to do his best to persuade them to move to the eastern end of New Guinea. If he succeeds he will have rendered an important service, as the Roman Catholic missionaries, I regret to say, have shown in some of the other islands of the Western Pacific that they are utterly unscrupulous, grasping, and treacherous. The end justifies the means. They tell the natives that the Protestants teach the wrong religion, that of the devil. Romilly, who has had considerable experience of them, gives them a bad character. I have given Musgrave a letter to the missionary father and a translation. I find my French is very rusty. I believe Musgrave can talk a little. At any rate he will be able to report what they are up to. His journey there will be rough but pleasant; the return journey, I fear, will be trying, as the schooner will have to beat against a strong south-easter, which always freshens in the afternoon. He is a plucky fellow, and volunteered to go. I find him most useful, thoughtful, businesslike, and thoroughly upright. I am fortunate indeed in having such an assistant.

Askwith returned from his shooting expedition yesterday afternoon, having shot several wallabies, ducks, &c. I would not let Fort go, as there is so much to be done. It is fair to state that he declined to go on that account. He is very useful, most willing, and does his work thoroughly well; always cheerful. We are getting rather short of coal. The calculations made at Sydney were all wrong. I have written to Townsville for a hundred tons.

I see my way clearly about this whole New Guinea affair. It will not be unpleasant, and I find that I am here at a very good time. The S.E. trade is certainly a blessing. I begin to think I shall be able to stand it for two years, but not for longer. There are more chances of getting letters over than I expected. In time I shall have my own schooner and establish regular communication. I do not often go on shore, as it is so rough and windy; but if we did not have the wind, the heat would be trying.

Saturday, September 5, Port Moresby.—We started at 5.30 A.M. in the launch, with a whale-boat in tow, for Bootless Inlet, about seven or eight miles off, within the Barrier Reef. The S.E. wind was fresh but not too strong. The party consisted of self, Fort, Romilly, Askwith, Pullen, Chalmers, and a native pilot, who was of little use, as by standing up in the boat one can easily see the reefs and the shoal water. We took our breakfast with us. We found the launch very uncomfortable, and as there was a head sea we had to put on our waterproofs. Going round Pyramid Point we found the sea rough, and we tumbled about, shipping a few seas. The whale-boat was best off (happy thought! go in future in the whale-boat). On arrival at Bootless Inlet (called Bootless by the navigator who discovered the harbour there, because he found nothing to see when he got there), the captain asked me where shall we go now? I replied land, breakfast, and get back as fast as we can. He appeared surprised, as he thought we had come to see something. So had I. Well, we landed on a nice little island called Lion Couchant, from its resemblance to a sitting lion. The trees at this end gave the appearance of a mane. We landed on a nice beach, boiled our kettle, made tea, ate some cold duck, marmalade, and bananas. The crew had beef and mutton.

I walked over the ridge of island, found it very bare, with no soil, and tufts of grass with a few trees at the end, which had shed their leaves from the force of the S.E. winds. As the S.E. wind always freshens in the afternoon and I foresaw that it might be uncomfortable in the launch, I gave orders to embark. So we returned; the breeze lulled and we had a very slow voyage home. The whale-boat left us with sails set, and simply sailed right away. She got in before us by some time. We reached ship at 1.30 P.M., eight hours away, tired and hungry.

Sunday, September 6.—Got up at 6 A.M., had nearly

two hours' walk, then a bath and breakfast. I have rigged up a sort of private arrangement in front of my cabin. I have had a large table made, and around it have placed heavy canvas screens to intercept the glare from the sea, which is trying to my eyes, and prevent my being overlooked, unless the passers-by choose.

I have just concluded service; it was successful as usual. We had three hymns, and the men selected them, 215, 234, 264. They sing very well. I read most of the prayers; Fort a short Lesson and a Psalm.

Monday, September 7.—Musgrave surprised us yesterday afternoon by turning up about 1 P.M. in the *Ellangowan*. She had made a splendid passage to Yule Island and back. It is evident to me that with this incessant S.E. wind blowing there can never be any really calm sea. The Barrier Reef does not do much to shelter you, as the wind threshes across and regularly beats upon the ship.

I find that owing to unforeseen circumstances at Thursday Island, our little scheme of removing the Roman Catholic missionaries may fall through. I had intended leaving this morning for Redscar Bay, where I wished to have a look at some land which is said to be valuable. But Chalmers, who had promised to come with me, told Askwith he thought he would not go, not even to the eastward. This was serious, so I countermanded our departure until Tuesday and sent early a note to Chalmers to say that I would deeply regret if he abandoned the idea. He came to breakfast and gave in. So this is a relief, for I feel that without him I could do nothing.

I landed about 11 A.M. to call on the missionaries, and stayed to lunch. It was a very curious sight. We sat in the verandah, a large party from the ship. It was a very good lunch. We were waited upon by naked boys and men with simply a waist-cloth; one of them had clothes. In the back premises natives of all sorts swarm, women and children, the wives and families of the teachers. Mr. and Mrs. Lawes are most hospitable. They keep open house and entertain every one and any one. It was a beautiful day, and I felt quite reconciled to the place. Lawes' house is a large Australian pattern bungalow, one story, and built on piles; very wide verandahs and plenty of air. After lunch I proposed a walk, and it ended in my going up a hill 750 feet high. It was a capital walk and I thoroughly enjoyed it. I was not in the least tired. Returned on board about 4 P.M.

Tuesday, September 8.—Off the Skittles, near Redscar Bay.

We left at 7.15 A.M. for the westward, and after steaming about thirty miles, going very slowly, with Captain Lake in the foretop, we arrived at our destination at 12. We are anchored on the lee side of the Skittles—some fine rocks, which stand out of the sea. We are also protected from the S.E. trade (which is now blowing pretty hard) by a long reef. We remain for the night and go on shore in the morning. The land is very ugly. It is low and flat. We saw the top of Mount Owen Stanley on our way. By the bye, Forbes left us some days ago, and is now a short distance on his way. He returns on the 11th.

Here is a table that may interest you as it gives a fair estimate of the weather and climate:—

Date	Temperature		Weather
	Maximum	Minimum	
August 29	78°	76°	S.E. wind; clear day; dry air.
,, 30	82	76	Dead calm morning; slight breeze in afternoon; rain and hot at night.
,, 31	83	76	Cloudy and muggy in morning; N.W. wind; appearance of rain.
September 1	81	77	Cloudy and muggy; wind changed in afternoon to S.E.; rain in evening.
,, 2	78	78	Beautiful cool S.E. wind in morning; ¼ gale in evening, and thick weather.
,, 3	80	77	Cloudy morning; fresh S.E. breeze sprung up, very strong; in afternoon cleared up.
,, 4	79	77	Pleasant breeze in morning; bright weather, hazy to seaward; S.E. wind freshening in afternoon.
,, 5	79	77	Slight S.E. breeze; sunny; freshened as before in afternoon.
,, 6	81	77	do. do. do.

Wednesday, September 9.—We landed this morning at 7.30 in the whale-boat towed by the steam-launch. Chalmers, self, Romilly, Fort, Askwith, Chief Engineer Lindt, Anthony (my servant), and several sailors. We took a tent and food for spending a day on shore. We had to wait for the tide to rise, as there is a bar to the river Aroa. The rolling surf was not high, and we got in without getting wet. We left the tent and some of the men on a nice sandy patch at mouth of river, then proceeded up it for about two miles. The vegetation was tropical, palm trees of all kinds, tangled undergrowth, trees in some places meeting overhead. We rowed up, and it reminded me of our excursions up the backwaters of the Thames. It was cool and pleasant.

At last we reached the landing-place, where we found an old hag and an old man making sago. The man was cutting away with a wooden adze at the sago trees, which contain a fibrous sort of substance. The old woman took it to a sort of sieve close to edge of water, where she put in the fibre and added water. After kneading the pulp she pressed it through the sieve, and the sago came away with the water. It was received in a sort of trough, and then the sago, a fine powder, settled. We walked up to the village, where there is a mission teacher. He was out, but his wife, daughter, and son were at home. Their house consists of one large room on piles, very clean, roof and sides made of native thatch, cool and comfortable. There is a kitchen outside. The house stands in an enclosure fenced with reeds or thin poles stuck into ground. There were numerous houses in the village, all of the same kind, consisting of one room on piles with a verandah. There were very few people at home, but plenty of pigs and a few dogs. The men and women are away planting in the fields.

We drank some cocoanut milk and, after remaining a short time, started for another village four miles off, walking through a plain covered with tall coarse grass. On arrival, we found a similar village to the last, all the people away at their plantations. We found the teacher at home. The chief was in half mourning, i.e. more or less blackened, with his head adorned with cassowarie feathers. He wore no clothes, but had several armlets, made of reeds, on his arms, and a very tight waistbelt of a kind of fibre, which had the effect of dividing his body in two and gave him a fashionable waist. He squatted and I made him the usual present. He then ate cocoanut and afterwards chewed betel, and helped himself freely to lime water thick as cream. We walked about village. There are plenty of cocoanut trees planted by the natives. Their banana and yam plantations are some distance off. After resting a bit, we walked back to the first village, and there had a very good lunch provided by the missionary teachers. The wives and daughters, dressed in bedgowns, waited on us. The teachers and wives are Samoans; the men large and stately, one had a particularly fine face. They own land in their country and give up everything at the call of the missionaries. The lunch was good; simple, and fairly well cooked—fowls, yams, gravy, banana compote, tea. After we had lunched, they dined, then the sailors. The chief came in (the old man in mourning) and his wife, a lady old and plain, with a petticoat and ornaments. They fed copiously, and partook of betel and lime, picked their teeth, and made themselves quite at home. Numerous natives of all ages and sizes looked on. Then a head chief called, and I also made him a present. He complained that his land had been bought by a white man, and purchase had not been properly effected. I promised to see into the matter. He then made me a present; afterwards the other chief and the teachers' wives and the daughter gave me gifts, all of little value, but as a token of good will, and in accordance with custom. The return presents for teachers were given the day after, and included blue calico with white spots for the women teachers. They are plain but graceful creatures, simple and unaffected, and smile pleasantly when they see you are pleased. After awhile we left to walk down to our camp. On our arrival there, having walked some twelve miles, I had a bath and, after a time, dinner, which we enjoyed very much. I did not feel in the least tired, and was surprised to find that the heat was not oppressive, except when we were sheltered from the S.E. trade. I slept very well, although lightly, and woke in the morning refreshed.

Thursday, September 10.—I took a short walk on the sands of the sea-shore, then lay in a hammock, and after breakfast we started for the ship at about 9 A.M. We sailed for the Burra Burra Islands, where we arrived at 3 P.M., and remained the night.

Some of the men have gone off in a boat to shoot pigeons. Fort enjoys himself immensely, but is insane in the matter of clothes. He dresses as if in the Arctic regions. I warn him that he will soon find to his cost that this warm clothing takes it out of him. I dress in the lightest things, but always have a change ready, and a cummerbund to put on if it gets chilly.

Friday, September 11.—We anchored last night under the shelter of the Vari Vare Islands (not Burra Burra), and found it a much better anchorage than Port Moresby. In the morning got up at 5.30 A.M. for a walk on the island. We found that the islands are as usual without water, although they are covered with grass. In walking round, one of the sailors found a pigeon which had been wounded yesterday afternoon. We brought it with us and hope it may be saved. The party got some eighteen pigeons yesterday. They were cooked to-day and found tough; no, I am wrong, they made a very fair pigeon-pie. The tough one was a large grown pigeon, like a fowl, which had been set apart for my special delectation.

Saturday, September 12.—Last night, through some stupidity, the launch foundered; of course nobody in her. She has just been got up; it was done very well and expeditiously. Captain Lake, however, has his wits about him and is very careful. This morning two chiefs of inland tribes came to see me and the steamer. They had never seen a ship before. They were taken below to the ladies' cabin and were much pleased with the looking-glass. These chiefs had been looking after tribes which had just returned. The natives peer in at my cabin windows as I write. They have begun to call me the Queen's son.[1]

The *Lark* has just returned. The afternoon is very fine. I shall probably go on shore for a walk.

I did not go on shore, but did a lot of official papers and felt tired in the evening in consequence. Went to bed at 9 P.M. as usual.

Sunday, September 13.—This morning was calm and lovely. Fort and I went for a row in the dingey. I shall continue to row, as a way of taking exercise pleasantly and easily. The boat is a tub, badly finished, and the oars simply laughable.

As usual, at 10.30 we had the inspection of the ship's company. I sit at my table, and the officers and men parade, and their names are called out. At 11 A.M. our service, well attended, and good singing. This time

[1] See *New Guinea Notes*, p. 371.

one of the men played the fiddle ; he does it very well, only rather too slowly. He will improve. There is a talk of a concert, but it is so rough and boisterous in the evening that I do not see how it can come off; I am afraid we should not hear the music. Thankful are we to have this squally weather, as it keeps the thermometer down ; never higher than 80° in my cabin and 76° at night, with a fine breeze blowing over one. When I go down below I pity Romilly and the others in their stuffy cabins, because there is no means of getting the air down. The ship lies head to wind, and the ventilators are not constructed to catch wind.

Monday, September 14.—Up at daylight ; cocoa, and into dingey. We try sailing, but there is no wind, so give it up. I met Musgrave on shore, took a look at site for his house and walked about ; then back to ship, feeling refreshed. This afternoon Askwith lands to join Pullen and officers of *Lark* in an expedition inland under guidance of Chalmers. They will be away until Saturday.

Half gale as usual springing up at 4 P.M. ; gusts of wind, slight motion of ship ; all very pleasant. We have not taken to dining on deck. It is 'blustery,' but pleasant. We hear that Forbes is laid up with sore throat, also Lawes.

Tuesday, September 15.—Row as usual ; walk on shore. No *Herbert*; what can have delayed her? Go on shore at 10.30 to inquire into a reported robbery. Examine teacher, whose evidence is interpreted. Return on board ; at work again, looking over papers.

By the way, I remembered you on the 23rd, and

thought of my own birthday. I am sending you a card, not a New Guinea one; brought on purpose to send it to you. I wish you very many happy returns of the day.

I got the violets all right; and also the three cards for my birthday. Thank Val and Violet[1] for theirs. Remember me to your dear mother.

Have I told you of our cat? She pays me visits at intervals during the day, but I object to her sleeping in my cabin *on me!*

Wednesday, September 16.—As usual, this morning I was up at 5.30, after a good night. I got into the dingey and rowed ashore. Inspected waterworks, site for future town and botanical gardens. I attach much importance to planning everything out from the beginning. One sees the evil in Australia of the principle of hand to mouth, and want of foresight, in regard to such towns as Brisbane, Sydney, and others.

After breakfast a vessel sighted. Some said she was a foreigner. We all agreed she was not the long-expected *Herbert*, as she appeared too large and had three masts. Shortly she took in all sail and steamed into the harbour. She was the *Raven*, which the admiral had sent from Cooktown with despatches for me and mails. I was very pleased, because from the despatches I found that Clayton, of the *Diamond*, was coming to New Guinea with a gunboat and a schooner to make a demonstration. The captain of the *Raven* called officially, and we agreed that he need not return to Cooktown until Friday morning. He reported that the sea outside

---
[1] Sir Peter's daughters.

the reef was very heavy. I was still more delighted when on going to cabin I found two letters from you dated 24th and 31st August; also three letters from Victor, one from Mr. Wright, one from Philip[1] on business, and one from Kinloch Cooke. Numerous other letters of no interest from all sorts of people. I have had a good read of them all, and could not help crying with delight at reading dear old Victor's enthusiastic and happy letters, showing him to be becoming so self-reliant and able to take care of himself. Every one is so good to him, and it is most comforting to find that he is getting on so well in his form.

I am making a good start in New Guinea, but must devote next year to it. I do not now fear the climate. As for the blacks, they are easily met by firmness, justice, and caution. I am more than ever convinced that all the outrages are justifiable. I have heard horrible stories about the doings of the whites, and, please God, I shall let the light of day into them. A righteous cause I am engaged in, and that gives me zest in working it.

Fort is really very hard worked. The mere looking after the catering and general conduct of the ship is enough for one man. He has lots to write, and I keep him employed. He is a very good fellow, and I should miss him much. I shall not leave him behind me at Port Moresby, as it will be uncomfortable.

So far as I can foresee, my plans are as follows. Go to eastward and round to German boundary, part of

---

[1] Sir Peter's son Victor was at that time in England with his tutor, Mr. Wright. Mr. Philip Scratchley is Sir Peter's nephew and executor.

the time with Clayton, and get back here towards the middle of November; then go westward as far as Thursday Island, down to Yorktown, there change into a steamer for Sydney. You may not see me until Christmas Day, but on the other hand I shall stay with you until end of February and see you off to England. I shall then return here for four or five months, go to New Zealand or Tasmania for one, and then go back until you are coming out again. By that time everything will be finished.

Even if you were without Violet and Val I would not bring you here. The life is not suited to a lady, unless she has a calling for it like Mrs. Lawes. Poor woman, she is not very well. What self-denying lives she and Lawes are living. The surroundings are disgusting; naked barbarians (not savages, because, poor creatures, they are quiet enough if only fairly and justly treated) everywhere; dirty, without clothes, and living purely animal lives, but with great capabilities for a better and more useful life in the future. They must have energy, when you see a fleet of canoes going for a voyage of several hundred miles. Several hundred men and children (no women) taking some *thirty thousand pots* to the westward to be exchanged for sago and other things.

Thursday, September 17.—We are still at Port Moresby. I went for my usual row at daylight, and walked on the beach, with a delightful S.E. breeze blowing. After breakfast the *Herbert*, which we had so long expected, arrived.

I sent on board the *Herbert* to warn the captain that

no one was to land or stores to be put on shore without my written permit. I found, after a time, that there were three men on board who had come over without permits, and also a stowaway. I forbade the former landing until I had seen them, and cautioned the stowaway not to be allowed on shore, also that he was to go back. I then cancelled the permit of the steamer, and gave the owners another. They will all find that they have caught a Tartar in me.

The *Raven* left at daylight, and had some gun practice outside. *Herbert* commenced discharging cargo, including sheep, which were landed on an island in the harbour as an experiment. We received mails, and I was busy writing.

Friday, September 18, *Port Moresby.*—Discharging of cargo continued from the *Herbert.* Musgrave came off to say that Currie was intoxicated and disorderly. I arranged to send off a petty officer and two men to arrest Currie if necessary. It turned out afterwards that on seeing the men land, he thought it advisable to 'skedaddle' back to Hula. In discussing these matters afterwards, I was met with official difficulties. I said we had to deal with each case as it arose, and not to anticipate a difficulty in its settlement. Few men recognise the fact that there is no difficulty which cannot be dealt with, and that the word 'impossible' should not exist. I had also to deal with the case of the three men who had come over without any permits. They were brought on board. The leader of the party was a Swede, and a very decent fellow; his companions were Australians. One, I am happy to say, said he did not intend to stay. I gave permission to the others to land their goods and commence building their store.

Saturday, September 19, *Port Moresby.*—Rowed as usual before breakfast. Then a hard day's work with despatches and letters, as the *Herbert* was leaving early on Sunday. It was hot in the afternoon, but the cool breeze prevented the high temperature being unpleasant.

Sunday, September 20.—I could not have my row, as I was busy with letters until 9 o'clock, when I closed the mail bag. I had remained up writing last night until past midnight. It was delightfully cool. We are leaving to-morrow for our voyage to the eastward. We had our usual service, with the fiddle for the hymns—the singing much improved. As usual the men select the hymns, and they are always very good.

Monday, September 21.—Up at 5.30 A.M. and at 6 for a row. Forbes came off to say good-bye. He has quite recovered from his sore throat, and is satisfied that he will get on very well, although he does not expect to reach Mount Owen Stanley this season. He will be stopped by the rains.

We started at 10 A.M. We arrived off Tupuselei,[1] a village about twelve miles from Port Moresby. In the afternoon we went on shore for a walk of a few miles. It was pleasant; the inhabitants with their chief received us. The chief had called in the morning and received presents.

Tupuselei is smaller than the Port Moresby villages.

[1] See *New Guinea Notes*, p. 370.

The houses are built in the sea, the teacher's house being the only one on shore. These sea villages are like the lake villages which have been found at the bottom of the lakes in Switzerland. I fancy, however, that the latter were much stronger, as they have stood for centuries under the water. The New Guinea houses appear very rickety; at a distance they look like a bundle of sticks carrying a thatched house. The piles are hard wood from the mangrove swamps, and are worked into their places until they stand firm in the bottom of the sea. The piles are crooked and irregular, yet they stand the strong winds. The roofs and sides of the huts are thatched with the palm tree leaves. The floors are rough board laid on sleepers on top of piles.

A short distance inland we saw the remains of what must have been a temple—a sort of scaffolding with a platform. The poles of the scaffold were carved very rudely at the top and end in a sort of horn. There are no traditions about these structures, which are to be found in other villages and also inland.

Tuesday, September 22.—We landed this morning at daylight, walked inland a few miles to a village called Padiri on top of a hill, and were disappointed, as we expected to see the houses in the trees. There was only one and it was deserted. We were accompanied in our walk by the chief, the teacher, and sundry persons carrying our food. We were met by the village chief and a portion of the inhabitants, a large proportion being old hags, to whom we gave tobacco.

In selecting a suitable place on which to eat our breakfast, we came across a grave, which was simply a platform on four posts, on which the dead person was laid —somewhat after, only not in fact like, the Towers of Silence in parts of India. We avoided the dried-up mummy and went to another hill, where our natives followed us.

Wednesday, September 23.—After our return yesterday we got up steam and left for Kaile, another village on the coast. I should mention as an indication how friendly the natives near Port Moresby are—that is, showing how well they are under the influence of the missionaries—when we returned to the beach we found our men surrounded by a large crowd of men, women, and children in great excitement, laughing and talking. The men were running races for pieces of tobacco. They were more like boys. The natives of Tupuselei are fine powerful fellows.

We started early this morning for our excursion to the plantations. We had first to row about two miles along the beach to the entrance into a small creek where we landed. We were accompanied by several natives dressed up, carrying spears and shields—and most picturesque they looked. The walk to Veiburi, another hill village, was pleasant; the inhabitants received us with acclamation. After looking round the village we returned to the steamer, and started for Kapa Kapa, some ten miles off on the coast.

During our walk Askwith complained that he did not feel well, and on reaching the steamer showed indications of having caught the fever. Romilly we found also complaining, and Skinner, one of our petty officers. It became evident that they all three had the fever.

It was caused by their having gone on shore a fortnight ago in the dingey, and owing to the heavy surf they were not able to return. Consequently they had to remain on shore, sleeping in the teacher's house, but without changing their clothes. They had gone quite unprepared for sleeping on shore.

Thursday, September 24.—We decided to take a rest at Kapa Kapa, and not to land to-day. Seventeen chiefs came on board and received presents. We had a long talk with them, because it appeared that there was a quarrel between the hill tribes and those on the coast. I told the chiefs that I insisted upon there being no fighting, and that they were to make up their differences. They agreed to, but we shall see whether they will keep their promises. I noticed amongst the chiefs a very intelligent man—more like a Malay—the head chief of a village I am to visit to-morrow. He seemed to take a fancy to me. It is a great nuisance having to do all the talking by interpretation, because I always feel doubtful whether one's meaning is correctly conveyed to the natives, and *vice versâ*. I believe further on we shall be compelled to resort to double interpretation!

The days are beginning to pass quickly, as the routine of going on shore, making a march, visiting a village or two, and returning to the steamer, is becoming monotonous. I am also beginning to take an interest in sensational novels, of which we have a large stock on board—always a bad sign that I am becoming lazy. Writing is becoming an exertion, although I never really felt better.

Friday, September 25.—This morning we got up at 5.30 to walk to Rigo, a village seven miles off. The way led through the bush. The village was most interesting. There were regular streets in it, although they were very irregular as to the roadway. We found the remains of booths which had been erected on both sides of the main street for a village feast, also a large sort of Christmas tree, a big pole in the ground with festoons of vegetables. We returned by about 1 P.M., having done our fourteen miles without being over-tired. I rested all the afternoon.

Saturday, September 26.—Left this morning for Hula, the residence of Messrs. Guise and Currie. Did not go on shore, but Renaki, a very intelligent old chief, came on board and lodged his complaint. He asked me whether I was powerful enough to remove Currie and Guise. I said I was, and would do so on my way back.

Sunday, September 27.—Our service was badly attended because I had refused to allow any men to go on shore, as Hula does not bear a good character.

Monday, September 28.—We went on shore early to walk to a village called Kalo, about seven miles off. A pleasant trip. The walk lay through groves of cocoanut trees, and we passed through several interesting villages, where the grounds round the houses were enclosed, and banana and cocoanut trees planted in them. One of the chiefs' houses had a sort of spire, thatched roof, and sides. We saw a number of men suffering from skin diseases—a very unpleasant sight. We joined the launch in the creek close to the village, and went about five or six miles by sea to Kerepunu, where we found our steamer which had left Kalo in the morning. We did not land that afternoon.

Kerepunu, Tuesday, September 29.—Went on shore after breakfast to spend the day in the native teacher's house, which is on the beach and well exposed to the S.E. wind.

It is warmer here than at Port Moresby. The place is very pretty; the village is situated on one side of the entrance to a large inlet called Hood's Lagoon. Canoes, heavily laden with produce, and managed by women, are constantly passing to and fro, as there is a great deal of trade between Kerepunu and Kalo, the inlet being well sheltered by a reef. We lie very comfortably at anchor. It is one of the best anchorages on the coast.

I received large quantities of presents, yams, cocoa-nuts, and spears, from the native teachers and chiefs.

Koapena,[1] the chief at Aroma, arrived to meet me. He is a fine old fellow, over six feet high, about sixty years old. I believe he has been a great warrior in his youth. He is very good-tempered. He pulled the ornament out of his nose and presented it to me. This is considered a great compliment. The ornament is made out of a shell, and when in the nose gives the appearance of a moustache. When he laughs, which he does very often, and shrugs his shoulders, he has the appearance of a Papuan Mephistopheles.

Wednesday, September 30.—It was reported to me that four men went on shore without leave after dark and returned about half past nine o'clock; and that there was a great uproar in the village before they came

[1] A further account of Koapena will be found in *New Guinea Notes*, p. 371.

off. I sent at once to enquire what had happened, and was told that the men had been behaving improperly. I decided not to make an excursion into Hood's Lagoon, and went on shore after breakfast to take depositions of the natives in the matter. I decided to hold a court to try the men on the charge of behaving so as to cause or excite a breach of the public peace. I find that I have the power to constitute myself and Romilly into a court of justice, and try any one for almost any offence; but, as I have no jail at Port Moresby, there is a difficulty about punishment.

Thursday, October 1.—The trial came off to-day, but we did not give our judgment as the native witnesses were not very satisfactory. We had to resort to double interpretation. Of course the men pleaded 'not guilty' and made up a defence. The result will be that there will be no more going on shore. I was not sorry for the opportunity of having the trial, as it showed the natives that their complaints would be inquired into when addressed to me.

Friday, October 2.—We started at 9.30 A.M., but ran on to a sandbank close to the entrance of Hood's Lagoon. As I write there is an amusing scene on the shore: two sailors in charge of the hawser are practising jumping, and the natives looking on are trying to do the same, only they fail utterly, having no elasticity or spring in their legs. They seem immensely tickled by their own failure, and express their delight by giving their thighs a smack—it is their custom. They have a way, too, of giving a curious 'click' with their tongues when pleased. I am beginning to like them very much.

The result of our accident was that we had to wait for the tide, and then could only go a short distance to anchor. The weather is deliciously cool.

Saturday, October 3.—We started early for Paremata and arrived there about 9.30. We anchored close to the shore, and landed at 10.15 for a walk through the village to Maopa, where the old chief Koapena lives. Koapena came with us from Kerepunu, and whilst on board wandered everywhere—on deck, into the cabins, and below also; looking at himself in the glass in Romilly's cabin, sitting by Fort as he writes, putting elastic bands on his arms, behaving altogether like a child. We walked to his village, which is not much of a place, but he is the head of a tribe of about fifteen hundred. He has great authority all along the coast, and if he chose could be very troublesome to us, but he appreciates the advantages of having the white man with him. Altogether he is really a very fine specimen of a barbarian savage.

We returned to the sea-coast, and, after lunching with the mission teachers, I inquired into a robbery case. I also presented a native teacher with a silver watch for having saved the lives of fifty-six natives who had been wrecked close to the village.[1]

After presents to the chiefs, we returned on board. The teachers gave me the largest present I have had— pigs, yams, sweet potatoes, and spears. I, of course, returned suitable presents. By the way, as a return present to Koapena for his nose ornament, I took off my neck a policeman's whistle, which I had put on for the

[1] See *England's New Colony*, p. 201.

purpose, and put it round his neck. The old man was highly pleased. They appreciate presents given in this way. At parting he came to my cabin and insisted upon rubbing noses.

Sunday, October 4.—Having lost a day on the 2nd, we were obliged to leave to-day for South Cape, a distance of 140 miles. We could not in consequence have service. We left at 10.30 A.M., and did not reach South Cape until 9.15 A.M. on

Monday, October 5.—We had a rough passage of it, outside the reef all night. Still the *Blackall* is a very dry boat and ships no seas, only tumbles about like a cork on the waves. We went on shore after breakfast, and strolled on the beach. I am much taken with South Cape, but it is not so healthy, I fancy, as Port Moresby. It has the advantage of being well sheltered from the S.E. trade and N.W., so that there is smooth water in the anchorage at all times.

In the afternoon, after lunch, we had a row, and visited, or rather looked at from the shore, the ancient place where the natives used to hold cannibal feasts. They do not now, and are very harmless! There are very few natives on the island, which is a very long one with plenty of high hills. As we decided to start very early next day in order to go to the top of a hill 800 feet high, I determined to sleep on shore in Chalmers's house. So after dinner we all went ashore. I had a comfortable bedroom and slept well, waking long before daylight. Of course no one had brought a watch on shore, so that we had to wait for dawn.

Tuesday, October 6.—We climbed up to the top of

the hill—and a very rough walk it was: up a watercourse and through thick scrub, regular Australian alpine climbing. At the top we had a beautiful view and there was a refreshing breeze. After a light refection of raisins and a few dates we descended the hill and found our boat waiting for us. Off to the ship for breakfast. In the afternoon we went ashore to arrange sites for houses and for purchase; then visited a large lagoon afterwards. I like the place very much.

Wednesday, October 7.—In the morning landed early again and walked along boundary of land I had purchased from natives.[1] At 10 A.M. we left for Dinner Island and arrived there at 3 P.M. Here we were informed that another murder had been committed—a Captain Miller at Normanby Island. We found his grave at Dinner Island. His crew brought back his body to the place.[2]

---

[1] *Ante*, p. 287.

[2] Captain Miller was murdered on a small island off Normanby Island, on October 3, 1885, the facts of the case, according to native evidence, being as follows :—He went that morning in his schooner to Normanby Island. He had with him on board an Italian, a Manilla boy, a Chinaman, and an Australian black. His object was to erect a smoke-house, and fish for bêche-de-mer. The natives appeared friendly and collected stones for him. Suddenly two approached him from behind and killed him, one braining him with a tomahawk, the other cutting his throat. From the investigation, which was conducted by Sir Peter Scratchley on the spot, it was difficult to discover any motive for the murder. Miller had never been to the island before, and the outrage appeared to be actuated by mere bloodthirstiness. Afterwards, however, when at Port Moresby, the prisoner Diravera told the native interpreter that a brother of Nagodiri's and a cousin of Diravera's had been taken away with others in a labour vessel some years before; that the others had been returned, but that he, as well as others, had died in Queensland; that payment had been made for the others who had died, but that none had been made for his death; consequently, Nagodiri had determined to kill the first white man who came to the island, and asked Diravera to help him. Upon the arrival of H.M.S. *Dart*, which happened to be surveying

I am satisfied that these traders are often reckless, unscrupulous, brutal, and piratical. They cheat the natives and are apt to appeal to their revolvers. I cannot feel any sympathy for such men. They go where they have no business to. They are a thorn in my side, and I do not think the life of any white man should be risked in avenging their deaths.

Hearing that Captain Miller's cutter had gone to Teste Island, I decided to start early to-morrow morning to catch it up.

I do not think much of Dinner Island. It is an unhealthy place and not nearly so nice as South Cape. It is situated amidst a group of islands of all sizes, all clothed with tropical vegetation; and in the evening the views are very fine.

Thursday, October 8.—Rowed early in morning, and afterwards left for Teste Island. All the islands to the eastward have been discovered and named by Frenchmen. We arrived there at noon. I landed to

near Normanby Island, at the scene of the outrage, Diravera voluntarily came on board, bringing with him what he believed in all good faith was the proper payment for his share of the murder, viz., a few arm-shells, a native basket, some tobacco, and tortoise-shell. He was, however, made prisoner and handed over to Captain Clayton, of H.M.S. *Diamond*. After two days spent in vainly endeavouring to capture Nagodiri, it was decided to burn down the cluster of villages to which he belonged, but to spare the village to which Diravera belonged, as the latter had given himself up. The villages were accordingly burnt to the ground on October 14. Diravera was detained on board H.M.S. *Diamond* until the arrival of that vessel at Port Moresby. There he was kept prisoner, and employed in making roads and other occupations. Sir Peter Scratchley wrote a despatch to the Secretary of State for the Colonies, explaining the circumstances of the case—the low value of life among the natives, and their universally recognised custom of receiving payment as compensation for murder. He recommended that Diravera should be kept a prisoner at Port Moresby for some ten or twelve months, after which he should be returned to his native island.

take evidence concerning Captain Miller's death; walked over the plantations attached to mission; was given some pine-apples, and visited a trader. After strolling along the beach I returned on board.

Teste Island, Friday, October 9.—Having decided to remain here for a day, went ashore to explore. We had our usual party, and climbed up to the top of a sort of ridge or backbone of the island, which gave us a good view. The island appeared fertile. We then went down to beach and visited several villages. After breakfast I was bored by a visit from the trader, and I rather opened his eyes when I explained my views about him and his *confrères*. He wanted me to agree that the proper way of dealing with these wretched natives was to employ native police, shut our eyes, and have no written reports of their doings. I said to him, 'In fact, you would wish me to surprise the natives, deceive them by appearing to wish to trade, and then slaughter them.' He was astonished at my indignation. I told him he would not get Imperial officers to do this dirty work for the traders, and my advice to them was to go away.

Saturday, October 10.—We left for Dinner Island at 6 A.M. and arrived at 10 A.M. There we found Clayton, and the *Diamond*. He called shortly after arrival, and I returned his visit at 3 P.M. I was received in great state. The yards were manned, the marines were on deck as a guard of honour, they presented arms as I stepped on deck, and I walked into the captain's cabin. After an interval I returned, guard presented arms, and I walked down gangway into my boat. Then we got away a short distance, when the ship fired a salute of seventeen or nineteen guns, I forget which.

About 5.30 his Excellency got into the dingey with his secretary, clad in his usual boating costume of flannel pyjamas, for a row. It was blowing somewhat, and our fear was that we would drift on to the *Diamond*, when we should not have presented so very dignified an appearance as in the afternoon. At any rate this did not occur, and I was relieved. The *Raven* had come in the morning also, and we got our letters, but the mail was a small one and not satisfactory.

The *Raven* had joined in the ceremony by saluting me on their quarter-deck with the marines as I rowed past.

Sunday, October 11.—This morning Fort and I rowed round Dinner Island in about forty minutes. It is a small island, and therefore not a wonderful feat. When I saw Clayton's beautiful galley I was very envious, and I vowed that I would have a boat of my own, and also a nice rowing-boat instead of the clumsy, heavy dingey we have to use. These I shall order in Sydney for my next cruise. The order, regularity, and precision of the navy strike one rather forcibly after the A. S. N. half-collier-half-merchant-vessel way of doing things on board the *Governor Blackall*. We had service, Chalmers officiating. The attendance was good. He has a good manly clear voice, and reads very well. The singing was quite up to the mark.

The Doctor is quite well. His professional skill is not rated highly by his patients, and I think nature has had more to do with their recovery than anything else.

Monday, October 12.—We started early this morning for Normanby Island viâ China Straits; *Raven* leading, *Diamond* next, then the *Governor Blackall*. The scenery was really beautiful, and we appeared to be passing through a cluster of islands of all sizes. We met the *Dart* on our way as she was surveying. We stopped to speak her, and I went on board the *Diamond* to confer with Clayton. Captain Field, of the *Dart*, announced that he had on board one of the murderers of Captain Miller. The wretch was transferred to the *Diamond* and interrogated. I decided to go with Chalmers in the *Raven* to Lydia Island to obtain more evidence. We took on board some natives, whom we examined afterwards. Then we steamed onward to regain the *Diamond* and the *Governor Blackall*, arriving just before dark. We went to reconnoitre the scene of the murder. We found clusters of small native houses scattered along a long beach, looking very peaceful amidst cocoanut-tree groves.

Tuesday, October 13.—Yesterday afternoon, before our arrival in the *Raven*, boats were sent from the *Diamond* and *Blackall* to capture native canoes. Three natives were brought on board and put into the sail room, a well-ventilated place in the hold. I sent Fort to see that it was ventilated.

Up early and on board the *Diamond* to examine witnesses, captured men, and the self-confessed murderer. Then back to breakfast. Afterwards I went in the cutter with a covering boat and Clayton to inspect villages on other side of bay. In the afternoon we captured another supposed murderer, identified by an interpreter. His wife when she saw him taken off filled the air with her cries. I am getting tired of this detective and murderer-hunting business. However, one has to learn all that is possible about natives and their ways. Clayton naturally looks to me, as representing the civil power, to support him and his actions.

Wednesday, October 14.—We decided to retain the canoes which came from the village whence the self-confessed murderer had surrendered. The poor wretch looked very much scared when I examined him. He told the whole story, describing, in the most artless manner, exactly how he killed the man; he evidently thought very little of the deed. In fact, we find that, in the eyes of the natives, human life is of no real value; it is merely a question of a few arm shells. Diravera, the murderer, had brought with him what he considered compensation, and appeared surprised that we did not accept the arm-shells and let him go! It is in consequence of certain superstitions that life is so valueless. They are like the Chinese in that respect, so that we have a people with a very old civilisation resembling in that point savage tribes with no civilisation.

After consultation, it was decided that early this morning the villages on the other side of the bay, which had refused to surrender the second murderer, should be burnt. This business was carried out by the men of *Diamond* and *Raven*. A few rounds of shell were fired into the village, to show the natives that we had the power of harming them, if we chose. Then the covering party in boat fired a few volleys to clear the huts, and they were all soon in a blaze. After this police work had been done, we started for the scene of another murder at Slade Island.[1] There after parleying with the natives, who were friendly, we landed and sat on a log and heard their account of the business. It was a curious sight: about twenty natives, several women and children, insisted on sitting close to us. A tale was then unfolded, which to my mind made the murder excusable. After taking notes of the evidence, we decided that nothing could be done, and returned to our ships. They were dancing and 'tom-toming' in the village all night, as a feast was going on.

Thursday, October 15.—This morning we were up early to walk over the island. We ascended the hill, which was steep, and what was worse, the scrub was thick, and the red ants were very troublesome. As you pushed your way and brushed past the leaves of the trees, the ants got on to your arms, neck, and body, and then commenced biting you. They crept inside

---

[1] This was the case of a man named Reid, who was killed at Slade Island (Tupe-tupe), in December 1884. It appeared from the evidence of the natives examined, that Reid was continually interfering with native women. On the morning of his murder, going to his house he found that some things had been stolen. He charged a native boy, who was acting as his servant, with stealing them. The boy denying, Reid got angry, and struck him with the stock of his revolver. The boy cried bitterly, and his elder brother Makasoki took a spear, threw it, and wounded Reid in the back, as he thought his brother was going to die. Reid ran to the water, and Doboresi threw a spear, which struck Reid in the side. Reid tried to swim off to his cutter, when Makasoki, who had taken a rifle from a Chinaman's hut close by (the Chinaman being absent), fired, but did not wound Reid. Makasoki then handed the rifle to Aropata, a relation of his, who shot Reid through the head when he was getting over the side of his cutter.

my shirt, and altogether I voted that a walk of this kind was a nuisance. We have been singularly fortunate so far—the nasty creatures that crawl up you are not numerous, and we have seen no snakes. We are told that in the rainy season all these bush-lands are infested with leeches which crawl up you. I shall avoid walking during that season accordingly. After walking along the ridge we descended to the shore on the other side of island, and visited several villages. The people were very friendly, and we returned on board at 8 30 to breakfast.

A native had then to be examined. He was supposed to talk good 'pigeon' English, but this I discarded because it requires great practice to understand it. We then resorted to double interpretation. It is curious how the evidence of these natives agrees; you may examine four or five men separately, and at different times, when there can be no possible collusion. They all tell their stories simply and to the point. They conceal nothing and do not appear to be ashamed of anything.

We then started, at 10.30 A.M., for Moresby Island, where there was another murder to be investigated.[1]

After our arrival we went to shore in the galley, accompanied by the cutter manned by about a dozen men. As we approached the shore a shot-gun was fired, which put us on the *qui vive*, as we knew that the natives had taken possession of a number of guns from the plunder of Captain Friar's vessel.

We interviewed the natives on the shore from our

[1] The murder of Captain Friar, see *ante*, p. 305.

boat. We demanded the surrender of the skull of the murdered man, and of the gun and other things that had been taken from him. By degrees they were all brought. We then got them to tell their story, which they did in the usual way. After a time a light-coloured native, tall and rather stately, with red hair (red hair is somewhat common), came to the shore. He was recognised by Chalmers as a native by name Bailala.[1] After some talk we got him to tell what he knew, and he promised to come on board. When on board I examined him, and found that the murder had been regularly planned by a large number of villages. The names of the men concerned were given to us. We decided next morning to try to get them.

Friday, October 16, 1885.—At 8.45 A.M. we went in a boat to the shore to have a parley with the natives— the carpenter's head was given up. It was kept in the village in a basket as a trophy, and was brought to us. I was at breakfast and declined to see it, and afterwards handed it over to Clayton. Admiral Tryon thinks a great deal of getting back the heads. Clayton has committed both heads to the deep, and held a short service when doing so. After breakfast we again started in two boats to reconnoitre other villages. At 12 o'clock the *Raven* arrived from Dinner Island (suggestive of cannibalism) bringing the *Harrier* with mails.

In the afternoon we went to shore again, but failed to secure the murderers, so captured several canoes, including a fine war canoe. One of the houses was set on fire by a native interpreter who had misunderstood

---

[1] See note, p. 305.

our orders. Clayton said he would return some other time for the purpose of destroying villages.

I forgot to mention our parley with one of the murderers of Captain Friar. He was a splendid specimen of a savage, and boldly acknowledged the murder, giving his reasons for it. He declined to come on board, although promised that he would not be killed. We might have captured him at one time, but I agreed with Clayton that the risk was too great. After a time numerous natives armed with spears, who had accompanied our murderer, slunk off, and he was left alone with four or five men. We could then have shot him, and according to some people that was the proper way of dealing with him. They would have liked us to massacre the whole 'crowd' of them. Our savage went off after a time, walking along the beach as we pulled parallel to the shore, and again we might have shot him. I am opposed to all treachery, and although I feel that the killing of whites should be punished, I do not see my way to do so judicially and according to justice.

Saturday, October 17.—The *Raven* left this morning to return to his village the poor wretch we captured by mistake on October 13. Chalmers told me afterwards that the man's wife had already put on mourning (*i.e.* covered herself with a black sort of pigment from head to foot. The men do the same when mourning). When he arrived at the village her delight was great.

We started again at 7.15 A.M. and skirted round the shore to try and find a Chinaman who had been reported to be living on shore, and we were afraid, after having taken vengeance, that the natives might turn on the Chinaman. But we could not find him. So we returned to Dinner Island, where we found the *Dart* and the *Harrier*. I dined with Clayton on board the *Diamond*. In the evening a collier came with coals for us and the Admiral, so we had quite a fleet: H.M.S. *Diamond*, *Raven*, *Dart*, and *Harrier*, the *Governor Blackall*, *Jennie B.* (collier), and schooner *Daisy*, a thing never seen before in New Guinea.

Sunday, October 18.—This morning at 4 A.M. we were awakened by the look-out man of the *Diamond* shouting 'Man overboard!' I awoke at once. The cry came, 'Native has escaped!' It was the wretched murderer, who had watched his opportunity and jumped into the sea, intending to escape to the island and thence to the other islands, hoping to find his way home. It turned out that, as the man appeared quiet and reconciled, he had been given more liberty. Fort got hold of our watchman, jumped into the dingey, and gave chase. The *Diamond* had also lowered a boat, but Fort got the start. They pulled to the shore, and within a few yards Fort was able to capture the poor creature; he was then returned to the *Diamond*.

We had our service as usual. I officiated, as Chalmers had not returned.

In the evening had my row.

Monday, October 19.—It commenced to rain early.

We have been coaling all day. About 10 A.M. we started with a guard-boat to visit a village where a Bengalee or Manilla man, by name Bob Lumse, had been killed.[1] We reached the village in about three-quarters of an hour. It was smooth and calm weather. The natives being friendly, we landed at once and commenced inquiry into murder. The evidence was unsatisfactory, as it could not be shown that there was any provocation on the part of Bob Lumse. Another example of the utter disregard of human life amongst the natives of New Guinea. It will take a generation to teach them differently. It is no use talking about teaching the natives that they cannot kill white people or foreigners with impunity—you cannot avenge the murders without wholesale slaughter. We saw a place where cannibal feasts used to be held. I believe they are not now held owing to the influence of the mission.

Tuesday, October 20.—Rowed round Dinner Island in the morning, and afterwards completed my despatches and letters to send by the *Dart* to Sydney. In the afternoon walked round Dinner Island. This is not a great feat, as the island is small, only about half a mile long, and narrow.

---

[1] The village where Bob Lumse was killed was Magaikarona on Hayter Island, in the Bay of Goyouare. The chief was summoned and questioned with regard to the murder. He stated that Lumse did not deal fairly with the natives, and that they were constantly quarrelling; he called one of the accomplices of the murder, by name Kieu, who stated : ' For four Sundays we have been working for this man; to some he gave tobacco, to others tomahawks, to others no tomahawks, saying to these last that he would pay them after he had been to Dinner Island. One afternoon we had a great quarrel with Bob. Langeno felt very angry. The next morning very early Langeno came to him, as he was sleeping close to where Bob slept, and said, "Come and let us kill Bob"; he said, "No, why should we kill our friend?" He saw that Langeno was much disturbed and was very angry. Langeno then took a spear and pierced Bob's neck close to the windpipe; in drawing out the spear it was broken. The others speared Bob after he was dead. Bob's head was not cut off.'—*Extract from Official Records.*

I presented Dick, the mission teacher, with a watch, as a reward for his bravery in going off to Moresby Island to bring away Captain Friar's cutter. He is a fine native, a Lifu man.[1]

Wednesday, October 21.—Left for Killerton Island early. The *Diamond* and *Raven* accompanied us. Arrived at 10 A.M. and walked over the island, which is a good specimen of an island that has risen from the sea by coral formation. It is, I should say, unhealthy, as it is flat and there are lagoons inside. I interviewed four white men.

Went on board the *Raven*, in order to visit a village on the mainland which was reported to be hostile. Landed with Captain Ross and Chalmers. The chief came up to us crying, saying that all his people had run away because they thought we were coming to kill them. The chief cried very loudly, and was much agitated. On investigation we found that they had never expressed any desire to attack white men. We had a palaver, bought some curios. Chief sent a pig in compensation for an apparent attempt to cheat the mission teacher, which pig I accepted and presented to the officers and men of the *Raven*. Returned to my steamer.

Thursday, October 22.—Left Killerton at 6 A.M., arriving at Dinner Island at 10. Stayed there quarter of an hour and on to South Cape.

Friday, October 23.—Took a longer row this morning, and were caught in a squall of rain. It was hard work pulling against the wind and sea. Left at 9 for

---

[1] See *England's New Colony*, p. 201.

Dufaur Island to obtain information concerning Captain Webb's murder.[1] About 1 o'clock we sighted the *Ellangowan*, which was coming to meet us. We signalled her to anchor near us at Dufaur. We are just going to our anchorage as I write.

We anchored at Dufaur Island with the *Diamond* and *Raven*, the *Ellangowan* leading the way. Her flag, granted by the Admiralty, is a very good one. It is the blue ensign with Union Jack in corner, a dove carrying an olive branch, and the words 'Messenger of Peace' below.

We landed and had a talk with the natives, then walked a short distance inland up a dry creek; found the soil very rich. The whole place felt more like the tropics than any we had yet seen. We returned to the ship and agreed to start next morning early for Milport Harbour, where Captain Webb, his wife, and crew had been murdered.

Saturday, October 24.—Row in morning, then started. Shifted to the *Raven*, leaving the *Diamond* and *Blackall* to follow later on. We reached Milport Harbour about

---

[1] Webb and his wife were murdered at Milport Bay in July or August, 1884. From native evidence obtained by Mr. Romilly, it appeared that the murder was committed in cold blood and under circumstances of great brutality. After two days spent in vainly endeavouring to come to a parley with the natives, several of the villages on the hills surrounding the bay were shelled. This was the only punishment possible. The villages were perched on heights up which it would have been impossible to send an attacking party. Sir Peter Scratchley afterwards visited Toulon Island, where Webb had been staying previous to his murder. He was there informed that the natives of Milport Bay were the bitter enemies of the Toulon Islanders, and that they had warned Webb not to go to the bay, as he was regarded as a friend of the Toulon people, and would certainly be killed. Mr. Fort, in his official record of the investigation, adds that Webb bore a bad character for brutal and dishonest dealings with the natives.

twelve o'clock, and got into boats in order to try and interview the natives. We spent several hours in the operation, with no result. Our interpreter shouted to the natives, who were up in their little villages on the tops of inaccessible hills, and they took no notice whatever—they knew very well what we had come for. We could see them in the tree-tops looking down upon us. No doubt we could have shot some of them, as we had a guard-boat with us manned by picked men. We were only able to get speech of one man, and he did not belong to the harbour. He declared that all the tribe had had a hand in the murder. There were about five very small villages to be seen on the hill-tops. This man Webb was a horrid brute; he had often burnt down villages, shot boys for stealing tobacco, and he compelled his wretched wife to go with him, although Chalmers had begged him not to do so, as he was sure to get killed. He had actually set a savage dog upon her a few days before. The ruffian deserved his fate, and I have no sympathy with him. We could do nothing as the natives were far away.

Milport Harbour, Sunday, October 25.—We had our usual muster of the crew, and service afterwards. H.M.S. *Harrier* left, carrying the mails. Romilly, who had been ailing for some days, at last yielded to the urgent advice of all his friends and determined to go to Yorktown in the ship. In the afternoon I went for a row in the whale-boat, and Clayton came in his galley, in order to see whether we could open up communication with the natives. We patiently tried for two hours. We saw numbers of them in one of the hill-top villages. We shouted to them, through the interpreter, to come down, as we only wished to talk. They replied back that they were afraid. Then after a time they taunted us and said, 'Why do you not come up to us, if you wish to speak?' Just what we did not intend doing! So we left, and decided that the only thing remaining to be done was to fire on the villages with shell the next morning, in order to demonstrate to the native mind that we could reach them and damage their houses without going up to them. The firing was bad at first, as I expected. It was very much like firing at a battery on a hill. None of the shell would have harmed any one in a battery, and I doubt whether any of the natives remained after the first shell exploded. The scene was interesting but depressing, because I knew that, however necessary it might be to damage these wretched beings as a punishment, the effect would be to embitter them against the white man for years to come.

Monday, October 26.—I decided to leave at 11 A.M. for Aroma, leaving the *Diamond* and *Raven* at anchor. We were at sea all night and it was rather rough, but I found my cot comfortable. Askwith, who was worse again, slept in my cabin. I see clearly that he must be sent back to Australia to recover.

Tuesday, October 27.—Reached Paremata at 9 A.M., the captain having kept well out at night in order to be well away from the reefs. We anchored for the day, and told Koapena that we wanted him to go with us to Cloudy Bay the next day. Did not land, as it was blowing rather hard and there was a surf on the beach.

Wednesday, October 28.—We started at 9 A.M. for Cloudy Bay, arriving at 4.55 P.M. On our way we met the *Diamond* and *Raven*, and proceeded in our usual procession—*Raven* first, then the *Diamond*, and lastly the *Blackall*. We got to a very good anchorage for the night, with a nice breeze which cooled the air. Askwith appears to me to be no better, so I determined to send him to Townsville. He now wishes to go himself.

In the cool of the evening went for a row. Attempted to interview the natives, but none were to be seen. Cloudy Bay was the scene of another outrage which had been punished by H.M.S. *Beagle* some years ago. The native villages had been burnt, and we found in their place two or three small wigwam-looking structures. This proved that the punishment had driven the natives away. After dinner Koapena went on shore again, and found that the tobacco we had left hanging to a pole had been taken, but no natives were to be seen. No doubt they were not far off, but they had no intention of seeing even their friend. They feared a surprise and treachery.

Thursday, October 29.—We sent a boat ashore at daylight to try again for the natives, but they could not be found. Started for Aroma. Arrived in the afternoon. Did not land. I shifted with my bag to the *Diamond*, to remain on board until Saturday and allow the *Blackall* to start for Port Moresby at 5.30, in order that she might reach the port early to-morrow and commence preparations for crossing over to Townsville.

Friday, October 30.—At daylight we landed with Clayton to perform the ceremony of hoisting the flag at

Moapa, Koapena's village.[1] I wished to do this as a reward for the good reception given to the whites by him at all times. The *Raven* and *Diamond* sent men. Altogether about fifty men with a band were landed, about half of them marines. There was little surf, but as the tide was out we had some difficulty in getting on shore. As usual I was mounted on a native teacher's back, and did not wet my feet. These teachers are generally very sturdy men. They mostly come from Raratonga near Samoa, and are large-limbed, fine men. The teacher here is Trion, to whom I gave a watch some time ago for having saved the lives of some natives who were shipwrecked near here and would have been killed.

The men formed up, and headed by the band we marched about two miles along the beach, accompanied by a large portion of the population—men, women, and children—who crowded round our men. On arrival at Moapa, which is a very large village of some 1,500 or more souls, the inhabitants turned out to receive us. The first operation was to send for Koapena, who appeared to be hiding. This was because he had not done as we had told him—to remove certain skulls of Chinamen who had been murdered a long time before on the coast. Clayton very properly declined to hoist the flag so long as these trophies were hanging in the centre of the village. Koapena then told Chalmers that he and his teachers could remove the skulls. This was done and they were buried. Then the ceremony of the flag was proceeded with. The men formed up in front of the

[1] See also *New Guinea Notes*, p. 372.

flagstaff, which I had caused to be erected the day before near Koapena's house. The flag was hoisted. Three rounds of blank cartridge as a feu-de-joie, a short speech, three cheers for the Queen, a distribution of tobacco and a few axes to chiefs. Then we marched home, or rather to the beach, through cocoanut plantations, with an escort from the population. On the way Koapena called for a halt, and gave the men cocoanuts fresh from the trees, and they evidently enjoyed the draughts of milk. I think it mawkish stuff. By the way, when the men were drawn up, Koapena, without any prompting, went down both the front and rear ranks and shook hands with each man. The dignified and stately way with which he went through the operation was very striking. He is a grand old savage. We returned on board, and although the sea had moderated got rather wet. I at once had my bath and then breakfast, and am now writing my diary. A delightful breeze is blowing through a huge gunport, and I cannot believe I am off the coast of New Guinea. It is cooler than Sydney. We start for Port Moresby at 4 to-day, and should get there about daylight to-morrow. My intention is to remain on shore whilst the *Governor Blackall* goes to Townsville and back. It will be a pleasant change for me, as I am sick of being at sea.

. . . . . .

Port Moresby, November 14.—We arrived here on October 31, and on November 4 I started for a trip inland with Fort and Chalmers. We got back all well on the 11th inst. Distance there and back under 100 miles. It was rather rough work, but the knowledge I have gained of the country repays me. My ideas are getting settled, and I shall be able to lay down my programme with confidence. I have not been able to attempt a line of my diary. In this climate I cannot do more than a certain amount of work, and I make it a rule to give up writing or any business if I feel at all fagged.

I may say I feel remarkably well, and unless bad luck should attend me, you will be able to welcome me back in good health—thinner of course, but of that I am glad, as it makes me more active.

Fort was a regular brick on the trip. No man could have been more kind or behaved better.

I am enchanted with the New Guinea natives. Anything could be done with them, the boys particularly. They have such nice faces, are so bright, intelligent, and willing.

We start to-morrow to try Guise and Currie. The *Harrier* is now waiting there to deport them, if I find I can do it. We then pass on to Dinner Island, where the *Raven* is waiting to escort me to the New Guinea coast. The Admiral is most obliging.

Thursday, November 19.—Got up at 5 A.M. to send off letters, which were to wait here (Dinner Island) for the *Harrier*. Then rowed ashore to select site for a coal-shed, as I have decided to make Dinner Island one of the stations for an officer. It is very convenient, and being surrounded by dozens of islands will become a centre of great importance. After rowing about a short time to get some exercise, returned on board. We started shortly after 7 A.M., the *Raven* having left at

6 P.M. The men-of-war are very exact; they always start to the minute.

After going about twenty miles in Milne Bay, we anchored opposite to the mouth of a river. We went off in the whaler to explore it. The scenery was beautiful, quite tropical; the river must have been at least 150 yards across and nine feet in depth. After going up about two miles we landed at a small village. The natives were very friendly, but appeared to be poor. After doing some trading and getting a few specimens for Forbes, we started to return, and on our way called at another village, where the chief came off at once. We ascertained that a long time ago a boat containing white men had gone up the river named Dava Dava. So our illusion that we were the first white men who had been up it was dispelled. No name has been given to the river. I shall explore it when I return to New Guinea next year. On our return to the *Blackall* we found that the *Raven* had passed us and gone on to Discovery Bay, so named by Moresby.

The appearance of the coast is very beautiful. Hills and mountains 2,000 feet high slope down to the edge of the sea, covered with dense tropical bush, with here and there clearings where cocoanut trees grow in abundance. After steaming another five miles we came suddenly upon lovely scenery, and soon we found ourselves in Discovery Bay, where the *Raven* was at anchor.

We found, on landing, a semicircular bay, with the native huts standing amidst cocoanut trees. We walked along the sea-shore, and found it very hot work, as the bay is sheltered from the wind. It is said that there is gold to be found inland close to the shore. This would give Discovery Bay a great importance. In attempting to cross a creek on a catamaran—it was only a few yards across—I fell into the water on my back, but escaped with a partial wetting. These catamarans consist of three long pieces of trees lashed together with some fibre. The natives are very dexterous with them; paddling either sitting or standing. They appear graceful whilst paddling; women also look very well on them.

The women here do not tattoo and are better-looking. All the population was very friendly. There were dozens of canoes trading with the ship. There was little to be got, however, that was worth having; although the men forward buy almost anything and pay ridiculous prices. In fact, the natives bring every kind of rubbish, thinking, no doubt, the white man a great fool for buying the things. Bits of tortoiseshell of no value, matting, cocoanuts, inferior spears, paddles, nautilus shells (which I believe fetch a good price amongst the jewellers who buy them to set up), sugarcane, leaves of plants, yams, &c.

After our walk and the wetting we returned to the ship, and started for another bay a few miles off. This we found very similar to Discovery Bay. The country was flatter and ran back to lofty ranges, said to be 2,500 to 3,000 feet high. The scenery after a time palls upon one, as there is much sameness about it.

The above was the last entry made by Sir Peter Scratchley in his Diary. Two days later (November 21) he was taken ill while proceeding in the *Governor Blackall* from Killerton Island to Bentley Bay, on his way to inspect the boundary of the British territory at Mitre Rock. The first symptoms of his illness seemed merely to denote a somewhat severe bilious attack, but it was soon apparent that he was suffering from New Guinea fever, although not, as it seemed, in a dangerous form. He insisted on continuing his voyage to Mitre Rock, which was reached on November 25, but, after remaining there for a short time, he became so much worse, that it was determined to return direct to Cooktown, where the *Governor Blackall* arrived on December 1. Early that morning he seemed better, but towards noon he became completely prostrated by the intense heat, and for some hours was scarcely conscious. All speed was therefore made to reach Townsville, *en route* for Sydney and cooler latitudes; but Sir Peter Scratchley gradually sank, and died at sea at nine minutes past one o'clock on the morning of December 2, 1885.

CHAPTER XX.

NEW GUINEA NOTES.[1]

At Port Moresby the mission is by far the most striking feature. The religious services are very popular, and outward observances are strictly kept—little or no work being done on Sundays. The church is prettily situated; the interior is plain, and the natives sit on the ground to listen to services in the Motu tongue. On the occasion of our visit, the teachers and their wives, dressed in clean garments, were seated in the front, while the rest of the congregation, unwashed and in their ordinary undress, squatted behind. The chief, Boevagi, and another village headman occupied seats by the table in their capacity as deacons. Two infants were christened, one of whom had already a remarkable history; having been born during a hunt on the bank of a river, while the mother (wife of a teacher named Kumate) was alone in the camp. She washed the child herself, put it in a net bag on her back, and walked the same day ten miles into Port Moresby!

The congregation was attentive and sang the hymns heartily; they are very quick at learning tunes. When the Sacrament is administered, cocoa-nut milk is used for wine. The Rev. W. Lawes has not only translated hymns and short pieces, such as the Commandments, into Motu, but even the four Gospels. His school has been a great success, many learning the three R's in Motu, and by their own desire gaining some knowledge of English. I saw copper-plate writing which could scarcely have been surpassed in an English National School.

Coloured teachers are placed in various villages along the coast, often at the request of the natives themselves, who see

[1] See Preface.

the advantage of having an arbitrator in their quarrels. These teachers come from all parts of the Pacific, chiefly from Eastern Polynesia, and after some training in the London Mission College go to Port Moresby to learn Motu before being sent to a mission station. A great point is made that they should marry young, which as a rule they do.

A Jesuit mission has been sent to Yule Island, northwards from Port Moresby, under the special patronage of the Pope, who is said to take great interest in these Islands. This mission seemed likely to extend its work to the mainland and so interfere with the London Missionary Society. Sir Peter Scratchley offered to transport the mission and build the Father a house on any spot they might select upon the east coast. This proposal was accepted, subject to Père Navarre's approval.[1]

Peace is one great result of the mission-teaching in New Guinea. Wherever teachers have been placed, traders can safely go and travellers meet with hospitality. When the Rev. James Chalmers arrived Mr. Lawes had formed a mission at Port Moresby; but little was known of the inland tribes, and the coast tribes were engaged in perpetual warfare. Mr. Chalmers went amongst them everywhere, with a walking-stick, preaching always 'maino' (peace). In a short time his influence was felt, and now is paramount along the coast and far inland. Strangers are asked if they know 'Tamate,'[2] and if so, are treated with kindness. Tribes that have never seen a white man enquire for him and are anxious to hear if he is well.

He is regarded as a 'mighty sorcerer' in many districts, the native belief generally being reverence for an unseen power whom it is dangerous to provoke. Thus the spirits of the mountain are held in dread. All kinds of small things, such as fire-flies, are invested with spiritual attributes, but all are spirits of evil. There is no comfort or brightness in the native religion. A dim Supreme Being, called Aobada, whose province it is hard to determine, appears to hold the chief place, and then a succes-

---

[1] See *Sir Peter's Diary*, p. 312.

[2] Mr. Chalmers is affectionately spoken of as 'Tamate' by his native flock, and is known by this name far and wide in New Guinea.

sion of dreaded evil spirits, including the ghosts of the dead, follow in dismal order. All is darkness and fear.

The mission buildings stand on the top of a low hill. Below, two villages of the Motu tribe are situated upon the beach between the mainland and a small rock, a miniature Monte Carlo in appearance, which at high tide becomes an island. At a short distance, beneath a palm grove and also upon the beach, stands another group of houses. Each of these villages has its own name, although the district is known as Hanuabada (Great Village). There are two distinct dialects spoken, because at each end of the village, as at Lealea and Boera (two other villages on the coast), people of the Koitapuan tribe have settled, who have only lately commenced to intermarry with the Motuans. The Koitapuans were originally an inland tribe, but were driven down to the sea by the Koiari. They appear to have settled peaceably in villages on the coast, being revered as sorcerers and friends of the mountain spirits, but keep aloof from their neighbours of the same township. Although living so close together even the children of the two tribes never play with each other. The Koitapuans submit to no authority, there being no chief of paramount power either amongst the Motuans or themselves. In fact these tribes have no political system. Each man comes and goes exactly as he likes. The custom of their forefathers is the only binding tie, to which they adhere with rigid conservatism. Indeed the want of chiefs is one of the great difficulties in settling the government of New Guinea.

The houses on this part of the coast, as also in the villages inland, are built upon piles, varying from four to eight feet in height. A few steps up a rude ladder lead to a platform on which some of the family generally recline. A baby, and often a young pig, in nets suspended from the eaves, are gently swinging to and fro. Fishing-nets lie in a corner with shells attached for weights. Nautilus shells with grass streamers or hideous carved pieces of wood hang before the bamboo door, which is low and narrow, and leads into the common-room, where all the family sleep. The common-room is about twelve feet by eighteen, with a bare flooring of rough planks, generally the sides of old canoes. Through the chinks the garbage is thrown upon the plentiful remnants of cocoa husks below, for the pigs to eat or sea to carry away. In the middle of the room is the fireplace, a pile of ashes on some boards, with a spark protector of bamboo sticks hung about three feet above. On the central pole is hung a tom-tom, while here and there on the grass walls are suspended gourds for lime, bamboo pipes, tomahawks, adzes, spare grass petticoats, and net bags. In one corner swings a netted hammock. The others are occupied by yams, taro, pots for trading or water, and drinking-gourds of cocoa-nut. If the family is large these are placed on a shelf opposite the door. A few light rafters serve as resting-places for spears, arrows, or paddles. There is no window, but a movable shutter can generally be opened on the sea side, and plenty of air enters through the walls and the holes in the floor. The ground beneath the houses is thoroughly explored throughout the day by dogs and pigs. Both are very peculiar animals. The dogs are lean and mangy, curs which cannot bark, but howl and whine dismally. Some of the larger dogs, however, are fleet, and are used for hunting 'wallaby,' but they do not seem to receive much care or any food from their masters. The pig, on the contrary, is the pet of the village. He goes wherever he likes and pokes his snout into everything. Before the missionaries introduced the black and white species all were of the same variety, longitudinally striped in youth with reddish brown and black, and becoming dark grey with advancing years; but now in Hanuabada all kinds may be met with, grouting in every direction. Feasting on pig is to the Papuan perfect delight. No more succulent morsel is known to him than pork, a delicacy only to be indulged in upon great occasions, or to be given as a present to distinguished visitors, who are expected not only to pay for it, but to eat it on the spot in company with the donors. The young pigs are treated with the greatest care, tended like babies, and even suckled by the women. Small enclosures littered with the softest grass are made lest they should stray, and men carry them about in their arms for an airing, or to exhibit to admiring friends. Even an Irishman's pig might envy the pampered porkers of Hanuabada.

When a sheep was landed for the mission-house the natives did not seem to remember ever having seen a similar animal. They assembled round it as it quietly lay on the beach, and one boy was given the rope round its neck to hold. The poor beast, cramped with the sea journey, lay still even after the cords round its legs had been cut, and the natives could only judge that it must be a 'hairy pig;' but as soon as I lifted it up, the animal kicked out merrily, with a back leg motion such as no pig in Hanuabada ever possessed. The whole village ran shouting along the beach, and the boy dropped the rope in a second. It was only when no damage ensued that they slowly returned, and finally followed in a highly excited state when a sailor hoisted the sheep on his shoulder and carried it off to be cooked.

The natives certainly affect severe simplicity in the matter of dress. The only article common to all the men is a thin string, a third of an inch in breadth, passed tightly round the waist and between the legs. A band of grass, which serves as a pocket for tobacco, knives, and decorations of croton leaves, is for the most part worn upon the upper part of the arm. Some have head-bands of red braid or small rounded pieces of shells, while a few wear necklaces of shells or teeth, and curved bones through the nose. Their hair, thick, matted, and long, is drawn up by a comb of bamboo cane. The women wear petticoats of woven grass, sometimes stained to a red hue. The married and betrothed have short hair; the majority are tattooed with a V-shaped mark and other designs upon the breast. Their figures are squat and not so erect as those of Hindoo women, as they generally carry weights on the back and not on the head.

The native villages are of some size, one having 114 and another 65 houses. No house contained more than ten people.

It might be supposed that these people are sunk in mere savage barbarism. On the contrary they have for unknown ages been remarkable in mercantile ventures At the time of our arrival they were busily preparing for a great trading expedition, before the south-east monsoon, to friendly villages in the west, binding together large canoes and building grass bulwarks and tall masts, or preparing pottery ware.

About twenty large canoes called 'lakatoi' start from all this portion of the coast, manned by about 600 men. The Motu men take the precedence by starting first, and then canoes from other villages follow. Allowing the average number of fifty pots for each man, made by his wives and relations during the previous six months, these expeditions convey westwards, for about 200 miles, the large number of 30,000 pots, and bring back about 150 tons of sago. The enterprise of people, so backward in other respects, in trusting themselves to the open sea on mere rafts, and trading to such a distance, is extraordinary. They remain at Elema, Orokolo, and other places towards the west till the north-west monsoon begins, and then return with the sago. No women are allowed to accompany the expedition. The result is that almost all the children are born about the same time, being conceived during the three months succeeding the return of the traders. There are other strange restraints on over-population besides this. Thus, twins are always destroyed, the natives saying that they do not know who the father is, as they believe that each child must have a separate father, and moreover consider it like a pig to have more than one offspring at a birth. It is said that at a village called Motu Motu, husbands live apart from their wives after childbirth until the children are weaned. Illegitimate children too are destroyed, if the mother is unmarried, because they can have no place in the tribe and no one knows who may be the father.

When the time for preparing the 'lakatoi' has arrived, some enterprising man lights a fire at early morn in the village street, and, on being asked his purpose, proclaims that he has a canoe and is ready to start for the west. Others offer themselves as crew, or bring other canoes, masts, sails, and gear. A joint-stock company is soon formed and receives excellent credit, for the traders leave their wives and children behind as security, and punctually repay the wallaby, bananas, yams, or cocoanuts which have been provided for the family in their absence. The 'lakatoi' are gradually formed with many ceremonial observances, and shortly before leaving take several trial trips.

We saw them thus sailing about the bay with tall sails curiously shaped like the claws of an immense crab. Men guided them with numerous paddles, while others attended to the sail, hauled up by a long rattan rope working in a slit at the top of the mast. Girls, intent upon betrothal, for which this is the great opportunity, danced with interlaced arms upon the bows, shifting their bodies about with a continuous swing, which sent their grass petticoats whirling like the skirts of a ballet-girl. Crowds watched from the beach, and every one shouted, entering with great zest into the doings of their favourite boats. Every portion of the expedition, even the seasons at which various parts of the 'lakatoi' are made, is arranged according to precedent.

The pottery manufactured for this trade is entirely made by women. No machinery or rudimentary potter's wheel has come into use, but the women judge the size of the pots so accurately, and fashion them so deftly, that though rude they are admirably shaped. Red and grey clay is broken up into powder, in old canoe sides or hollowed planks, and when mixed with fine silver sand and water is kneaded into a large lump, from which the top and lip of the pot are first fashioned by hand, shell, and a flat stone. The remainder of the lump, from which the base is made, is supported in half an old pot, and pressed outwards to its shape. Then the roughness of the whole exterior and interior is smoothed by patting with stone, scraping with shell, and moistening with fingers, and finally the trade mark of the family is cut with sharp shell. The finished pots are now dried in the sun and then baked in a fire, being laid lip to lip in a circle with the bases outwards, and heated by burning wood, carefully placed over them in wigwam fashion. As soon as they become red-hot they are taken out between two long sticks, and sprinkled from a bunch of cocoa fibre with tannin, of blackish hue, extracted from mangrove bark. Another heating on a slow fire completes the process before the pots are stored for exportation.

Tobacco will probably prove an important article of trade in the future. The mission at Port Moresby lives by tobacco. It is the small coin of the country, which is used in payment of every little service. Without it the missionaries could not get water or vegetables, or have messages carried; while to the native it is the greatest luxury of life, excepting pig. European tobacco pipes are not valued in these districts as they are in the south where they have been introduced by traders. The native pipe is made of a thick piece of bamboo about two or three feet long. The joint at one end is left intact, a hole being made in the joint at the other. Near the closed end a hole is pierced in the side, into which a piece of twist rolled in leaf like a cigarette is inserted. Smoke is drawn into the tube by inhaling at the hole in the joint, and when the tube is full the cigarette is withdrawn, and the smoker fills his mouth with smoke from the side hole, puffing it out immediately. The same person seldom takes a second whiff, but hands the pipe to his neighbour, and in three whiffs it is finished. Every one smokes; men and women, old and young, even children of eight or nine years old.

Many natives visited the *Governor Blackall* almost every day whilst she was anchored in the harbour. Some were more self-important than others, but they speedily forgot their dignity if the cook produced a saucepan of rice, for which they greedily scrambled. Apparently they considered the ship to be a free place for promenading, and they walked about in the most unconcerned manner, but always on the watch for something to steal. One chief, while being shown round the ship, saw a box of fusees on a table outside Sir Peter's cabin. Slowly and solemnly he stalked by, and as he passed, closed his hand firmly over the treasure. I happened to see him from behind, and, tapping his shoulder, held out a hand for its return. He gave it back at once, his companions laughing at his ill-success. Hands would be softly passed through port-holes, to seize anything within reach. One of the staff amused himself by arranging some tempting articles on strings, and, lying in his berth, rapped with his stick the knuckles of those who tried to take them. The discomfited adventurers soon saw the joke, and brought up their friends to suffer, taking huge delight if they too were rapped. Longing eyes were cast on large bunches of bananas, hung under the awning to ripen, but no one was sufficiently venturesome to cut a whole bunch down. Single bananas could, however, be deftly abstracted.

It was interesting to watch the effect of various European productions upon our visitors. They retained wonderful composure, and seemed to take everything for granted, though so much must have been quite new to them. The engine-rooms and furnaces generally seemed to inspire awe, but they delighted especially in a standard mirror placed in Sir Peter's chief cabin, and would have stayed all day watching a bath being filled and emptied. One chief walked up to the mirror and attempted to go through it. As he avoided his reflection, it moved of course in front of him. He got angry, the image did likewise. He stretched out his hand, and so did the image, but when he felt the smooth surface, comprehension dawned upon him, he roared with laughter, and danced gaily up and down before the glass. Then he fetched his friends to see the new wonder, and thoroughly enjoyed their perplexity. I afterwards presented him with a small trade glass. His delight at receiving an article similar to that which he had so much admired knew no bounds. He gurgled joyfully as he looked at himself in it, hurried about to show it to his three wives, the eldest of whom promptly annexed it, and then returning suddenly embraced me warmly and rubbed noses. The man was thickly daubed with cocoa-nut oil, and had patches of coarse hair over his body, as the bush natives do not carefully depilate like those on the coast.

Amongst other things, our white skins particularly struck their fancy, and curious eyes peered through the port-holes of the bath-rooms, for they could scarcely believe that we were white all over. Shaving was also a process which greatly interested them.

Several carefully examined the shoes worn by different members of our party, which were taken off for their inspection. They looked, felt, and blew into them, and touched the socks to see if there were really feet there. When socks also were removed their delight was tempered with alarm, as they thought we were stripping off our skins.

The natives generally came to the ship in cranky-looking canoes. These are formed by laying a thick pole parallel to the hollowed trunk of a tree. The pole is connected with the trunk by four, five, or six smaller poles lashed at one end to the trunk, and at the other to cross-sticks driven into the pole. These cross-sticks are hammered in while the pole is green, and become firmly fixed as the wood seasons. The connecting poles serve to carry paddles, spears, or other articles which are too long to slip through the interstices.

Some of the native traditions are curious. One concerning the Kekeni rocks (marked 'Skittles' in charts), off the 'Toutou' opening to the Aroa river, says that these rocks came down the stream from inland and stopped up the mouth of the river. The fishes tried to pass and could not. The Kekeni would listen neither to the prayers of the small, nor to the protests of the big, so the latter in wrath met together, and bit through the base of the rocks until the pent-up water broke them down, and carried them with a rush to their present position.

We anchored close to these rocks when we visited the Kabadi villages, where white men were almost unknown. The river Aroa can never be valuable for navigation, as its current is very strong, and its course choked and shallowed by shifting sand-banks, on which numerous alligators lay basking in the sun. They were very quick in waddling to the water on our approach, especially when tickled by small shot, which could not possibly harm their thick hides. Snags and fallen trees add to the difficulties of the river, and during the S.E. monsoon the bar is impracticable except at high tide. The banks are thickly covered with tropical jungle, great palms, and mangrove trees.

When we reached Vanuabada, the chief village of the

Kabadi district, it was already dark, but several natives came to the landing-place to conduct us to the teacher's house, which consisted of one story containing one large room, raised on piles, and reached by a ladder; the floor was covered with mats from Samoa, of which island he and his wife were natives. About thirty of the villagers flocked in to stare at us, and remained until we laid ourselves on the floor to sleep, when one by one they reluctantly departed.

Next morning we examined the village at daybreak, and found it very superior to Hanuabada. The houses were at some distance from each other, built on piles in a clear carefully-swept space of sandy soil, beneath the shade of immense cocoa-nut palms. The inhabitants were evidently more disposed to dress than the people at Port Moresby, a wider band being worn, and several wearing old shirts. They appeared cleaner, and generally a finer-looking people than the Motuans, several of the faces having a peculiarly Jewish type.

One of the great objections to the settlement of any white men in New Guinea is fever, which is very sudden and overpowering in its action. In journeying inland from the coast a belt of miasma must be crossed before healthy country can be reached. This fever decimates the teachers, kills the traders, and even sweeps away native villages. In attacks of fever the muscles are apt to become contracted, and the natives employ shampooing with much success to relieve the stiffness. The shampooers are generally women, who knead the limbs softly and tenderly, feeling the muscles, not pounding and pressing. They will continue the process for hours, one woman on each side, using the ball of the thumb and the centre joint of the finger upon the muscles of the leg, arm, and back.

About ten miles inland from Port Moresby there is a creek lined with plantations of bananas, sago-palm, and sugar-cane belonging to the Koiari, some of whom we once met on the war-path to avenge the death of six of their men. These warriors were daubed with black and ashes, armed with spears, and supplied with peculiarly shaped shields, with a tortoiseshell back, on which were boars' tusks, red and blue seeds, and two white shells with black eyes. This shield being small is held in the mouth to add to the ferocious appearance of the warriors. We got them to show their tactics, which consist in darting backwards and forwards with great speed, not running, but executing a kind of double-shuffle.

The Koiari tribe were not at enmity with the Motu tribe, and were very friendly to us. If there had been any disputes, carriers could not have been obtained. It is very difficult to get carriers to go far, and frequent changes soon leave the traveller at the mercy of a new tribe, speaking an entirely different language. In most districts there seems to be a custom that if a tribe undertakes the charge of a visitor, the men who travel with him are responsible for his safety, and, if any harm happens to him, are liable to punishment by the tribe on their return.

Amongst the numerous expeditions made by Sir Peter Scratchley was one to Tupuselei, a village which is actually built *in* the sea, the houses being raised on poles quite 400 yards from the beach, and only accessible in canoes. The inhabitants are consequently quite secure from any attack by inland tribes. Not far from Tupuselei is a place called Padiri.

Although this district is so close to Port Moresby, the inhabitants, who are of the Koiari tribe, differ in many habits and customs from their neighbours; thus, at Port Moresby the dead are buried, while at Padiri the bodies are left on platforms to dry in the wind and sun.

At Kerepunu, our next halting-place, an important visitor came on board—Koapena, chief of the Aroma district. He is the only man in New Guinea who is a real chief, having established his power firmly over a proud and haughty race living in a fertile district of forty-two villages, and rules with a rod of iron. His influence is felt and known all along the coast, so that it was important to gain his good-will. Having been duly impressed with the power of the whites since Captain Digby, of H.M.S. *Sappho*, had given him an exhibition of a man-of-war's crew exercising at general quarters, and how a shell could be fired, Koapena was most anxious to be friendly, and at once evinced his intention unmistakably. He was taken to be introduced to the great chief, and, as Sir Peter rose up in his deck cabin to greet him, stooped down over him and rubbed noses. Sir Peter made a grimace, but, as he said afterwards, he saw that he was in for it, and resistance was useless.

Koapena, in his native grandeur, was certainly a fine man. We took his measurement and found he was six feet one inch high (without his frizzed hair), thirty-nine inches round the chest, thirty-eight inches round the haunch, seventeen in the calf, and twelve in the arm. His hand was enormous; his dress not worthy of mention, save some deep tattoo marks on his back, said to represent sundry enemies he had killed. As soon as Sir Peter heard that Koapena was coming, he hung a policeman's whistle round his neck. This was solemnly taken off, and handed to Koapena, who esteemed it as a token of great personal favour from the 'Queen's son,' and, though rather afraid to blow it, seemed proud to wear the decoration.

Koapena was evidently anxious to be anglicised, and had an unlimited capacity for smoking. Whenever he wanted a cigar, he squatted down outside Sir Peter's cabin, grinning and watching every movement, until the desired weed was thrown to him. Not that he really consumed many. Accustomed to the puffs of a native pipe, he could not manage a long smoke, and tried to smoke a cigar in the native style. Thus, he took a whiff of smoke, and then applied himself for several minutes to chewing areca nut and betel leaves, and absorbing quantities of lime. Meanwhile the cigar went out, and had to be lighted again before the smoking could continue. One box of matches for a cigar was almost a meagre allowance for Koapena.

He must have been very dull on board, particularly as he could not understand how we slept so long. Natives wake up at all hours, talk awhile, and perhaps sleep again; at the first sign of dawn they are wide awake.

At Aroma, Koapena took Sir Peter to his chief village, Maopa, whither, at large feasts, all the surrounding villages have to bring food. It is approached by a long avenue of cocoa-nut trees, and contains houses, some of which are three stories high. Sir Peter wished the Union-jack to be hoisted there and placed under Koapena's charge, but above a certain platform he descried the skulls of some murdered Chinamen. It was difficult to obtain their removal, but Koapena was plainly told that unless they were removed the flag would not be hoisted. Subsequently he gave in, and on Sir Peter's return, in company with H.M.S. *Diamond* and *Raven*, on October 30, 1885, a number of officers and men landed and marched from Keppel Point to Maopa for the purpose of hoisting the flag. As the natives would not touch the skulls, Koapena asked the teachers to take them down and bury them. An immense crowd of natives had assembled, amongst whom a low murmur was heard when the audacious deed was done. All then marched to the chief's house, where a flagstaff had been set up, close to which Sir Peter, Captain Clayton, and other officers took their stand, and, after an address to the natives, the flag was run up.

The excitement and enthusiasm were great, nearly 3,000 natives being present, and as the sailors marched back, they were accompanied by men, women, and children, in a triumphal procession. About half-way to the ships Koapena asked that a halt might be made for refreshment. As soon as the signal was given, lads swarmed the cocoa-nut trees by scores and threw down the fruit, while others opened them below and handed them round with the greatest glee. The whole ceremony passed without a hitch.

APPENDICES.

APPENDICES.

APPENDIX A.

I.

NAVAL DEFENCE—AUSTRALIAN OPINION.

Mr. Morgan (South Australia) moved, seconded by Mr. Palmer (Queensland), who stated that he only did so for the purpose of raising discussion :

That in the opinion of this Conference, the time has arrived when joint action should be taken for the more efficient naval defence of the Australian Colonies and New Zealand, and for the protection of the large number of valuable vessels now engaged in the Australian carrying trade.

With this view, united representations should be made to the Imperial Government, requesting a sufficient naval force should be maintained in Australian waters, to be used exclusively for the defence and protection of the Australian Colonies and New Zealand.

Subject, as in the last paragraph mentioned, the naval force, as so employed, to be under the exclusive control of the Admiralty.

Any scheme of naval defence should also include the naval defence of the harbours of the capitals of the different Colonies, and the fortifications of King George's Sound or some other port in Western Australia, and the maintenance of a sufficient force for holding the same.

In view of the present and daily increasing wealth and importance of the Australian Colonies and New Zealand, and the magnitude of the interests involved, this Conference is of opinion that it would be unreasonable to expect the Imperial Government to bear the whole expense of the largely increased force which it will become necessary to maintain if the above scheme is carried out ; but, as Imperial interests are also largely involved, the Imperial Government should contribute to the extent of one moiety.

The representatives assembled at this Conference undertake to recommend to their respective Governors to make representation to the Imperial Government on the basis of the foregoing resolution, and to request the concurrence of the Imperial authorities therein.

They (with the exception of Western Australia) agree to the payment of one moiety of the expense of carrying out such a scheme as is here suggested, including the building and maintenance of the fortifications at King George's Sound—such moiety to be contributed ratably by all the Colonies and New Zealand (except Western Australia) on the basis of population.

The adoption of these resolutions does not in any way affect the question of the land fortification and defence of particular ports, which will be left as now to the discretion of the Colonies interested.

After considerable discussion Mr. Giblin (Tasmania) moved, as an amendment, seconded by Mr. Palmer (Queensland),— That all the words after the word 'Conference' in the first line be omitted, with a view to inserting the following words :—

Considering the large Imperial interests involved, the naval defence of these Colonies should continue to be the exclusive charge of the Imperial Government, and that the strength of the Australian squadron should be increased.

That the members of this Conference pledge themselves to use all legitimate endeavours to procure the efficient fortifications and land defence of the several ports of the Australian Colonies, at the cost of the several Colonies interested.

APPENDIX A.

Motion put,—That the words proposed to be omitted stand part of the question.

AYE.	NOES.
South Australia.	New South Wales, Queensland, Victoria, Tasmania.

Western Australia declined to vote.

Further motion put,—That the words proposed to be inserted be inserted.—*Carried unanimously.*

The amended resolution was then put as follows:—That in the opinion of this Conference, considering the large Imperial interests involved, the naval defence of these Colonies should continue to be the exclusive charge of the Imperial Government, and that the strength of the Australian squadron should be increased. That the members of this Conference pledge themselves to use all legitimate endeavours to procure the efficient fortifications and land defence of the several ports of the Australian Colonies, at the cost of the several Colonies interested.—*Agreed to unanimously.*

Memo.—The representatives of South Australia wished it to be understood that, although not voting against the amended motion, they were of opinion that—in order more effectually to secure the employment of an Australian squadron for the exclusive defence of Australian ports—the Colonies ought to contribute to the cost of maintaining such squadron.

II.

'PROTECTED BARBETTE' SYSTEM OF MOUNTING AND WORKING COAST GUNS.

MEMORANDUM BY SIR W. G. ARMSTRONG AND CO.

Before entering upon a description of the arrangement and advantages of the 'protected barbette' system, it may be well to state that though this system is applicable to either muzzle or breech loading guns, its advantages are more fully developed in the use of the former, and the preference is given to them, for the following reasons:—

1. It is now conceded that there are no inherent advantages in breech-loading guns which cannot be obtained with muzzle-loaders; but that if two guns have the same proportions of bore and rifling, and fire the same charges, the same ballistic results can be obtained whether the gun be loaded at the muzzle or at the breech. The choice between the two systems depends therefore upon the relative convenience in working, and adaptability to situation and circumstances.

2. The advantages of simplicity of construction, absence of small details, and non-liability to derangement by exposure or rough usage, are greatly in favour of the muzzle-loader.

3. On board a ship, where constant supervision is available, and cleaning of the guns forms part of the daily routine, and where, on account of the limited space, muzzle-loading with guns of the present length presents serious difficulties and great exposure of the men, breech-loading guns are employed with great advantage.

4. In a coast battery, where the guns are left exposed to the weather, often for long periods without any supervision or attention, it becomes imperative to adopt the simplest possible construction, to avoid all loose pieces and details which require to be kept in a store; and, in fact, to have a gun that will remain for years in good condition simply by excluding the air from

the bore, and be serviceable after a few minutes' cleaning whenever required.

5. Choosing then the muzzle-loader for coast-service, the objects kept in view in designing the 'protected barbette' system have been the following:—

(a.) To obtain for the men working the gun the greatest possible protection.

(b.) To reduce the number of men required to a minimum.

(c.) To provide the most effective and economical arrangement of emplacement.

Taking the last of these points first in consideration, it is claimed for the earthwork barbette that it may be made to give the most efficient protection at the least cost, as compared with either plated or masonry constructions; and that when damaged it admits of the most ready repair. Except at enormous cost, plated defences that would be of any avail against modern guns cannot be carried out; they are open to the very grave objection that the derangement or distortion of a single plate may be sufficient to impede if not entirely to stop the working of a gun, that the required repairs cannot be carried out between the intervals of attack, and that the materials for such repairs have to be obtained from a distance and transported and erected at great cost and with much labour.

The objections to masonry defences are of a similar character, and very nearly as cogent.

On the other hand, there are very few situations where the materials for an earthwork do not exist, either close at hand or within a moderate distance. Their construction involves little skilled labour; and the labour of a strong body of men, under cover of night, will generally suffice to efficiently repair any damage received during the day.

The question of cost of emplacement becomes the more important in face of the evident advantages gained by isolating the guns of a line of coast defence as much as possible. The power of a line of defence is by no means diminished by a judicious separation and arrangement of the guns, as their fire can be concentrated upon a passing ship or other point of attack just as readily as if they were side by side in one battery, while the attacking fire is weakened by division, and its probable efficiency reduced by the diminished size of the object at which it has to direct its aim.

A very slight depression on the surface of the ground is sufficient to completely mask a gun, if it is placed on rising ground and at a height above the general level. It is therefore desirable, wherever possible, to place the earthworks on points of considerable height above the sea-level; and the face of the work should slope away evenly and as gradually as possible, so as to give the greatest thickness of earth cover and to leave no salient point to attract attention or guide the aim.

The 'protected barbette' earthwork has been designed to fulfil, as far as possible, all the conditions laid down above. The interior of the earthwork is a rectangular emplacement, lined on three sides with brick or rubble walling, to support the earthwork, the nature and extent of the walling depending upon the nature of the site. The front wall has a height at its lowest point of $6\frac{1}{2}$ or 7 feet, while the height gradually rises in the return walls of the traverses on the right and left to any required height, according to the requirements of the situation. In one of the traverses, either right or left as may be most convenient, a strongly arched gallery is formed, in which the mechanical loading arrangement is fixed, and in which the men loading the gun are perfectly protected. This gallery may if convenient communicate with the magazines, so that the ammunition may be brought up to the gun under cover without being in any way exposed in the open.

The front end of the platform of the gun rests upon a strong pivot fixed close to the front wall of the emplacement, and at about the middle of its length. The gun is loaded when run out, and in this position the centre of gravity is almost directly over the pivot, so that the whole mass is in the most advantageous position for being trained, which is done in the case of guns of 7 tons weight by handspikes inserted in sockets in the rear of the platform, two men being able to run one of these guns round as fast as they can walk. For guns over 7 tons weight mechanical gear is used for training, and is so arranged as to give a rapid movement when changing the gun from one position to another, or a slower motion when laying the gun accurately.

For loading, the gun is trained round till its axis is parallel with the face of the parapet, the muzzle pointing towards the arched gallery in the traverse. The muzzle of the gun is then depressed until it rests in a fixed support, thus ensuring the same angle of depression. The loading apparatus, which is fixed in the arched gallery in a line coincident with the axis of the gun when trained round and depressed as described above, consists of a long hollow beam or lever balanced on a central pivot, on which it oscillates freely. This lever is hollow, and the staff of a long rammer passes down its centre. The two ends of a flexible wire rope which passes over a drum placed on a frame which carries the pivot of the loading lever are secured to the end of the rammer staff and passed over guide pulleys on the bottom side of the lever, so that by turning the drum in one direction the rammer is drawn forward out of the lever, and is again withdrawn by reversing the motion of the drum. The front end of the loading lever is formed into a box which receives the cartridge and projectile, and a counterweight is provided at the other end to assist in balancing the lever on its centre. Before loading, the front end of the lever (nearest the muzzle of the gun) is depressed to a convenient height from the ground and secured there by a chain or catch. The lid of the box is then raised and the cartridge and projectile deposited therein. If not too heavy the projectiles are lifted by hand, or, if too heavy to be handled, then are brought up to the box suspended from a specially designed lever trolley, and then laid in place. The lid of the box is then closed, the chain or catch released, and the counterweight, supplemented by the action of one man at each end of the lever, brings the front end of the lever up to the muzzle of the gun, the axis of the lever being a prolongation of that of the gun. The drum carrying the wire rope is now revolved as described above, and the rammer is drawn forward, pushing the charge before it into the gun. As soon as the charge is home the rammer is rapidly withdrawn, the end of the lever is brought down into position to receive another charge, while the gun at the same time is elevated till it clears the edge of the parapet, trained round into any required position and laid in the ordinary way.

In the event of any damage to or derangement of the lever and its gear, which from its protected situation and simple construction is not likely to occur, the cartridge and projectile may be lifted to the muzzle of the gun when depressed into loading position, either by hand or by a small crane hinged to the inside face of the parapet wall, and passed home into the gun by an ordinary hand rammer in the usual way, the men performing this operation being almost as perfectly protected as they are while working the mechanical loading lever.

It will be evident that reversing the arrangement described above, and bringing the breech of the gun opposite the loading gallery, and depressing the breech instead of the muzzle, this system of loading may be applied to breech-loading guns; but for the reasons given before, the muzzle-loaders are much preferred for coast defence generally, and specially for this arrangement of mounting and working.

The 'protected Barbette' system has been very favourably received, and a large number of guns are already mounted in different countries on this system. The 100-ton guns now being erected at Gibraltar and Malta are mounted on this plan, only that on account of the great size and weight of the guns and their projectiles all the movements for training the gun, working the loading appliances, and bringing up the shot, &c., are carried out by hydraulic appliances.

W. G. ARMSTRONG & CO.

III.

ORGANISATION AND CONSTITUTION OF THE LOCAL MILITARY FORCES OF SOUTH AUSTRALIA.

Volunteer Military Force.

The Volunteer military force is, to all intents and purposes, a Volunteer militia. Drill is compulsory, and the men are paid for attendance.

It is raised and organised under 'The Volunteer Act, 1865-66,' and the General Rules and Regulations made thereunder.

The Governor in Council, by this Act, may raise a Volunteer force not exceeding 1,000 men, exclusive of officers; also, a Reserve force (formed of men who have served for a period of at least three years in the Volunteer force) of similar strength.

The officers of the Volunteer and Reserve forces are appointed by the Governor in Council on the recommendation of the Commandant.

Any officer of the local military forces may at any time be called upon to retire, or his services be dispensed with, on account of misconduct, want of efficiency, &c.

Previous to appointment to the position of an officer, every candidate has to pass an examination.

Promotions are made by seniority tempered by selection.

Regulations are framed for the retirement of officers after reaching a certain age, fixed according to the rank held.

Non-commissioned officers are appointed by the Commandant after test examinations.

Discipline.

The Governor in Council may make, repeal, alter, or vary such general rules and regulations as may be expedient for the maintenance, discipline, and training of the Volunteer and Reserve forces, and by such rules and regulations may define offences and fix the punishment thereof by fine or imprisonment; but no fine is to exceed ten pounds, except for breach of engagement when called out for service, the fine for which shall not exceed fifty pounds (50*l*.) ; and no period of imprisonment shall exceed the term of forty-two days.

The Governor in Council, or the officer commanding the Volunteer force, may, at any time, order a Court of Inquiry to assemble.

Any commissioned officer in command of any body of men of the Volunteer or Reserve forces, may summarily order any member of such body to be imprisoned for any period not exceeding one day, or may inflict a fine not exceeding two days' pay.

The Commandant has the power of summary dismissal ; also the power of reducing non-commissioned officers to the ranks.

Enrolment, &c.

A Volunteer enrols for three years, and is not allowed to resign unless on account of ill-health or wishing to leave the Colony. If, however, a member has to go in search of work, or removes to another part of the Colony, he is placed on permanent leave, and would not, as long as absent from head-quarters, be required to join the colours unless the force were called out for active service.

Persons are not enrolled in the Volunteer force under 17 or above 35, except trumpeters and buglers. They are subjected to an examination by a medical officer of the force as to chest measurement, sight, and physique generally ; there is no particular standard as to height.

Time-expired men can re-enrol for a second or third period of service in the Volunteer force or reserve if approved by the Commandant, who is the only officer who has power to enrol, and receives a special commission as enrolling officer.

A re-enrolled or reserve force man wears distinguishing badges.

The officer commanding the force may order such parades as he may consider necessary, provided that no part of the cavalry or infantry shall be called out for more than thirty-six whole or seventy-two half-days in one year, nor the artillery more than forty-eight whole or ninety-six half-days in a year, and the reserve not more than twelve times in one year. A half-day's parade must not be less than two hours or exceed four hours, for which half a day's pay is granted.[1]

A day's pay is given for any period over four hours; but if men parade for either a full or half day, and the parade has to be broken off on account of weather, they will receive their pay.

A member of the force absent without leave from parade not only loses his pay for that parade, but is fined an equivalent amount; if absent for five consecutive parades without leave, unless on account of ill-health, he is liable to a fine of 5*l*., or ten days' imprisonment. Volunteers are likewise subject to fines, or in default imprisonment, for drunkenness and other offences against discipline.

Liabilities.

The Governor in Council, in the event of an invasion of the Colony, or of imminent danger thereof, may embody and call out the whole or any part of the Reserve or Volunteer force for actual military service in the Colony.

When called out for actual military service these forces (except as regards the infliction of corporal punishment or death) are subject to the Army Discipline Act.

RIFLE VOLUNTEER FORCE.
(*Late Rifle Association.*)

The Rifle Volunteer force is raised and organised under '*The Rifle Companies Act,* 1878.'

The Volunteer military force is practically all concentrated at Adelaide; the Rifle Volunteer force is composed of small companies, of not less than twenty, formed in townships throughout the Colony; hence there is an unusual number of officers in proportion to the number of rank and file.

---

[1] Officers from 15*s*. to 8*s*. 6*d*. per whole day. Non-commissioned officers and privates from 8*s*. to 5*s*. per whole day. Half these amounts for half days.

The officers are elected by the men, but subject to the approval of the Governor in Council.

All officers and sergeants are required to pass a test examination within one year of appointment, or resign. Examinations are likewise required previous to promotion to higher ranks.

The Governor in Council has supreme control over the Rifle Volunteer force, and may dissolve the force, or any company, or dispense with the services of any officer, if need be. Subject to the above control the Rifle Volunteer force is governed by a council of nine members, elected annually at a meeting of delegates from rifle companies convened by the inspecting officer.

The council may make rules not inconsistent with the Act, which rules, when approved by the Governor in Council and gazetted, have the force of law.

In like manner the Governor in Council may make regulations.

An inspecting officer is appointed by the Governor in Council. This officer is the channel of communication between the Government and the Council; is an *ex officio* member of the Council; keeps the official list of the force, affidavits of members, &c.; approves resignations, transfers, &c.; issues certificate of enrolment to companies; issues arms, accoutrements, ammunition, prize money, capitation grant, &c.; submits the names of officers for approval; conducts examination of officers and sergeants; is responsible that capitation grant is only given to 'efficients'; inspects each company twice per annum, and has the power of reducing any non-commissioned officer to the ranks.

Enrolment, &c.

Any able-bodied man may enrol in this force, if approved by the captain of the company, by taking an affidavit before a justice of the peace.

Any member of the force may resign, on the expiration of three months, after having given written notice to the inspecting officer.

Members of this force do not receive any pay, except a capitation grant of thirty shillings to each 'efficient.' The

Government also provide each member with a Martini-Henry rifle (on loan), accoutrements, and one hundred rounds of ammunition per annum, targets for the companies, and 200*l.* per annum prize-money. Members are allowed to purchase ammunition from the Government magazine at cost price.

Members have to drill ten times a year, in addition to two inspections and the ordinary class-firing.

Discipline is preserved and enforced by the rules made by the Council and approved by the Governor in Council. Fines and expulsion are made use of.

Members provide their own uniform, the pattern for which is fixed by the Council, who also decide upon the distribution of the Government prize-money, and arrange everything connected with the annual rifle matches.

Liabilities.

The Governor in Council, in the event of invasion, rebellion, &c., has power to call out the Rifle Volunteer force for actual military service in the Colony. The force would then be under the command of the officer commanding the South Australian military forces; and, similarly to the Volunteer military forces, would be subject to the Army Discipline Act.

Any member neglecting to obey such call would be subject to a penalty of 50*l.* and three months' imprisonment.

M. F. DOWNES, Colonel R.A., Commandant.

ADELAIDE: *December* 15, 1881.

IV.

ANSWERS FURNISHED BY COMMANDANT, SOUTH AUSTRALIA, TO QUESTIONS ADDRESSED TO HIM BY SIR PETER SCRATCHLEY.

1. *Question.*—*As to the difficulty of enforcing the stringent regulations in force for the Government of the South Australian Volunteer Military Force.*

Answer.—

I do not find the slightest difficulty in enforcing the regulations under which the Volunteer Military Force serves. The secret of this is, that the men are fully aware that they will be enforced, and, consequently, few break the rules. Also, those proposing to join the force now know well the nature of the service for which they intend to engage, and would not do so unless they were disposed to conform to the regulations. When the force was, in a fit of enthusiasm, first formed in 1877 many joined on the spur of the moment to whom all discipline was obnoxious. During the first twelve months I weeded out such in large numbers, and for a time the newspapers teemed with complaints of 'martinet discipline,' 'forcing volunteers to maintain the discipline of regulars,' and such like. All this has for three years or more been a thing of the past. The force is thoroughly respected, and respects itself. For more than six months I have had practically to stop recruiting, otherwise my numbers would exceed the strength allowed by Parliament.

If allowed, I could soon raise 500 more men in Adelaide alone. Very many of those whose term of three years has expired have re-enrolled for another term or passed into the Reserve force.

2. *Question.—As to the number, &c., of convictions before Police Courts.*

Answer.—

I enclose a return of all those who have been summoned before the Police Court since I came.

3. *Question.—As to the desirability or otherwise of granting a Capitation Allowance to Rifle Companies.*

Answer.—

If it is considered that the primary object of the rifle companies is to encourage rifle shooting, there is no need of a capitation grant. If, however, as I consider, 'discipline' (by which I understand the knowledge of drill and all the moral influences combined which tend to make a soldier) is of primary, and rifle-shooting but of secondary, importance, then the capitation grant will afford a powerful aid towards promotion of the former.

APPENDIX A.

Vide regulations lately issued by the South Australian Government to govern the allotment of the capitation grant which has been just sanctioned by the Parliament for the Rifle Volunteer force.

However, if a force of this nature is about to be formed, I would not commence by giving the capitation grant. The first rush of enthusiasm for a novelty will do a great deal in the way of discipline, if rightly guided, as well as of rifle shooting. Then when zeal begins to languish—when, as will invariably be the case, the cry is raised, 'Give us some more privileges'—the Government can yield to the cry on the one hand, and, on the other, have a most favourable opportunity of tightening up the screw and making the force the more reliable as a military body.

I consider that the rifle companies are doing a good work in South Australia, especially in the country districts, by not only giving men some idea of a salutary discipline and the knowledge of arms, but by finding employment for many of the idle hours for which otherwise the public-houses would be the only source of amusement. And it appears to me that this movement, combined with the system of drill now enforced in all the Government schools, will greatly popularise the use of arms to the rising and future generations, and thus promote throughout the country a strong spirit and capability of 'defence'—not 'offence'—which might otherwise altogether languish away through disuse, and in consequence of never seeing anything of a military nature.

It is a movement, I think, well suited to the genius and instincts of the Anglo-Saxon race when forming new Colonies.

4. *Question.—As to the desirability of appointing a Travelling Instructor for the Rifle Companies.*

Answer.—

I do not think travelling instructors would answer for the rifle companies; it would entail great expense to Government, and few non-commissioned officers are strong enough to withstand for any length of time the incessant temptation to which they would be exposed by the hospitality of members of the companies. Neither could they enforce attendance, and the drills would become very perfunctory. They themselves would be apt to get very slack in carrying out their duties with no one to overlook them.

The Government of South Australia have just sanctioned the appointment of an Officer Instructor to the rifle companies. This officer's principal duty will be, at the time of the inspections (twice a year), to visit each company and give elementary lectures to officers and men, besides assistance on parade; to assist companies within reach at their ordinary parades, the dates of which are all previously sent to me; also during the year to give courses of lectures open to all in Adelaide, and form classes of officers for instruction.

I think that by these means, and by the examination of officers and sergeants, which is now compulsory, I shall have no difficulty in obtaining the amount of elementary knowledge required.

M. F. DOWNES, Col. R.A., Commandant.

ADELAIDE: *December* 1881.

V.

QUEENSLAND VOLUNTEER FORCE.

EXTRACTS FROM REPORT OF MILITARY COMMITTEE (MARCH 7, 1882).

THE Committee are unanimously of opinion that the present condition of the force is not satisfactory; that the attendance of officers and men at drill and parade is, as a rule, very irregular; that the force, generally, is losing ground; and that it cannot, under the present system, be made efficient for the purposes of defence. This opinion is supported by the testimony of the officers commanding corps, batteries, and companies, as contained in their replies to the questions addressed to them by the President. The Commandant and the officers commanding the several branches of the force are also of the same opinion,

The unsatisfactory condition of the force, it is alleged, has been brought about by a variety of causes, of which the following may be specially mentioned :—(*a*) uncertainty in the action of the Legislature of the Colony; (*b*) the abolition of Land Orders; (*c*) the subsequent introduction, for one year only, of direct payment; (*d*) the sudden withdrawal of this payment; (*e*) the knowledge that volunteers in the Colonies of New South Wales and South Australia were receiving pay; and (*f*) the inability of the officers to enforce the regulations, which were framed to apply to a system based on the principle of paying for services rendered.

The experience of Queensland, that a fairly satisfactory defence force cannot be maintained by a purely volunteer system, is not singular. In the province of South Australia it was found necessary, many years ago, to introduce the system of payment; and in the Colony of New South Wales, notwithstanding the large community from which volunteers could be drawn, the Legislature has been obliged to introduce a somewhat similar, but more expensive system. The feeling of enthusiasm which prompts the enrolment of volunteers gradually dies out, and, in times of peace, when there seems to be no immediate necessity for the existence of a force for the protection of the country, there arises, sooner or later, a reluctance on the part of those who have enrolled themselves to devote time and energy without receipt of an equivalent. This is more especially the case in countries like Queensland, where the population is comparatively small, and the force must necessarily be recruited almost entirely from the wage-earning portion of the community, who cannot afford to give up any substantial part of their time without some pecuniary recompense. In view of this condition of things, and of the feelings common to all classes, that time and energy, unless in cases of special emergency, cannot fairly be demanded for the benefit of the country without some return for the work done, competent military authorities are unanimous in testifying as to the necessity of reverting to payment if a defence force is to be made really efficient. With this opinion the Committee think that the system at present existing in this

Colony is of little, if any, protective value. The Committee are of opinion that it would be useless to continue it, and that satisfactory results can be obtained only by introducing a pay system. They are, however, fully impressed with the absolute necessity of exercising very great economy in introducing changes. They assume that the circumstances of the Colony would not, for the present, warrant the establishment of a permanent paid body of men, which is obviously the most perfect form of defence force; and that the object now to be attained is to secure, at the least possible expense to the State, a number of men that will be fairly serviceable in the case of need, and thus render profitable the large expenditure that has already been incurred in the purchase of material and in the construction of works of defence.

After anxious and careful consideration of the conditions that exist in the other Australian Colonies, and of the various systems there in force, the Committee are of opinion that the circumstances of this Colony more nearly resemble those of the Province of South Australia than those of any other country, and that the organisation of the military forces that has prevailed for some years in that Province, and has been found to work with very satisfactory results, could, with some modification, be adopted with success in Queensland, without increasing the annual expenditure for defence purposes to any serious extent.

In South Australia the Volunteer force is divided into three classes: (1) a Volunteer Militia, confined to the metropolis, who are paid for attendance, and for whom drill is compulsory; (2) a Reserve Force, formed of men who have served for a period of at least three years in the Militia; and (3) Rifle Companies, of not less than 20 men, formed in townships throughout the Province.

The Committee recommend that a similar classification be adopted in Queensland, and that the Volunteer force should be remodelled as follows:—

1st. That a branch of the force, to be called Volunteer Militia, who shall be paid a moderate sum for their services, be concentrated in Brisbane under the supervision of a permanent staff of officers and instructors, the officers and men being placed under stricter military discipline, and being compelled to attend a specified number of daylight and moonlight drills, as well as a period of continuous training in camp every year.

2nd. That the country and coast corps be maintained, as far as practicable, at their present authorised strength, under the name of Volunteer Artillery Batteries and Rifle Companies, and subject to regulations exacting less frequent attendance at drills, and having for their primary object the attainment by the men, under salutary discipline, of a fair knowledge of arms.

3rd. That a reserve force, of the same strength as the Militia, be hereafter established, to be composed of men who have served as efficients with the Militia for a specified term of years, and to be affiliated to that branch of the force.

To give effect to the foregoing recommendations, the Committee propose that the present volunteer regulations be rescinded, and that a new set of regulations be adopted—under legislative sanction if necessary—embodying the following provisions:—

For the Volunteer Militia.

1. That there shall be established a force of . . . a standard being fixed of age, height, and physique.

2. That each member shall enrol for three years, and that he shall not be allowed to resign unless on account of ill health or being compelled to leave Queensland or to reside in a remote part of the Colony.

3. That there shall be 4 full-day, 8 half-day, and 12 moonlight drills, besides 6 days' continuous training in camp in each year; and that the standard of efficiency shall be so fixed that no member shall be classed as efficient unless, besides attending the regulated course of musketry or gunnery instruction and class-firing, he shall have attended at least two-thirds of the daylight and one-half of the moonlight drills, and have taken part in four out of six days of camp training.

4. That members shall be paid according to the following scale:—

	£	s.	
Lieutenant-Colonels	16	0	per annum
Majors	12	0	,,
Captains	10	0	,,
Lieutenants	9	0	,,
Sergeant-Majors and Quarter-master Sergeants	8	0	,,
Sergeants	7	10	,,
Bombardiers, 2nd, and Lance Corporals	7	0	,,
Corporals	6	10	,,
Privates	6	0	,,

One third of such payments to be made by equal quarterly instalments after services rendered; another third to be paid for attendance at camp; and the remaining third to be paid at the end of each year as a bonus for efficient service.

5. That the appointment of commissioned officers be by the Governor in Council; that no person shall be so appointed who has not passed a satisfactory test examination; and that promotions shall be made by seniority, tempered by selection, according to merit.

6. That non-commissioned officers shall be appointed by the Commandant after test examinations.

For Volunteer Artillery Batteries and Rifle Companies.

1. That volunteer batteries and rifle companies, of not less than 25 officers and men, may be formed and maintained in different townships throughout the Colony, so that the aggregate number of men enrolled does not for the present exceed 660.

2. That the officers of batteries and companies may be elected by the men, subject to the approval of the Governor in Council.

3. That all officers, both commissioned and non-commissioned, shall pass a test examination within one year after their appointment; and that promotions shall not be made until after such examination has been passed.

4. That each member shall, in addition to attending his

ordinary class-firing, be required to attend at least ten drills, besides two inspections, in each year.

5. That members shall be at liberty to resign upon giving three months' previous notice in writing of their intention.

In recommending that, for the present at all events, the paid members of the force should be concentrated in Brisbane, the Committee have been influenced by military considerations alone. Experience has proved that a paid force, to prove efficient, must be trained and administered under the immediate supervision of qualified military officers; and an extension of the pay system to the country districts and coast towns would render it necessary to increase the paid staff to such an extent as the results obtained would not fairly warrant. . . .

With regard to the officers of the paid force, the Committee recommend that the present plan of appointing officers after election by the men, be abolished; and that, in remodelling the force, only those officers should be selected who are thoroughly qualified. Candidates for new appointments and promotions should be required to pass test examinations, and to display a satisfactory knowledge of field fortification, reconnaissance, and minor tactics.

In order that the officers may be properly educated, the Committee strongly recommend the establishment of a school of instruction, in which the Commandant and the other staff officers shall perform the duties of instructors, each officer being required to go through a course of instruction suitable to the branch of the service in which he is serving, for which he should be granted certificates of proficiency. The Committee also recommend that, as necessary adjuncts to the school of instruction, there should be established, in some convenient position in Brisbane, under the control of the Commandant, a military library and reading and lecture rooms; and that a small annual grant should be made to provide for the purchase of books and other expenses in connection with the reading-room. Much good would also result if lectures and discussions on military subjects were encouraged.

In the case of artillery batteries and rifle companies, the

Committee recommend that the elective principle for the appointment of commissioned officers be maintained. The success of these bodies of men will mainly depend upon the personal influence of the officers, and, by making provisions that elections shall be subject to the approval of the Governor in Council, sufficient protection will be secured against the appointment of unsuitable persons.

The Committee are of opinion that the maintenance of annual camps of instruction is indispensable for the success of the paid force. In these camps the whole of the force have the advantage of combined training and work, under strict discipline, extending over a number of days, from which beneficial results may ensue. The Committee, however, do not recommend that the unpaid forces be required to attend at the camps of instruction, or that such camps should be established in the country or coast districts. The main object of a camp is to complete the efficiency of trained bodies by combined training and work during a limited period. This cannot be secured when the number of men is small, and where, as would be the case with artillery batteries and rifle companies, the knowledge of drill is necessarily imperfect.

As one of the main objects of the instruction of both the paid and unpaid branches of the force should be to secure proficiency in the use of the weapons entrusted to them, the Committee are of opinion that the utmost possible provision and inducement should be made for the attainment of such proficiency. They, accordingly, recommend that money should be voted annually for the erection and maintenance of suitable targets at all places where artillery batteries and rifle companies are established. Liberal grants should also be made for prizes at annual competitions; and the number of rounds of small ammunition to be devoted to class-firing should be increased from the present amount of 60 rounds per man to, at least, 100 rounds. . . . .

The ammunition available for small arms is very insufficient. The Committee are of opinion that the reserve should never be allowed to fall below 500,000 rounds.

The Committee find that large quantities of ammunition, purchased by money voted for volunteer purposes, are sold to the police and other persons; and that the moneys derived from such sales are paid into the credit of the general revenue. The Committee suggest that the annual estimate should, if possible, be so framed as to make it apparent how much of the vote for ammunition is expended for volunteer purposes alone.

. . . .

In conclusion, the Committee concur in the recommendation of the Military and Royal Commissions of New South Wales, that an imperial officer of standing should be appointed as inspecting officer of the Australian local forces and military adviser to the several Governments. This Colony's share of the cost of employing such an officer would be insignificant, whilst the advantages to be gained by his presence in the colonies are so obvious that it is unnecessary to detail them.

VI.

NEW SOUTH WALES COMMISSION.

I.

RECOMMENDATIONS OF THE MILITARY COMMITTEE WITH REGARD TO THE APPOINTMENT, PROMOTION, AND EDUCATION OF OFFICERS.

(i.) With regard to the Permanent Artillery officers, the Committee are of opinion that preference of appointment should be given to officers who have served in the Royal Artillery, but that the junior grades should be open to ex-Imperial officers of other branches of the service, and especially to candidates identified with the Colonies. The Committee submit these proposals on the understanding that the regulations in regard to qualifying examinations, with limit as to time, are strictly carried out.

As to the education of officers the Committee are unanimous in recommending that a school for instruction, with the necessary instructors, be formed in order that officers may attain a defined standard of military knowledge. Instruction to be conducted by qualified officers, and to include such subjects as reconnaissance, field-sketching, surveying, field fortification, minor tactics, elementary chemistry, and mathematics.

(ii.) With respect to the officers of the other branches of the local forces the Committee recommend—

    (*a*) That the nomination or elective principle for the appointment of commissioned officers be abolished, and that the present laws, as to candidates being obliged to produce a certificate of having passed either the Civil Service test examination or one of a higher degree, should continue in force.

    (*b*) That, prior to promotion, officers should, as at present, pass an examination as to fitness for higher command; and that some knowledge of field fortification, reconnaissance, and minor tactics be required.

(iii.) Whilst the Committee, with a view to economy, recommend, for the present, one school of instruction, they consider that all officers of the local forces should be required to go through a course suitable to the branch in which they are serving, embracing such subjects as minor tactics, field fortifications, surveying, and reconnaissance; and for which they should be granted certificates of proficiency.

(iv.) The Committee strongly recommend that a military library and a reading and lecture room should be established in some convenient position in Sydney, subject to the control of the commandant, and that an annual grant should be made for the purchase of books and the expenses of the reading-room. In the opinion of the Committee much good would result if lectures and discussions on military subjects were encouraged.

II.

SUGGESTIONS OF THE MILITARY COMMITTEE ON SUNDRY SUBJECTS RELATING TO THE ORGANISATION AND EQUIPMENT OF THE LOCAL FORCES.

The Committee desire to allude to a proposal which has been brought before the Committee by Colonel Anderson, to the effect that a general assembly of the Australian local forces should take place at some convenient place during Easter week of 1882. It is believed that there would be no difficulty in assembling from five to six thousand men for general manœuvres. It is scarcely possible to exaggerate on military grounds alone the importance of such a muster, as affording an opportunity for showing the military training and mobility of the several local forces of Her Majesty's Governments in Australia. The effect of demonstrating the military strength available for the defence of any one Colony attacked is not to be overlooked as a powerful argument in favour of the proposal.

Supply of Ammunition.—The supply of ammunition in time of war is a subject which the Committee consider should not be overlooked by the Royal Commission, and the majority recommend that steps should be taken to purchase a plant for the purpose of making up small arm ammunition. Colonel Downes suggests the establishment of a central arsenal for all the Colonies.

Supply and Distribution of Water and Ammunition in the Field and Ambulances.—The supply and distribution of water and ammunition to troops in the field, and the establishment of ambulances, are matters of the highest importance, which should engage the attention of the Colonial military authorities.

Commissariat Supplies.—The Committee see no difficulty in arranging for the commissariat supplies to troops in the field, and consider it unnecessary to make any recommendation on the subject.

VII.

VICTORIAN GOVERNMENT DEFENCE SCHEME.

RESOLUTIONS PASSED BY THE OFFICERS OF THE VOLUNTEER FORCE AT A GENERAL MEETING.

1. That the officers of the Volunteer Force adhere to the opinion so frequently expressed by them during the last ten or twelve years that a complete reorganisation of the system of defence for the Colony should be made, and that it is most desirable to take advantage of the opportunity offered by the proposed discussion in Parliament of the Government Defence Scheme to get the question satisfactorily settled on a permanent basis.

2. That the officers present decidedly approve of the proposed system of obtaining the services of Imperial officers and non-commissioned officers 'seconded,' for five years for the purpose of giving instruction to the officers and non-commissioned officers of the new force, and of establishing a military school for the education and training of future officers; but they are of opinion that the Imperial officers 'seconded' other than the Commandant should not be entitled to take command.

3. That the Volunteer officers strongly recommend that a special appropriation for the Defence Scheme be provided for five years at least.

4. That in the opinion of the officers present the Government Defence Scheme is capable of improvement in some of its details.

5. That it would be an improvement if provision be immediately made for the establishment of a Reserve.

6. That provision be made in the new Defence Bill for the completion by compulsory enrolment of the number of men provided for on the Government Scheme, should the voluntary enrolment be insufficient, and that power be taken by the Governor in Council to increase the number if necessary to 10,000 men in time of war.

7. That the allowance to commanding officers for maintenance, uniforms, incidentals, &c., be 30s. per head on the established strength, in addition to 20s. per head for efficients in Infantry corps, and 30s. per head for efficients in other branches of the service.

8. That the men be paid for attendance at parades and drills on the following scale :—

	£.	s.	d.
Maximum—20 half days, at 4s.	4	0	0
6 whole days, at 8s.	2	8	0
36 night drills, at 2s.	3	12	0
	10	0	0

That the payment be made quarterly, and that men shall be paid for the parades and drills they attend, irrespective of the number present. That the minimum scale for pay and efficiency might be :—

	£.	s.	d.
15 half days, at 4s.	3	0	0
3 whole days, at 8s.	1	4	0
24 night drills, at 2s.	2	8	0
	6	12	0

and that the pay for officers and non-commissioned officers be similarly arranged on the basis of the amounts proposed by Major Sargood.

9. That in the opinion of this meeting it is desirable that the cavalry be increased to 180 men, with the same proportion of officers as in the Imperial service.

10. That the Naval Reserve be continued as at present, both as to work and pay.

11. That it is considered unnecessary to fix any minimum attendance for parades and drills.

12. That the proportion of officers should be not less than in the Imperial service.

13. That the proposed ages for the retirement of officers be increased by five years.

14. That in the temporary absence of the Commandant the senior Victorian officer should take command.

15. That if a general inspecting officer for all the Colonies be appointed, he should be 'seconded,' as in the case of the Commandant.

16. That it is desirable that the control of the V.R.A. Ranges be left in the hands of the Victorian Rifle Association.

(Signed) J. M. TEMPLETON, Major, Chairman.

Report of the Non-Commissioned Officers of the 2nd Battalion Metropolitan Rifles.

Memo.—The non-commissioned officers of the 2nd Battalion Metropolitan Rifles have submitted a report to their commanding officer, Major Templeton, from which the following extracts are taken :—

'The Volunteer Force, as at present constituted, is of little value for the defence of the Colony.

'It is deemed desirable to pay the men for their attendance at drills, &c.'

Then follow several suggestions similar to those from the officers, and the report closes as follows :—

'In the opinion of the non-commissioned officers of the 2nd Metropolitan Battalion Red Rifles, if the alterations here recommended with reference to the rate of pay and the hours of drill be adopted, the Government Scheme of reorganisation will produce a really effective force for the defence of the Colony.'

(Signed) SERGEANT GLEADHILL, R.R., Secretary.

MELBOURNE: *5th September*, 1883.

VIII.

MILITARY TORPEDO CORPS.

MAJOR ELLERY'S MEMORANDUM.

The following suggestions refer solely to *defensive* as distinct from *offensive* torpedoes, and appliances.

A very clear distinction on this point is desirable, and it will be absolutely necessary that everything pertaining to fixed torpedoes for the defence of our channels shall be kept separate from *offensive* torpedoes, or such as it may be necessary to improvise for the temporary protection of floating defences; and that all stores, appliances, &c., fixed or floating, for training or actual torpedo defence, shall, as in the case of Great Britain and the other colonies, pertain solely at all times to the Defensive Torpedo Corps it is now proposed to organise.

Suggestions.

1. That a Defensive Torpedo Corps, of from 80 to 100 officers and men, be organised under the 'Discipline Act.'

This force should consist of three sections—namely, scientific, artisan, and boatman sections. The first section is already available in the present Torpedo and Signal Corps; the second can be readily raised in and around Melbourne; and the third from among seafaring men, and the fishermen in and around Queenscliff.

For the training of this corps, I propose there should be weekly drills at a depôt to be formed at Williamstown, and quarterly practice in the channels to be defended. As the part of the boat section which may be raised at Queenscliff could not well attend the weekly drills at Williamstown, it will be necessary to make special arrangements for drilling such members at Swan Island in the intervals between quarterly drills.

2. That a training depôt be formed at Williamstown, where there should be the requisite appliances for practice in all

branches of the work. These must comprise a shed and yard for fitting up torpedoes prior to their removal to Swan Island depôt, a torpedo-laying steamer, one or two boats, &c.

3. The main depôt at Swan Island should provide for the storage of the cables as well as the torpedoes and fittings, and also of the necessary stock of gun-cotton.

4. That the material and appliances necessary to carry out a torpedo defence of the West and South Channels on the modified scheme at present contemplated should be at once procured by importation from England or manufacture in the colony, and that, in order to determine what is still required, that I be furnished with a list of all torpedo material for defensive operations now in possession of the Government.

5. That all the necessary material and appliances shall be placed under the charge of the reorganised Torpedo and Signal Corps.

6. That drawings and specifications for all such material and appliances as can be economically and efficiently made in the colony be prepared, and tenders called for the immediate supply of the same.

Suggested Constitution of the re-organised Torpedo and Signal Corps.

1 Major Commanding	per annum	£150
2 Captains	at £60 ,,	120
3 Lieutenants	at 40 ,,	120
5 Sergeants	at 20 ,,	100
3 Corporals	at 15 ,,	45
20 Scientific Section Electricians, &c.	at 16 ,,	320
50 Privates, viz.: 25 Artisans } 25 Boatmen }	at 12 ,,	600
1 Bugler	at 12 ,,	12
1 Drill Instructor and Storekeeper	at 10s. per day	180
1 Coxswain	at 7s. 6d. per day	138
Uniforms		150
Contingent Expenses		200
		£2,135

This force might be increased to 100 strong in times of preparing for defence by being supplemented by 13 rank and

APPENDIX A. 405

file of the Permanent Artillery, who might also assist, in time of peace, in the care and maintenance of the Torpedo Depôt at Swan Island.

N.B.—It is very desirable that the drill instructor and storekeeper be obtained from the Torpedo School at Chatham.

IX.

NAVAL ASSISTANCE AFFORDED TO THE AUSTRALIAN COLONIES, NEW ZEALAND, AND TASMANIA, DURING THE PAST FIVE YEARS (1881-86).

IN THE MATTER OF GUNS, TORPEDOES, WARLIKE STORES, AND SERVICES CONNECTED THEREWITH, SO FAR AS KNOWN IN GUNNERY BRANCH.

1881.

H.M.S. *Wolverene* was transferred as a free gift to the New South Wales Government, and the armament, ammunition, and other War Office stores on board the vessel were at the same time presented to the colony. The full value of these stores was estimated at 8,700*l*.

A supply of friction tubes was made to the Colony of New Zealand in repayment with consent of the Admiralty.

Admiralty consent was given for the supply to the Victorian Government of four Nordenfelts out of an order given to Mr. Nordenfelt on Admiralty behalf by the War Department.

1882.

Twenty copies of Vol. II. of the Torpedo Manual were supplied to New Zealand. It is not known that any claim for repayment was put forward.

1884.

In the early part of 1884, the Agent-General for Victoria requested that a 15-inch 19-foot torpedo might be supplied for the Colonial torpedo vessel *Childers*, and at their Lordships'

E E

instance a torpedo of this nature was sold to the Victorian Government for 420*l*.

At the request of the Agent-General for Victoria, the Commodore in Australia was authorised to transfer an 18-ton gun (10-inch M.L.) from H.M.S. *Nelson* to the Victorian war-vessel *Cerberus* in place of one damaged. It is understood that the War Department has dealt with this question as a repayment service.

In April and May of this year, when preparations were being made in view of a possible war, the Commander-in-Chief, Australia, supplied (on repayment) to the Colony of New Zealand eight 64-pr. M.L. guns, some submarine mines, and other warlike stores from the Naval Reserves at Sydney. The Colonial Government subsequently expressed a wish to return the guns, and this was acceded to.

The value of the stores supplied amounted to 5,084*l*. 13*s*. 4*d*., including 3,000*l*. for the guns to be returned.

1885.

Certain War Office stores, of which precise details are not yet to hand, were at the same time supplied by Admiral Tryon to the Queensland Government, and will be either paid for or returned. The Colonial gunboat *Gayundah* has also, at the request of the Governor, been permitted to draw stores (on repayment) from Sydney Depôt.

The supply of torpedoes to the Governments of New South Wales, New Zealand, South Australia, and Tasmania was facilitated by the Admiralty during the summer of 1885, and the torpedoes purchased by the various Colonies have been inspected during manufacture and tested by Admiralty officers in a similar manner to those ordered by the Imperial Government. Facilities for freight were also afforded.

1881–1886.

Drawings and advice as to torpedo gear, air-compressing machines, &c., have been on various occasions furnished to the Australian Colonies when required, and confidential manuals and reports have been from time to time supplied to New Zealand, Queensland, New South Wales, and Victoria, Tasmania, and South Australia.

Pensioned torpedo artificers have been recently selected for the service of Queensland and New Zealand, and have received instructions in their duties on board H.M.S. *Vernon*. Similar instructional facilities were afforded in the case of Mr. Matthieson, R.E., appointed Torpedo Director of Tasmania.

Permission was granted in the summer of 1885 for a party of two officers and four men in the Queensland service to undergo a torpedo course on board H.M.S. *Nelson*.

Various applications on behalf of colonies for War Office stores and assistance connected therewith have been referred to the War Department, and have been dealt with by that Department.

X.

ASSISTANCE GIVEN TO THE AUSTRALIAN COLONIES NEW ZEALAND, AND TASMANIA, IN THE MATTER OF GUNS AND OTHER MILITARY STORES, DURING THE FIVE YEARS 1881-86.

Year	Details	Value	Total Value
	GIFTS ISSUED AT REDUCED PRICES.	£ s. d.	£ s. d.
1881-82	WESTERN AUSTRALIA: Certain military stores left behind on the disbandment in October 1880 of the pensioner force in the Colony	1,500 0 0	1,500 0 0
,,	NEW SOUTH WALES: The armament, ammunition, and military stores of H.M.S. *Wolverene*	8,700 0 0	8,700 0 0
1884-85	TASMANIA: Two 80-pr. R.M.L. converted guns with carriages and ammunition complete, required for the defence of Hobart	576 13 2	
,,	300 additional rounds of ammunition for the 80-pr. guns	240 0 0	
1885-86	The free conversion of 5' 8" smooth-bore guns into 64-pr. R.M.L. guns	745 0 0	1,561 13 2
	STORES ISSUED AT REDUCED PRICES.		
1884-85	QUEENSLAND: Four 9-pr. 8 cwt. R.M.L. ordnance, with carriages, limbers, projectiles, &c., issued at a total charge of 700*l.*	700 0 0	700 0 0
1885-86	NEW ZEALAND: Six 9-pr. R.B.L. guns, with carriages, limbers, projectiles, &c., at a total cost of 900*l.*	900 0 0	900 0 0

XI.

STATEMENT OF THE VALUE OF WARLIKE STORES ON REPAYMENT TO THE AUSTRALIAN COLONIES, NEW ZEALAND, AND TASMANIA, FOR WHICH CLAIMS HAVE BEEN MADE DURING THE FIVE YEARS ENDING MARCH 31, 1886.

ISSUED FROM ENGLAND.

Stores	Queensland	Western Australia	South Australia	New South Wales	Victoria	Tasmania	New Zealand
Guns.	£	£	£	£	£	£	£
1881–82	—	—	—	—	—	—	—
1882–83	—	—	—	—	—	—	—
1883–84	—	—	—	—	—	—	—
1884–85	—	—	—	—	2,122	—	—
1885–86	700	—	—	—	—	—	—
Rifles.							
1881–82	363	—	2,100	151	614	69	—
1882–83	3,151	—	2,155	—	—	605	—
1883–84	396	331	423	347	4,747	—	—
1884–85	96	54	1,255	347	2,194	550	—
1885–86	6,723	616	182	15,701	16,052	1,407	—
Small Arm Ammunition.							
1881–82	—	—	2,955	—	4,390	35	3,951
1882–83	1,429	—	6,314	4,896	42	670	—
1883–84	—	—	—	—	9,574	25	1,670
1884–85	3,294	—	71	694	737	292	—
1885–86	5,816	793	2,259	102	81	763	2,558
Other Military Stores.							
1881–82	1,589	—	2,891	2,762	156	744	3,559
1882–83	1,147	—	1,935	4,560	—	746	3,707
1883–84	1,356	—	3,108	9,916	10,266	73	—
1884–85	296	286	3,052	11,309	7,879	1,348	91
1885–86	3,804	30	3,726	15,611	7,250	736	5,243
Total	30,160	2,110	32,486	66,486	66,104	8,063	20,779

APPENDIX B.

1. COMMODORE ERSKINE'S PROCLAMATION.

Having received instructions from Her Majesty's Government to proclaim and establish a British Protectorate over the southern shores of New Guinea:

By virtue of the power and authority to me given, I hereby direct that the following regulations are to be strictly complied with, pending the arrival of the High Commissioner:

1. Mr. Deputy Commissioner Romilly, on my departure from the New Guinea coast, will assume temporary charge of the Protectorate, and will exercise the powers and authority vested in him as a Deputy Commissioner.

2. Port Moresby is to be the sole port of entry for goods, &c., within the limits of the Protectorate.

3. Captains of all ships, on arrival at Port Moresby, are hereby required to produce their manifest and papers for the inspection of the Deputy Commissioner, and no spirituous liquors are to be landed without his written consent.

4. A copy of the proclamation is to be handed to the captain of any vessel arriving, together with a copy of these regulations.

5. No firearms, gunpowder, dynamite, or any explosives are to be landed under any circumstances.

6. No settlement or acquisition of land is on any account to be permitted.

7. The captain of any vessel arriving at Port Moresby is hereby required to declare and report if he has any infectious disease on board.

Given under my hand, on board Her Majesty's ship *Nelson*, at Port Moresby, New Guinea, this fourteenth day of November, 1884.

(Signed) JAMES E. ERSKINE.

II. LEASES.

The different applications were for—

1. D'Arrow Island, which is apparently in the hands of a syndicate.
2. (*a*) Deliverance Island, on the north-west coast, latitude 9° 30' S., longitude 141° 35' E.
    (*b*) Bramwell Island, opposite Fly River.
    (*c*) A large tract of land on the Chester River.

The claim to the three last-mentioned places was based on the ground of original discovery.

3. Aro Island.

These applications were all based on the ground of occupancy or original exploration.

(Signed) G. SEYMOUR FORT.

III. LIST OF LANDS APPLIED FOR BY THE NEW GUINEA COMPANY.

Yule Island.—Long. 146° 30' E. This site is sought for the chief station of the company, on which it will erect agricultural mission, farming and trading depôts, &c., as recommended in the 'papers' read at the Royal Colonial Institute, of Signor D'Albertis, Wilfred Powell, Esq. (December 1878, and November 1883.)

Kabadi District.—Long. 146° 40' E. Starting from the eastern bank of Ethel River in line with and about half a mile north of Hall Sound; thence in a straight line east to the Aroa River; thence along the western bank of the Aroa River to the sea-coast.

Coombes River.—Long. 146° 22′ E. Starting from the coast inland along the western bank of this river to the base of Mount Yule; thence along such base of Mount Yule to the Marata River, with a return south to the coast along the eastern bank, and east by the sea-front.

Fly River.—Long. 143° E. From the sea-coast along this meridian N. to the southern bank of the Fly River; thence to the east and west by the said river inner-banks, and along the sea-coast to 143° E.

N.B.—The small island of 'Bampton' or 'Mibu' should be conceded with this plot for security, on which the agricultural mission, trading stores, and schools and workshops on the mainland for Moatta and neighbourhood would then be erected.

Baxter River.—Long. 142° E. From the sea-coast along this meridian N. to the southern bank of the Baxter River; thence around E. and S. within the boundaries of the said river to its mouth, and thence along the coast to 142° E.

N.B.—With this allotment the 'Talbot Island' should be conceded, as, like Plot D, the land is low and swampy, unfitted, without great outlay, to carry erections of a permanent character to constitute, as would be desired, an important and extreme western station; besides, it would be necessary for security, as the district will probably for some time be exposed to native raids and aggressive disturbance.

Bootless Inlet.—Long. 147° 17′ E. Starting at the coast, say two miles west and east of the inlet, carrying the intermediate frontage; thence inland to the Laroki River, with such length of allotment E. and W. thereupon, with the intermediate land, as can be accorded back to the west and east starting-points.

Or, as an alternative plot.—Any other eastern point near Yule, which in the opinion of H.M. High Commissioner would be a desirable station for a township or city eventually, on which the company could create a port, erect wharfages, buildings, and occupy or apportion the inland beneficially for colonisation.

(Signed) NEW GUINEA SYNDICATE.

August 13, 1885.

IV. CONDITIONS UNDER WHICH PERMITS TO TRADE, FELL TIMBER, ETC., WERE GRANTED.

(*a*.) That you keep me and my officers informed of your proceedings on the coast of New Guinea, from time to time sending me the names of the vessels employed.

(*b*.) That the permission hereby given you to remove the timber confers no right to fell any more timber without a fresh permit; this fresh permit, however, cannot be issued until I, or one of my officers, have visited the place where the timber is to be felled.

(*c*.) That you conduct your operations entirely at your own risk, and on the understanding that I, as Her Majesty's Special Commissioner, or any of my officers, undertake no responsibility whatever.

(*d*.) That you agree to obey such Regulations as may from time to time be issued by me for the government of the British territory in New Guinea.

1. I enclose for your information and guidance a copy of the Arms Regulations of 1884, issued by Her Majesty's High Commissioner for the Western Pacific.

2. I have further to inform you that I reserve to myself the right of cancelling this permission; calling upon you to leave the island should you or your agents at any time perform any act which I should consider detrimental to the maintenance of good order and government within the limits of the British territory in New Guinea.

3. You are requested to understand that this case is treated as a special one, and that the exemption from a licence or export duty will not apply to future cases.

(Signed) P. H. SCRATCHLEY.

PRINTED BY
SPOTTISWOODE AND CO., NEW-STREET SQUARE
LONDON

MESSRS. MACMILLAN & CO.'S PUBLICATIONS.

'A book over which it is a pleasure to linger.'—The TIMES.

BY PRINCE ALBERT VICTOR AND PRINCE GEORGE OF WALES.

THE CRUISE OF H.M.S. 'BACCHANTE,' 1879-1882.

Compiled from the Journals, Letters, and Note-Books of PRINCE ALBERT VICTOR AND PRINCE GEORGE OF WALES. With Additions by the Rev. JOHN NEALE DALTON, Canon of Windsor. With Maps, Plans, and Illustrations. Two Vols. Medium 8vo. 52s. 6d.

The TIMES says:—'The work is no mere boyish log of a three years' voyage. We certainly have the faithfully-kept log of day after day's sailing, but that is redeemed from monotony by the genuine and evident interest which the two Royal sailor boys took in every detail of their work. . . . Every page bears evidence of their diligence in collecting information, statistical and other, of the progress and present condition of Victoria and the other colonies.'

MADAGASCAR: an Historical and Descriptive Account of the Island and its former Dependencies. Compiled by SAMUEL PASFIELD OLIVER, F.S.A., F.R.G.S., late Captain Royal Artillery. With Maps. 2 vols. medium 8vo. £2. 12s. 6d.

By J. R. SEELEY, M.A., Regius Professor of Modern History in the University of Cambridge.

LECTURES AND ESSAYS. 8vo. 10s. 6d.

THE EXPANSION OF ENGLAND. Two Courses of Lectures. Crown 8vo. 4s. 6d.

OUR COLONIAL EXPANSION. Extracts from 'The Expansion of England.' Crown 8vo. 1s.

By E. A. FREEMAN, D.C.L., LL.D., Regius Professor of Modern History in the University of Oxford, Fellow of Oriel College, and Hon. Fellow of Trinity College, Oxford.

GREATER GREECE AND GREATER BRITAIN: George Washington the Expander of England. With an Appendix on Imperial Federation. Crown 8vo. 3s. 6d.

THE METHODS OF HISTORICAL STUDY. Eight Lectures read in the University of Oxford in Michaelmas Term, 1884, with the Inaugural Lecture on 'The Office of the Historical Professor.' 8vo. 10s. 6d.

THE CHIEF PERIODS OF EUROPEAN HISTORY. Six Lectures read in the University of Oxford in Trinity Term, 1885, with an Essay on 'Greek Cities under Roman Rule.' 8vo. 10s. 6d.

HISTORICAL ESSAYS. 8vo. First Series. 10s. 6d. Second Series, 10s. 6d. Third Series, 12s.

THE GROWTH OF THE ENGLISH CONSTITUTION FROM THE EARLIEST TIMES. Fourth Edition. Crown 8vo. 5s.

HISTORICAL AND ARCHITECTURAL SKETCHES; chiefly Italian. Illustrated by the Author. Crown 8vo. 10s. 6d.

SUBJECT AND NEIGHBOUR LANDS OF VENICE. Being a Companion Volume to 'Historical and Architectural Sketches.' With Illustrations. Crown 8vo. 10s. 6d.

ENGLISH TOWNS AND DISTRICTS. A Series of Addresses and Essays. With Illustrations and a Map. 8vo. 14s.

OLD ENGLISH HISTORY. With Five Coloured Maps. New Edition, revised. Extra Fcp. 8vo. 6s.

By the RIGHT HONOURABLE JOHN BRIGHT, M.P.

SPEECHES ON QUESTIONS OF PUBLIC POLICY. Edited by Professor THOROLD ROGERS, Second Edition. 2 vols. 8vo. 25s. With Portrait.
Author's Popular Edition. New Edition. Extra fcp. 8vo. 3s. 6d.

PUBLIC ADDRESSES. Edited by J. E. T. ROGERS. 8vo. 14s.

SPEECHES ON QUESTIONS OF PUBLIC POLICY. By RICHARD COBDEN, M.P. Edited by the Right Hon. JOHN BRIGHT, M.P., and JAMES E. THOROLD ROGERS. Extra fcp. 8vo. 3s. 6d.

MACMILLAN & CO., LONDON.

MESSRS. MACMILLAN & CO.'S PUBLICATIONS.

By JOHN RICHARD GREEN, M.A., LL.D.

THE MAKING OF ENGLAND. With Maps. 8vo. 16s.

THE CONQUEST OF ENGLAND. With Maps and Portraits. 8vo. 18s.

HISTORY OF THE ENGLISH PEOPLE. In 4 vols. 8vo.
Vol. I. EARLY ENGLAND, 449–1071—Foreign Kings, 1071–1214—The Charter, 1204–1291—The Parliament, 1307–1461. With Eight Coloured Maps. 8vo. 16s. Vol. II. The Monarchy, 1461–1540—The Reformation, 1540–1603. 8vo. 16s. Vol. III. Puritan England, 1603–1660—The Revolution, 1660–1688. With Four Maps. 8vo. 16s. Vol. IV. The Revolution, 1683–1760—Modern England, 1760–1815. With Maps and Index. 8vo. 16s.

A SHORT HISTORY OF THE ENGLISH PEOPLE. With Coloured Maps, Genealogical Tables, and Chronological Annals. Crown 8vo. 8s. 6d. 122nd Thousand.

By WILLIAM GIFFORD PALGRAVE.

A NARRATIVE OF A YEAR'S JOURNEY THROUGH CENTRAL AND EASTERN ARABIA. 1862–63. Seventh and Cheaper Edition. With Map, Plans, and Portrait of Author, engraved on Steel by JEENS. Crown 8vo. 6s.

ESSAYS ON EASTERN QUESTIONS. 8vo. 10s. 6d.

DUTCH GUIANA. With Map and Plan. 8vo. 9s.

MR. JOHN MORLEY'S COLLECTED WRITINGS. A New Edition. In Nine Volumes. Globe 8vo. Price 5s. each.
VOLTAIRE. One Vol.
DIDEROT AND THE ENCYCLOPÆDISTS. Two Vols.
ROUSSEAU. Two Vols.
ON COMPROMISE. One Vol.
MISCELLANIES. Three Vols.

ON THE STUDY OF LITERATURE. The Annual Address to the Students of the London Society for the Extension of University Teaching. Delivered at the Mansion House, February 26th, 1887. By JOHN MORLEY. Globe 8vo. Cloth. Price 1s. 6d.
*** ALSO AN EDITION, IN PAMPHLET FORM, FOR DISTRIBUTION, PRICE TWOPENCE.

By the Rev. J. P. MAHAFFY, M.A., Fellow of Trinity College, Dublin.

SOCIAL LIFE IN GREECE, FROM HOMER TO MENANDER. Fifth Edition, enlarged. Crown 8vo. 9s.

RAMBLES AND STUDIES IN GREECE. Illustrated. Third Edition, revised and enlarged. Crown 8vo. 10s. 6d.

AN EASTER VACATION IN GREECE. With Lists of Books on Greek Travel and Topography, and Time Tables of Greek Railways and Steamers. By JOHN EDWIN SANDYS, Litt.D., Fellow and Tutor of St. John's College, and Public Orator in the University of Cambridge. With a Map of Greece and a plan of Olympia. Crown 8vo. 3s. 6d.

DEMOCRACY; and other Addresses. By JAMES RUSSELL LOWELL. Crown 8vo. 5s.
Contents :—Democracy—Garfield—Dean Stanley—Fielding—Coleridge—Books and Libraries—Wordsworth—Don Quixote—Address delivered at 250th Celebration of Harvard College.

GREATER BRITAIN. A Record of Travel in English-speaking Countries during 1866–67. (America, Australia, India.) By the Right Hon. Sir CHARLES WENTWORTH DILKE. Eighth Edition, with Additions. Crown 8vo. 6s.

LETTERS, TRACTS, AND SPEECHES ON IRISH AFFAIRS. By EDMUND BURKE. Arranged and Edited by MATTHEW ARNOLD, with a Preface. Crown 8vo. 6s.

MACMILLAN & CO., LONDON.

www.ingramcontent.com/pod-product-compliance
Lightning Source LLC
Chambersburg PA
CBHW030544300426
44111CB00009B/847